Arthur Miller

DEATH OF A SALESMAN

Arthur Miller

DEATH OF A SALESMAN

[Edited with Complete Introduction, Biography, Author's Background, Complete Text, Study Questions, Select Criticism and Bibliography]

Mansi Sachdeva
B.A. English (Hons), Delhi University;
M.A., M. Phil. (English), IGNOU

ANMOL PUBLICATIONS PVT. LTD.
NEW DELHI - 110 002 (INDIA)

ANMOL PUBLICATIONS PVT. LTD.

H.O.: 4374/4B, Ansari Road, Darya Ganj,
New Delhi-110 002 (India)
Ph.: 23278000, 23261597

B.O.: No. 1015, Ist Main Road, BSK IIIrd Stage
IIIrd Phase, IIIrd Block
Bangalore - 560 085 (India)
Visit us at: www.anmolpublications.com

Death of a Salesman

First Published, 2009

PRINTED IN INDIA

Printed at Mehra Offset Press, Delhi.

Contents

Preface

Death of Salesman is one of the greatest works of Arthur Miller and encompasses both his personal as well as theatrical traditions. In this great play, you will find the glimpse of Yiddish theater, where family plays key role. This play revolves around two sons who have been estranged from their father. This great play was premiered in the year 1949.

Arthur Miller was born on 1915 and died on 2005. He was one of the respectable and leading American playwrights and was born in New York City. He was born in a women's clothing manufacturer family. In the year 1930, due to huge financial collapse, they were completely ruined. Miller started working in a ware house, after graduating from the high school.

Author

Chapter 1

Introduction

Arthur Miller's Death of a Salesman stems from both Arthur Miller's personal experiences and the theatrical traditions in which the playwright was schooled. The play recalls the traditions of Yiddish theater that focus on family as the crucial element, reducing most plot to the confines of the nuclear family. Death of a Salesman focuses on two sons who are estranged from their father, paralleling one of Miller's other major works, All My Sons, which premiered two years before Death of a Salesman.

Although the play premiered in 1949, Miller began writing Death of a Salesman at the age of seventeen when he was working for his father's company. In short story form, it treated an aging salesman unable to sell anything. He is berated by company bosses and must borrow subway change from the young narrator. The end of the manuscript contains a postscript that the salesman on which the story is based had thrown himself under a subway train.

Arthur Miller reworked the play in 1947 upon a meeting with his uncle, Manny Newman. Miller's uncle, a salesman, was a competitor at all times and even competed with his sons, Buddy and Abby. Miller described the Newman household as one in which one could not lose hope, and based the Loman household and structure on his uncle and cousins. There are numerous parallels between Abby and Buddy Newman and their fictional counterparts, Happy and Biff Loman: Buddy, like Biff, was a renowned high school athlete who ended up flunking out. Miller's relationship to his cousins parallels that of the Lomans to their neighbour, Bernard.

While constructing the play, Miller was intent on creating continuous action that could span different time periods smoothly. The major innovation of the play was the fluid continuity between its segments. Flashbacks do not occur separate from the action but rather as an integral part of it. The play moves between fifteen years back and the present, and from Brooklyn to Boston without any interruptions in the plot.

Death of a Salesman premiered on Broadway in 1949, starring Lee J. Cobb as Willy Loman and directed by Elia Kazan (who would later inform on Arthur Miller in front of the House Un-American Activities Committee). The play was a resounding success, winning the Pulitzer Prize, as well as the Tony Award for Best Play. The New Yorker called the play a mixture of "compassion, imagination, and hard technical competence not often found in our theater." Since then, the play has been revived numerous times on Broadway and reinterpreted in stage and television versions. As an archetypal character representing the failed American dream, Willy Loman has been interpreted by diverse actors such as Fredric March (the 1951 film version), Dustin Hoffman (the 1984 Broadway revival and television movie), and, in a Tony Award-winning revival, Brian Dennehy.

Chapter 2

Biography of Arthur Miller

Arthur Miller was one of the leading American playwrights of the twentieth century. He was born in October 1915 in New York City. He was the son of a women's clothing manufacturer who was ruined during the economic collapse of the 1930s. Living through young adulthood during the Great Depression, Miller was shaped by the poverty that surrounded him. The Depression demonstrated to the playwright the fragility and vulnerability of human existence in the modern era. After graduating from high school, Miller worked in a warehouse so that he could earn enough money to attend the University of Michigan, where he began to write plays.

Miller's first play to make it to Broadway, The Man Who Had All the Luck (1944), was a dismal failure, closing after only four performances. This early setback almost discouraged Miller from writing at all, but, luckily for American theater, he gave himself one more try. Three years later, All My Sons won the New York Drama Critics' Circle Award as the best play of 1947, launching Miller into theatrical stardom. All My Sons, a drama about a manufacturer of faulty war materials, was strongly influenced by the naturalist drama of Henrik Ibsen. Along with Death of a Salesman (his most enduring success), All My Sons and The Man Who Had All the Luck form a thematic trilogy of plays about love triangles involving fathers and sons. The drama of the family is at the core of all of Miller's major plays, but nowhere is it more prominent than in the realism of All My Sons and the impressionism of Death of a Salesman.

It was by writing his masterpiece, Death of a Salesman

(1949), that Miller secured his reputation as one of the nation's foremost playwrights. Death of a Salesman mixes the tradition of social realism that informs most of Miller's work with a more experimental structure that includes fluid leaps in time as the protagonist, Willy Loman, drifts into memories of his sons as teenagers. Loman represents an American archetype, a victim of his own delusions of grandeur and obsession with success, which haunt him with a sense of failure.

Miller won a Tony Award for Death of a Salesman as well as a Pulitzer Prize. The play has been frequently revived in film, television, and stage versions that have included actors such as Dustin Hoffman, George C. Scott and, most recently, Brian Dennehy in the part of Willy Loman.

Miller followed Death of a Salesman with his most politically significant work, The Crucible (1953), a tale of the Salem witch trials that contains obvious analogies to the McCarthy anti-Communist hearings in 1950s America. Three years later, in 1956, Miller found himself persecuted by the very force that he was warning against when he was called to testify before the House Un-American Activities Committee. Miller refused to name people he allegedly saw at a Communist writers' meeting a decade before, and he was convicted of contempt. He sought further action and later won an appeal.

Also in 1956, Miller married actress Marilyn Monroe. The two divorced in 1961, the year of her death. That year Monroe appeared in her last film, The Misfits, which is based on an original screenplay by Miller. After divorcing Monroe, Miller wed Ingeborg Morath, to whom he remained married until his death in 2005. The pair had a son and a daughter.

Miller also wrote the plays A Memory of Two Mondays and the short A View from the Bridge, which were both staged in 1955. His other works include After the Fall (1964), a thinly veiled account of his marriage to Monroe, as well as The Price (1967), The Archbishop's Ceiling (1977), and The American Clock (1980). His most recent works include the plays The Ride Down Mt. Morgan (1991), The Last Yankee (1993), and Broken Glass (1993), which won the Olivier Award for Best Play.

Although Miller did not write frequently for film, he did pen an adaptation for the 1996 film version of The Crucible starring Daniel Day-Lewis and Winona Ryder, which garnered him an Academy Award nomination. Miller's daughter Rebecca married Day-Lewis in 1996.

Chapter 3

Timeline

1915 Born October 17 in New York City, second son of Isadore and Augusta Miller.

1929 Depression causes financial difficulties in father's clothing business. Family moves to Brooklyn.

1934 Enters the University of Michigan, Ann Arbor. Studies journalism.

1936 First play, Honors at Dawn, produced. Wins Hopwood Awards in Drama for No Villain (1936) and Honors at Dawn (1937), and Theater Guild Bureau of New Plays Award for They Too Arise.

1938 Receives Bachelor of Arts from University of Michigan. Begins work with the Federal Theater Project.

1940 Marries Mary Grace Slattery.

1944 Visits army camps collecting material for screenplay, The Story of G.I. Joe. Situation Normal (prose account of this tour) published. The Man Who Had All the Luck published and produced in New York; wins Theater Guild National Prize.

1945 Novel, Focus, published.

1947 All My Sons produced and published in New York; wins New York Drama Critics' Circle Award.

1949 Death of a Salesman published and produced; wins Pulitzer Prize and N.Y. Critics' Circle Award.

1950	Adaptation of Ibsen's An Enemy of the People produced.
1953	The Crucible produced and published.
1954	Is refused passport by State Department to attend opening of The Crucible in Brussels.
1955	A Memory of Two Mondays and the one-act version of A View from the Bridge produced and published in New York.
1956	Two-act version of A View from the Bridge produced in London. Divorces Mary Slattery. Appears before House Un-American Activities Committee. Marries Marilyn Monroe.
1957	Convicted of contempt of Congress for refusing to name suspected communists. Collected Plays published. 1958 Conviction reversed by Supreme Court.Elected to the National Arts and Letters Institute.
1960	Filming of The Misfits. Separates from Marilyn Monroe. 1961 The Misfits released. Divorces Marilyn Monroe. The Misfits published as a novel.
1962	Marries Austrian-born photographer Ingeborg Morath.Birth of daughter Rebecca Augusta Miller.
1964	After the Fall and Incident at Vichy produced by the Lincoln Centre Repertory Theater.
1965	Elected International President of PEN (Poets, Essayists, and Novelists).
1967	I Don't Need You Any More, a collection of short stories, published.
1968	The Price published and produced in New York.Serves as delegate to Democratic National Convention.
1969	In Russia published with Inge Morath. 1970 Fame produced in New York.
1972	The Creation of the World and Other Business produced in New York. Serves as delegate to the Democratic National Convention.

1974 Up from Paradise (musical version of The Creation of the World) produced in Ann Arbor, Michigan.

1977 The Archbishop's Ceiling produced at the Kennedy Centre in Washington, D.C. In the Country published with Inge Morath.

1978 Visits China with Inge Morath. The Theater Essays of Arthur Miller published.

1980 The American Clock produced in New York. Playing for Time presented on television.

1982 Two one-acts, Some Kind of Love Story and Elegy for a Lady, open at the Long Wharf Theater in New Haven. 1983 Directs Death of a Salesman in China with Chinese cast.

1984 Revival of Death of a Salesman opens on Broadway with Dustin Hoffman as Willy Loman.

1985 Broadcast of 1984 production of Death of a Salesman on television.

Later Career

In 1964 Miller's next play was produced. After the Fall is a deeply personal view of Miller's own experiences during his marriage to Monroe. The play reunited Miller with his former friend Kazan: they collaborated on both the script and the direction. After the Fall opened on January 23, 1964 at the ANTA Theater in Washington Square Park amid a flurry of publicity and outrage at putting a Monroe-like character, called Maggie, on stage. Also in the same year, Miller produced Incident at Vichy. In 1965, Miller was elected the first American president of International PEN, a position which he held for four years. During this period Miller wrote the penetrating family drama, The Price, produced in 1968. It was Miller's most successful play since Death of a Salesman.

In 1969, Miller's works were banned in the Soviet Union after he campaigned for the freedom of dissident writers. Throughout the 1970s, Miller spent much of his time experimenting with the theater, producing one-act plays such as Fame and The Reason Why, and traveling with his wife, producing In The Country and Chinese Encounters with her. Both his 1972 comedy The Creation of the World and Other Business and its musical adaptation, Up from Paradise, were critical and commercial failures.

In 1983, Miller traveled to the People's Republic of China to produce and direct Death of a Salesman at the People's Art Theater in Beijing. The play was a success in China and in 1984, Salesman in Beijing, a book about Miller's experience in Beijing, was published. Around the same time, Death of a Salesman was made into a TV movie starring Dustin Hoffman as Willy Loman. Shown on CBS, it attracted 25 million viewers. In late 1987, Miller's autobiography, Timebends was published. Before his autobiography was published, it was well known that that Miller would not talk about Monroe in interviews; in Timebends Miller talks about his experiences with Monroe in detail. During the early 1990s Miller wrote three new plays, The Ride Down Mt. Morgan (1991), The Last Yankee (1992), and Broken Glass (1994). In 1996, a film of The Crucible starring Daniel Day Lewis and Winona Ryder opened. Miller spent much of 1996 working on the screenplay to the film. Mr. Peters' Connections was staged off-Broadway in 1998, and Death of a Salesman was revived on Broadway in 1999 to celebrate its fiftieth anniversary. The play, once again, was a large critical success, winning a Tony Award for best revival of a play. On May 1, 2002, Miller was awarded Spain's Principe de Asturias Prize for Literature as "the undisputed master of modern drama." Previous winners include Doris Lessing, Günter Grass and Carlos Fuentes. Later that year, Ingeborg Morath died of Lymphatic cancer at the age of 78. The following year Miller won the Jerusalem Prize. In December 2004, the 89-year-old Miller announced that he has been living with a 34-year-old artist Agnes Barley at his Connecticut farm since 2002, and that they intended to marry. Miller's final play, Finishing the Picture, opened at the Goodman Theater, Chicago, in the fall of 2004. He stated that the work was based on the experience of filming The Misfits. Miller died at his home in Roxbury of congestive heart failure on the evening of February 10, 2005 (the 56th anniversary of the Broadway debut of Death of a Salesman) at the age of 89, surrounded by his family.

Legacy

Miller's career as a writer spanned over seven decades, and at the time of his death in 2005, Miller was considered to be one of the greatest dramatists of the twentieth century, among the likes of Harold Pinter, Eugene O'Neill, Luigi Pirandello, Samuel Beckett, Jean-Paul Sartre, Bertolt Brecht, and Tennessee Williams. After his death, many respected actors, directors, and producers paid tribute to Miller, some calling him the last great practitioner of the American stage, and Broadway theaters darkened their lights in a show of respect. Miller's alma mater, the University of Michigan opened the Arthur Miller Theater in March, 2007. Per his express wish, it is the only theater in the world that bears Miller's name.

Miller's friend Professor Christopher Bigsby is currently working on Arthur Miller: The Definitive Biography, based on boxes of papers Miller made available to him before his death in 2005. The book will be published in November 2008, and is reported to reveal unpublished works in which Miller "bitterly attack[ed] the injustices of American racism long before it was taken up by the civil rights movement".

Chapter 4

Tragedy and the Common Man

In this age, few tragedies are written. It has often been held that the lack is due to a paucity of heroes among us, or else that modern man has had the blood drawn out of his organs of belief by the skepticism of science, and the heroic attack on life cannot feed on an attitude of reserve and circumspection. For one reason or another, we are often held to be below tragedy-or tragedy above us. The inevitable conclusion is, of course, that the tragic mode is archaic, fit only for the very highly placed, the kings or the kingly, and where this admission is not made in so many words it is most often implied.

I believe that the common man is as apt a subject for tragedy in its highest sense as kings were. On the face of it this ought to be obvious in the light of modern psychiatry, which bases its analysis upon classic formulations, such as the Oedipus and Orestes complexes, for instance, which were enacted by royal beings, but which apply to everyone in similar emotional situations.

More simply, when the question of tragedy in art in not at issue, we never hesitate to attribute to the well-placed and the exalted the very same mental processes as the lowly. And finally, if the exaltation of tragic action were truly a property of the high-bred character alone, it is inconceivable that the mass Of mankind should cherish tragedy above all other forms, let alone be capable of understanding it.

As a general rule, to which there may be exceptions unknown to me, I think the tragic feeling is evoked in us when we are in the presence of a character who is ready to lay down his life, if need be, to secure one thing—his sense of personal dignity. From Orestes to Hamlet, Medea to Macbeth, the underlying struggles that of the individual attempting to gain his "rightful" position in his society.

Sometimes he is one who has been displaced from it, sometimes one who seeks to attain it for the first time, but the fateful wound from which the inevitable events spiral is the wound of indignity, and its dominant force is indignation. Tragedy, then, is the consequence of a man's total compulsion to evaluate himself justly.

In the sense of having been initiated by the hero himself, the tale always reveals what has been called his tragic flaw," a failing that is not peculiar to grand or elevated characters. Nor is it necessarily a weakness. The flaw, or crack in the character, is really nothing—and need be nothing, but his inherent unwillingness to remain passive in the face of what he conceives to be a challenge to his dignity, his image of his rightful status. Only the passive, only those who accept their lot without active retaliation, are "flawless." Most of us are in that category. But there are among us today, as there always have been, those who act against the scheme of things that degrades them, and in the process of action everything we have accepted out of fear or insensitivity or ignorance is shaken before us and examined, and from this total onslaught by an individual against the seemingly stable cosmos surrounding us—from this total examination of the "unchangeable" environment—comes the terror and the fear that is classically associated with tragedy.

More important, from this total questioning of what has previously been unquestioned, we learn. And such a process is not beyond the common man. In revolutions around the world, these past thirty years, he has demonstrated again and again this inner dynamic of all tragedy.

Insistence upon the rank of the tragic hero, or the so-called nobility of his character, is really but a clinging to the outward forms of tragedy. If rank or nobility of character was indispensable, then it would follow that the problems of those with rank were the particular problems of tragedy. But surely the right of one monarch to capture the domain from another no longer raises our passions, nor are our concepts of justice what they were to the mind of an Elizabethan king.

The quality in such plays that does shake us, however, derives from the underlying fear of being displaced, the disaster inherent in being torn away from our chosen image of what or who we are in this world. Among us today this fear is as strong, and perhaps stronger, than it ever was. In fact, it is the common man who knows this fear best.

Now, if it is true that tragedy is the consequence of a man's total compulsion to evaluate himself justly, his destruction in the attempt posits a wrong or an evil in his environment. And this is precisely the morality of tragedy and its lesson. The discovery of the moral law, which is what the enlightenment of tragedy consists of, is not the discovery of some abstract or metaphysical quantity.

The tragic night is a condition of life, a condition in which the human personality is able to flower and realise itself. The wrong is the condition which suppresses man, perverts the flowing out of his love and creative instinct. Tragedy enlightens and it must, in that it points the heroic finger at the enemy of man's freedom. The thrust for freedom is the quality in tragedy which exalts. The revolutionary questioning of the stable environment is what terrifies. In no way is the common man debarred from such thoughts or such actions.

Seen in this light, our lack of tragedy may be partially accounted for by the turn which modern literature has taken toward the purely psychiatric view of life, or the purely sociological. If all our miseries, our indignities, are born and bred within our minds, then all action, let alone the heroic action, is obviously impossible.

And if society alone is responsible for the cramping of our lives, then the protagonist must needs be so pure and faultless as to force us to deny his validity as a character. From neither of these views can tragedy derive, simply because neither represents a balanced concept of life. Above all else, tragedy requires the finest appreciation by the writer of cause and effect.

No tragedy can therefore come about when its author fears to question absolutely everything, when he regards any institution, habit or custom as being either everlasting, immutable or inevitable. In the tragic view the need of man to wholly realise himself is the only fixed star, and whatever it is that hedges his nature and lowers it is ripe for attack and examination. Which is not to say that tragedy must preach revolution.

The Greeks could probe the very heavenly origin of their ways and return to confirm the rightness of laws. And Job could face God in anger, demanding his right and end in submission. But for a moment everything is in suspension, nothing is accepted, and in this stretching and tearing apart of the cosmos, in the very action of so doing, the character gains "size," the tragic stature which is spuriously attached to the royal or the high born in our minds. The commonest of men may take on that stature to the extent of his willingness to throw all he has into the contest, the battle to secure his rightful place in his world.

There is a misconception of tragedy with which I have been struck in review after review, and in many conversations with writers and readers alike. It is the idea that tragedy is of necessity allied to pessimism. Even the dictionary says nothing more about the word than that it means a story with a sad or unhappy ending. This impression is so firmly fixed that I almost hesitate to claim that in truth tragedy implies more optimism in its author than does comedy, and that its final result ought to be the reinforcement of the onlooker's brightest opinions of the human animal.

For, if it is true to say that in essence the tragic hero is intent upon claiming his whole due as a personality, and if this struggle must be total and without reservation, then it automatically demonstrates the indestructible will of man to achieve his humanity. The possibility of victory must be there in tragedy. Where pathos rules, where pathos is finally derived, a character has fought a battle he could not possibly have won. The pathetic is achieved when the protagonist is, by virtue of his witlessness, his insensitivity or the very air he gives off, incapable of grappling with a much superior force. Pathos truly is the mode for the pessimist. But tragedy requires a nicer balance between what is possible and what is impossible. And it is curious, although edifying, that the plays we revere, century after century, are the tragedies. In them, and in them alone, lies the belief—optimistic, if you will, in the perfectibility of man. It is time, I think, that we who are without kings, took up this bright thread of our history and followed it to the only place it can possible lead in our time—the heart and spirit of the average man.

Chapter 5

Key Facts

Full Title

Death of a Salesman: Certain Private Conversations in Two Acts and a Requiem

Author

Arthur Miller

Type of Work

Play

Genre

Tragedy, social commentary, family drama

Language

English (with emphasis on middle-class American lingo)

Time and Place Written

Six weeks in 1948, in a shed in Connecticut

Date of First Publication

1949

Original Publisher

The Viking Press

Climax

The scene in Frank's Chop House and Biff's final confrontation with Willy at home

Protagonists

Willy Loman, Biff Loman

Antagonists

Biff Loman, Willy Loman, the American Dream

Setting (Time)

"Today," that is, the present; either the late 1940s or the time period in which the play is being produced, with "daydreams" into Willy's past; all of the action takes place during a twenty-four-hour period between Monday night and Tuesday night, except the "Requiem," which takes place, presumably, a few days after Willy's funeral

Setting (Place)

According to the stage directions, "Willy Loman's house and yard [in Brooklyn] and various places he visits in New York and Boston"

Falling Action

The "Requiem" section, although the play is not really structured as a classical drama

Tense

Present

Foreshadowing

Willy's flute theme foreshadows the revelation of his father's occupation and abandonment; Willy's preoccupation with Linda's stockings foreshadows his affair with The Woman; Willy's automobile accident before the start of Act I foreshadows his suicide at the end of Act II.

Tone

The tone of Miller's stage directions and dialogue ranges from sincere to parodying, but, in general, the treatment is tender, though at times brutally honest, toward Willy's plight

Themes

The American Dream; abandonment; betrayal

Motifs

Mythic figures; the American West; Alaska; the African jungle

Symbols

Seeds; diamonds; Linda's and the womon's stockings; the rubber hose

Chapter 6

Context

Arthur Miller was born in New York City on October 17, 1915. His career as a playwright began while he was a student at the University of Michigan. Several of his early works won prizes, and during his senior year, the Federal Theater Project in Detroit performed one of his works. He produced his first great success, All My Sons, in 1947. Two years later, Miller wrote Death of a Salesman, which won the Pulitzer Prize and transformed Miller into a national sensation. Many critics described Death of a Salesman as the first great American tragedy, and Miller gained eminence as a man who understood the deep essence of the United States. He published The Crucible in 1953, a searing indictment of the anti-Communist hysteria that pervaded 1950s America. He has won the New York Drama Critics Circle Award twice, and his Broken Glass (1993) won the Olivier Award for Best Play of the London Season.

Death of a Salesman, Miller's most famous work, addresses the painful conflicts within one family, but it also tackles larger issues regarding American national values. The play examines the cost of blind faith in the American Dream. In this respect, it offers a postwar American reading of personal tragedy in the tradition of Sophocles' Oedipus Cycle. Miller charges America with selling a false myth constructed around a capitalist materialism nurtured by the postwar economy, a materialism that obscured the personal truth and moral vision of the original American Dream described by the country's founders.

A half century after it was written, Death of a Salesman

remains a powerful drama. Its indictment of fundamental American values and the American Dream of material success may seem somewhat tame in today's age of constant national and individual self-analysis and criticism, but its challenge was quite radical for its time. After World War II, the United States faced profound and irreconcilable domestic tensions and contradictions. Although the war had ostensibly engendered an unprecedented sense of American confidence, prosperity, and security, the United States became increasingly embroiled in a tense cold war with the Soviet Union. The propagation of myths of a peaceful, homogenous, and nauseatingly gleeful American golden age was tempered by constant anxiety about Communism, bitter racial conflict, and largely ignored economic and social stratification. Many Americans could not subscribe to the degree of social conformity and the ideological and cultural orthodoxy that a prosperous, booming, conservative suburban middle-class championed.

Uneasy with this American milieu of denial and discord, a new generation of artists and writers influenced by existentialist philosophy and the hypocritical postwar condition took up arms in a battle for self-realization and expression of personal meaning. Such discontented individuals railed against capitalist success as the basis of social approval, disturbed that so many American families centered their lives around material possessions (cars, appliances, and especially the just-introduced television)—often in an attempt to keep up with their equally materialistic neighbors. The climate of the American art world had likewise long been stuck in its own rut of conformity, confusion, and disorder following the prewar climax of European Modernism and the wake of assorted -isms associated with modern art and literature. The notions of Sigmund Freud and Carl Jung regarding the role of the human subconscious in defining and accepting human existence, coupled with the existentialist concern with the individual's responsibility for understanding one's existence on one's own terms, captivated the imaginations of postwar artists and writers. Perhaps the most famous and widely read dramatic work associated with existentialist philosophy is

Samuel Beckett's Waiting for Godot. Miller fashioned a particularly American version of the European existentialist stance, incorporating and playing off idealistic notions of success and individuality specific to the United States.

The basis for the dramatic conflict in Death of a Salesman lies in Arthur Miller's conflicted relationship with his uncle, Manny Newman, also a salesman. Newman imagined a continuous competition between his son and Miller. Newman refused to accept failure and demanded the appearance of utmost confidence in his household. In his youth, Miller had written a short story about an unsuccessful salesman. His relationship with Manny revived his interest in the abandoned manuscript. He transformed the story into one of the most successful dramas in the history of the American stage. In expressing the emotions that Manny Newman inspired through the fictional character of Willy Loman, Miller managed to touch deep chords within the national psyche.

Chapter 7

Narrative Technique in Arthur Miller's Death of a Salesman

In telling his story Miller returned to a narrative technique he had found useful before. The father's guilt in All My Sons becomes apparent to the audience and to the antagonist after being hinted at in a succession of fragmentary references to a hidden crime. Though in Death of a Salesman the son already knows his father's sin, the audience again learns the truth in a climactic revelation that follows a series of covert allusions. "There's one or two things depressing him," Biff says in the opening scene, beginning the series; later he adds, "I know he's a face and he doesn't like anybody around who knows!" Linda, blindly loyal, suspects nothing: "what has [Biff] got against you?" she asks her husband. Bernard, a neighbour, inquires into the secret shared by father and son: "what happened in Boston, Willy?" Willy's response, "I can't tell you," sums up his reticence on the topic.

Suggestive references of this kind, however, are relatively unimportant in this work. The chief narrative method of developing tension, temperament, and fact is dramatized memory, which allows Miller to represent time as a melding of the past and the present into one rather than a sequence of events. This subjective approach to delayed exposition brings to light not only crucial past events but also the emotional charges associated with them; Willy Loman wig wags between current and past guilt feelings. The memories, generally concerned with the disintegration of his family and his professional aspirations, are released by events in the past that are dramatized on stage in his mind. Thus, after he is fired by Howard in Act II, Willy remembers his refusal of a vocational opportunity that might have led to success in Alaska instead of the present humiliation of being fired. And Biff's unfavorable report on an attempt to get financial backing from Bill Oliver turns Willy's mind back to the hotel room in which Biff discovered him with his mistress — a discovery that the father fears has initiated his son's failures.

Transitions in place and time are cleverly implemented by ingenious stage effects, a skeletonized house-set, multiple playing areas (apron, forestage, and two levels of the house), and the repetition of key words or topics (motifs) before, during, and after each recollection. C Miller's skill in executing imaginative, meaningful transitions is apparent in the opening scene, which introduces the subject of family disharmony. A conversation with Linda about his driving that day reminds Willy of the old "Chevy" he owned when his boys still loved and obeyed him. As he "loses himself in reminiscences," sitting in his kitchen, interest moves to another playing level, the upstairs bedroom, where the brothers too have been discussing their father's careless driving.

Then, when they recall their popularity with girls in their youth, they in turn are interrupted by Willy "mumbling" downstairs to an imaginary Biff on the same subject: "the girls pay for you?...Boy, you must really be makin' a hit." Musical motifs, lighting arrangements, and scenic changes complete the preparation for the first vision, which opens, appropriately, with Willy admiring his popular teen-age sons as Biff polishes the "Chevy." During this transition, as in others, recurring themes are grouped in psychologically significant combinations. While Willy visualizes a joyful, affectionate family group, another intimate but less innocent scene from a still earlier time — again involving a "girl" — breaks in on the word "make""

Willy [to Linda]: There's so much I want to make for

The Woman: Me? You didn't make me, Willy. I picked you.

Willy's family-dream returns, with Linda mending stockings (his mistress had asked for "a lot of stockings".); but, since innocence has been corrupted, shame colors the recollection. Now the mention of girls and cars, punctuated by "The Woman's laugh," denotes Biff's (and by implication, Willy's) irresponsibility, not worth. Changed to waking nightmare, the daydream disappears and leaves Willy alone in his kitchen, guiltily denying responsibility for his son's failure.

Two motives impel Willy to conjure the "reminiscences." First, he seeks escape from his problems by reliving a happier time ("how do we get back to all the great times? Always some kind of good news coming up"). Disturbed by recurring troubles, however, he involuntarily recalls bad news; then he seeks the origin of his and Biff's difficulties. "Why?" he continually asks "what — what's the secret? Why? Why! Bernard, that question has been trailing me like a ghost for the last fifteen years." Yet the same lack of self-awareness that caused his failure as a father keeps him from learning the "secret" contained in the visions. In contrast to Biff, who finally accepts his limitations, Willy remains unalterably determined that his son shall show the world "all kinds of greatness." His hallucinations thus measure the blind intensity of his ambition, which is strong enough to withstand not only galling indignities in the present but also agonizing internal re-creations of his inadequacy in the past. As circumstances become more threatening and as his remembrances become more real, leading Willy back to the central trauma of his life, his resistance to fact the truth grows correspondingly more desperate. He stubbornly refuses to admit defeat; for example, when Charley offers him work as a way to salvage his pride, he "furiously" refuses. The effect of his growing anxiety is to steadily increase tension as the action progresses: Willy's agitated justifications gradually cumulate great excitement. When dealing with an intense character who concentrates his energies "upon the fixed point of his commitment," Miller writes, a playwright must design "scenes of high and open emotion, and plays constructed toward climax rather that the evocation of a mood alone or of bizarre spectacle."

Chapter 8

Themes, Motifs and Symbols

The American Dream

Willy believes wholeheartedly in what he considers the promise of the American Dream—that a "well liked" and "personally attractive" man in business will indubitably and deservedly acquire the material comforts offered by modern American life. Oddly, his fixation with the superficial qualities of attractiveness and likeability is at odds with a more gritty, more rewarding understanding of the American Dream that identifies hard work without complaint as the key to success. Willy's interpretation of likeability is superficial—he childishly dislikes Bernard because he considers Bernard a nerd. Willy's blind faith in his stunted version of the American Dream leads to his rapid psychological decline when he is unable to accept the disparity between the Dream and his own life.

Willy's life charts a course from one abandonment to the next, leaving him in greater despair each time. Willy's father leaves him and Ben when Willy is very young, leaving Willy neither a tangible (money) nor an intangible (history) legacy. Ben eventually departs for Alaska, leaving Willy to lose himself in a warped vision of the American Dream. Likely a result of these early experiences, Willy develops a fear of abandonment, which makes him want his family to conform to the American Dream. His efforts to raise perfect sons, however, reflect his inability to understand reality.

The young Biff, whom Willy considers the embodiment of promise, drops Willy and Willy's zealous ambitions for him when he finds out about Willy's adultery. Biff's ongoing inability to succeed in business furthers his estrangement from Willy. When, at Frank's Chop House, Willy finally believes that Biff is on the cusp of greatness, Biff shatters Willy's illusions and, along with Happy, abandons the deluded, babbling Willy in the washroom.

Betrayal

Willy's primary obsession throughout the play is what he considers to be Biff's betrayal of his ambitions for him. Willy believes that he has every right to expect Biff to fulfill the promise inherent in him.

When Biff walks out on Willy's ambitions for him, Willy takes this rejection as a personal affront (he associates it with "insult" and "spite"). Willy, after all, is a salesman, and Biff's ego-crushing rebuff ultimately reflects Willy's inability to sell him on the American Dream—the product in which Willy himself believes most faithfully. Willy assumes that Biff's betrayal stems from Biff's discovery of Willy's affair with The Woman—a betrayal of Linda's love. Whereas Willy feels that Biff has betrayed him, Biff feels that Willy, a "phony little fake," has betrayed him with his unending stream of ego-stroking lies.

Motifs

Motifs are recurring structures, contrasts, or literary devices that can help to develop and inform the text's major themes.

Mythic Figures

Willy's tendency to mythologize people contributes to his deluded understanding of the world. He speaks of Dave Singleman as a legend and imagines that his death must have been beautifully noble. Willy compares Biff and Happy to the mythic Greek figures Adonis and Hercules because he believes that his sons are pinnacles of "personal attractiveness" and power through "well liked"-ness; to him, they seem the very incarnation of the American Dream.

Willy's mythologizing proves quite nearsighted, however.

Willy fails to realise the hopelessness of Singleman's lonely, on-the-job, on-the-road death. Trying to achieve what he considers to be Singleman's heroic status, Willy commits himself to a pathetic death and meaningless legacy (even if Willy's life insurance policy ends up paying off, Biff wants nothing to do with Willy's ambition for him). Similarly, neither Biff nor Happy ends up leading an ideal, godlike life; while Happy does believe in the American Dream, it seems likely that he will end up no better off than the decidedly ungodlike Willy.

The American West, Alaska, and the African Jungle

These regions represent the potential of instinct to Biff and Willy. Willy's father found success in Alaska and his brother, Ben, became rich in Africa; these exotic locales, especially when compared to Willy's banal Brooklyn neighborhood, crystallize how Willy's obsession with the commercial world of the city has trapped him in an unpleasant reality.

Whereas Alaska and the African jungle symbolize Willy's failure, the American West, on the other hand, symbolizes Biff's potential. Biff realizes that he has been content only when working on farms, out in the open. His westward escape from both Willy's delusions and the commercial world of the eastern United States suggests a nineteenth-century pioneer mentality—Biff, unlike Willy, recognizes the importance of the individual.

Symbols

Symbols are objects, characters, figures, or colors used to represent abstract ideas or concepts.

Seeds

Seeds represent for Willy the opportunity to prove the worth of his labour, both as a salesman and a father. His desperate, nocturnal attempt to grow vegetables signifies his shame about barely being able to put food on the table and having nothing to leave his children when he passes. Willy feels that he has worked hard but fears that he will not be able to help his offspring any more than his own abandoning father helped him. The seeds also symbolize Willy's sense of failure with Biff. Despite the American Dream's formula for success, which Willy considers infallible, Willy's efforts to cultivate and nurture Biff went awry. Realizing that his all-American football star has turned into a lazy bum, Willy takes Biff's failure and lack of ambition as a reflection of his abilities as a father.

Diamonds

To Willy, diamonds represent tangible wealth and, hence, both validation of one's labour (and life) and the ability to pass material goods on to one's offspring, two things that Willy desperately craves. Correlatively, diamonds, the discovery of which made Ben a fortune, symbolize Willy's failure as a salesman.

Despite Willy's belief in the American Dream, a belief unwavering to the extent that he passed up the opportunity to go with Ben to Alaska, the Dream's promise of financial security has eluded Willy. At the end of the play, Ben encourages Willy to enter the "jungle" finally and retrieve this elusive diamond—that is, to kill himself for insurance money in order to make his life meaningful.

Linda's and The Woman's Stockings

Willy's strange obsession with the condition of Linda's stockings foreshadows his later flashback to Biff's discovery of him and The Woman in their Boston hotel room. The teenage Biff accuses Willy of giving away Linda's stockings to The Woman. Stockings assume a metaphorical weight as the symbol of betrayal and sexual infidelity.

New stockings are important for both Willy's pride in being financially successful and thus able to provide for his family and for Willy's ability to ease his guilt about, and suppress the memory of, his betrayal of Linda and Biff.

The Rubber Hose

The rubber hose is a stage prop that reminds the audience of Willy's desperate attempts at suicide. He has apparently attempted to kill himself by inhaling gas, which is, ironically, the very substance essential to one of the most basic elements with which he must equip his home for his family's health and comfort—heat. Literal death by inhaling gas parallels the metaphorical death that Willy feels in his struggle to afford such a basic necessity.

Chapter 9

Plot Overview

As a flute melody plays, Willy Loman returns to his home in Brooklyn one night, exhausted from a failed sales trip. His wife, Linda, tries to persuade him to ask his boss, Howard Wagner, to let him work in New York so that he won't have to travel. Willy says that he will talk to Howard the next day. Willy complains that Biff, his older son who has come back home to visit, has yet to make something of himself. Linda scolds Willy for being so critical, and Willy goes to the kitchen for a snack.

As Willy talks to himself in the kitchen, Biff and his younger brother, Happy, who is also visiting, reminisce about their adolescence and discuss their father's babbling, which often includes criticism of Biff's failure to live up to Willy's expectations. As Biff and Happy, dissatisfied with their lives, fantasize about buying a ranch out West, Willy becomes immersed in a daydream. He praises his sons, now younger, who are washing his car. The young Biff, a high school football star, and the young Happy appear. They interact affectionately with their father, who has just returned from a business trip. Willy confides in Biff and Happy that he is going to open his own business one day, bigger than that owned by his neighbour, Charley. Charley's son, Bernard, enters looking for Biff, who must study for math class in order to avoid failing. Willy points out to his sons that although Bernard is smart, he is not "well liked," which will hurt him in the long run.

A younger Linda enters, and the boys leave to do some chores. Willy boasts of a phenomenally successful sales trip, but Linda coaxes him into revealing that his trip was actually only meagerly successful. Willy complains that he soon won't be able to make all of the payments on their appliances and car. He complains that people don't like him and that he's not good at his job. As Linda consoles him, he hears the laughter of his mistress. He approaches The Woman, who is still laughing, and engages in another reminiscent daydream. Willy and The Woman flirt, and she thanks him for giving him stockings.

The Woman disappears, and Willy fades back into his prior daydream, in the kitchen. Linda, now mending stockings, reassures him. He scolds her mending and orders her to throw the stockings out. Bernard bursts in, again looking for Biff. Linda reminds Willy that Biff has to return a football that he stole, and she adds that Biff is too rough with the neighborhood girls. Willy hears The Woman laugh and explodes at Bernard and Linda. Both leave, and though the daydream ends, Willy continues to mutter to himself. The older Happy comes downstairs and tries to quiet Willy. Agitated, Willy shouts his regret about not going to Alaska with his brother, Ben, who eventually found a diamond mine in Africa and became rich. Charley, having heard the commotion, enters. Happy goes off to bed, and Willy and Charley begin to play cards. Charley offers Willy a job, but Willy, insulted, refuses it. As they argue, Willy imagines that Ben enters. Willy accidentally calls Charley Ben. Ben inspects Willy's house and tells him that he has to catch a train soon to look at properties in Alaska. As Willy talks to Ben about the prospect of going to Alaska, Charley, seeing no one there, gets confused and questions Willy. Willy yells at Charley, who leaves. The younger Linda enters and Ben meets her. Willy asks Ben impatiently about his life. Ben recounts his travels and talks about their father. As Ben is about to leave, Willy daydreams further, and Charley and Bernard rush in to tell him that Biff and Happy are stealing lumber. Although Ben eventually leaves, Willy continues to talk to him.

Back in the present, the older Linda enters to find Willy outside. Biff and Happy come downstairs and discuss Willy's condition with their mother. Linda scolds Biff for judging Willy harshly. Biff tells her that he knows Willy is a fake, but he refuses to elaborate. Linda mentions that Willy has tried to commit suicide. Happy grows angry and rebukes Biff for his failure in the business world. Willy enters and yells at Biff. Happy intervenes and eventually proposes that he and Biff go into the sporting goods business together. Willy immediately brightens and gives Biff a host of tips about asking for a loan from one of Biff's old employers, Bill Oliver. After more arguing and reconciliation, everyone finally goes to bed.

Act II opens with Willy enjoying the breakfast that Linda has made for him. Willy ponders the bright-seeming future before getting angry again about his expensive appliances. Linda informs Willy that Biff and Happy are taking him out to dinner that night. Excited, Willy announces that he is going to make Howard Wagner give him a New York job. The phone rings, and Linda chats with Biff, reminding him to be nice to his father at the restaurant that night.

As the lights fade on Linda, they come up on Howard playing with a wire recorder in his office. Willy tries to broach the subject of working in New York, but Howard interrupts him and makes him listen to his kids and wife on the wire recorder. When Willy finally gets a word in, Howard rejects his plea. Willy launches into a lengthy recalling of how a legendary salesman named Dave Singleman inspired him to go into sales. Howard leaves and Willy gets angry. Howard soon re-enters and tells Willy to take some time off. Howard leaves and Ben enters, inviting Willy to join him in Alaska. The younger Linda enters and reminds Willy of his sons and job. The young Biff enters, and Willy praises Biff's prospects and the fact that he is well liked.

Ben leaves and Bernard rushes in, eagerly awaiting Biff's big football game. Willy speaks optimistically to Biff about the game. Charley enters and teases Willy about the game. As Willy chases Charley off, the lights rise on a different part of the stage. Willy continues yelling from offstage, and Jenny, Charley's secretary, asks a grown-up Bernard to quiet him down. Willy enters and prattles on about a "very big deal" that Biff is working on. Daunted by Bernard's success (he mentions to Willy that he is going to Washington to fight a case), Willy asks Bernard why Biff turned out to be such a failure. Bernard asks Willy what happened in Boston that made Biff decide not to go to summer school. Willy defensively tells Bernard not to blame him.

Charley enters and sees Bernard off. When Willy asks for more money than Charley usually loans him, Charley again offers Willy a job. Willy again refuses and eventually tells Charley that he was fired. Charley scolds Willy for always needing to be liked and angrily gives him the money. Calling Charley his only friend, Willy exits on the verge of tears.

At Frank's Chop House, Happy helps Stanley, a waiter, prepare a table. They ogle and chat up a girl, Miss Forsythe, who enters the restaurant. Biff enters, and Happy introduces him to Miss Forsythe, continuing to flirt with her. Miss Forsythe, a call girl, leaves to telephone another call girl (at Happy's request), and Biff spills out that he waited six hours for Bill Oliver and Oliver didn't even recognize him. Upset at his father's unrelenting misconception that he, Biff, was a salesman for Oliver, Biff plans to relieve Willy of his illusions. Willy enters, and Biff tries gently, at first, to tell him what happened at Oliver's office. Willy blurts out that he was fired. Stunned, Biff again tries to let Willy down easily. Happy cuts in with remarks suggesting Biff's success, and Willy eagerly awaits the good news.

Biff finally explodes at Willy for being unwilling to listen. The young Bernard runs in shouting for Linda, and Biff, Happy, and Willy start to argue. As Biff explains what happened, their conversation recedes into the background. The young Bernard tells Linda that Biff failed math. The restaurant conversation comes back into focus and Willy criticizes Biff for failing math. Willy then hears the voice of the hotel operator in Boston and shouts that he is not in his room. Biff scrambles to quiet Willy and claims that Oliver is talking to his partner about giving Biff the money. Willy's renewed interest and probing questions irk Biff more, and he screams at Willy. Willy hears The Woman laugh and he shouts back at Biff, hitting him and staggering. Miss Forsythe enters with another call girl,

Letta. Biff helps Willy to the washroom and, finding Happy flirting with the girls, argues with him about Willy. Biff storms out, and Happy follows with the girls.

Willy and The Woman enter, dressing themselves and flirting. The door knocks and Willy hurries The Woman into the bathroom. Willy answers the door; the young Biff enters and tells Willy that he failed math. Willy tries to usher him out of the room, but Biff imitates his math teacher's lisp, which elicits laughter from Willy and The Woman. Willy tries to cover up his indiscretion, but Biff refuses to believe his stories and storms out, dejected, calling Willy a "phony little fake." Back in the restaurant, Stanley helps Willy up. Willy asks him where he can find a seed store. Stanley gives him directions to one, and Willy hurries off.

The light comes up on the Loman kitchen, where Happy enters looking for Willy. He moves into the living room and sees Linda. Biff comes inside and Linda scolds the boys and slaps away the flowers in Happy's hand. She yells at them for abandoning Willy. Happy attempts to appease her, but Biff goes in search of Willy. He finds Willy planting seeds in the garden with a flashlight. Willy is consulting Ben about a $20,000 proposition. Biff approaches him to say goodbye and tries to bring him inside. Willy moves into the house, followed by Biff, and becomes angry again about Biff's failure. Happy tries to calm Biff, but Biff and Willy erupt in fury at each other. Biff starts to sob, which touches Willy. Everyone goes to bed except Willy, who renews his conversation with Ben, elated at how great Biff will be with $20,000 of insurance money. Linda soon calls out for Willy but gets no response. Biff and Happy listen as well. They hear Willy's car speed away.

In the requiem, Linda and Happy stand in shock after Willy's poorly attended funeral. Biff states that Willy had the wrong dreams. Charley defends Willy as a victim of his profession. Ready to leave, Biff invites Happy to go back out West with him. Happy declares that he will stick it out in New York to validate Willy's death. Linda asks Willy for forgiveness for being unable to cry. She begins to sob, repeating "We're free." All exit, and the flute melody is heard as the curtain falls.

Chapter 10

Character List

Willy Loman

An insecure, self-deluded traveling salesman. Willy believes wholeheartedly in the American Dream of easy success and wealth, but he never achieves it. Nor do his sons fulfill his hope that they will succeed where he has failed.

When Willy's illusions begin to fail under the pressing realities of his life, his mental health begins to unravel. The overwhelming tensions caused by this disparity, as well as those caused by the societal imperatives that drive Willy, form the essential conflict of Death of a Salesman.

Biff Loman

Willy's thirty-four-year-old elder son. Biff led a charmed life in high school as a football star with scholarship prospects, good male friends, and fawning female admirers. He failed math, however, and did not have enough credits to graduate. Since then, his kleptomania has gotten him fired from every job that he has held. Biff represents Willy's vulnerable, poetic, tragic side.

He cannot ignore his instincts, which tell him to abandon Willy's paralyzing dreams and move out West to work with his hands. He ultimately fails to reconcile his life with Willy's expectations of him.

Linda Loman

Willy's loyal, loving wife. Linda suffers through Willy's grandiose dreams and self-delusions. Occasionally, she seems to be taken in by Willy's self-deluded hopes for future glory and success, but at other times, she seems far more realistic and less fragile than her husband. She has nurtured the family through all of Willy's misguided attempts at success, and her emotional strength and perseverance support Willy until his collapse.

Happy Loman

Willy's thirty-two-year-old younger son. Happy has lived in Biff's shadow all of his life, but he compensates by nurturing his relentless sex drive and professional ambition.

Happy represents Willy's sense of self-importance, ambition, and blind servitude to societal expectations Although he works as an assistant to an assistant buyer in a department store, Happy presents himself as supremely important. Additionally, he practices bad business ethics and sleeps with the girlfriends of his superiors.

Charley

Willy's next-door neighbour. Charley owns a successful business and his son, Bernard, is a wealthy, important lawyer. Willy is jealous of Charley's success. Charley gives Willy money to pay his bills, and Willy reveals at one point, choking back tears, that Charley is his only friend.

Bernard

Bernard is Charley's son and an important, successful lawyer. Although Willy used to mock Bernard for studying hard, Bernard always loved Willy's sons dearly and regarded Biff as a hero. Bernard's success is difficult for Willy to accept because his own sons' lives do not measure up.

Ben

Willy's wealthy older brother. Ben has recently died and appears only in Willy's "daydreams." Willy regards Ben as a symbol of the success that he so desperately craves for himself and his sons.

The Woman

Willy's mistress when Happy and Biff were in high school. The Woman's attention and admiration boost Willy's fragile ego. When Biff catches Willy in his hotel room with The Woman, he loses faith in his father, and his dream of passing math and going to college dies.

Howard Wagner

Willy's boss. Howard inherited the company from his father, whom Willy regarded as "a masterful man" and "a prince." Though much younger than Willy, Howard treats Willy with condescension and eventually fires him, despite Willy's wounded assertions that he named Howard at his birth.

Stanley

A waiter at Frank's Chop House. Stanley and Happy seem to be friends, or at least acquaintances, and they banter about and ogle Miss Forsythe together before Biff and Willy arrive at the restaurant.

Miss Forsythe and Letta

Two young women whom Happy and Biff meet at Frank's Chop House. It seems likely that Miss Forsythe and Letta are prostitutes, judging from Happy's repeated comments about their moral character and the fact that they are "on call."

Jenny

Charley's secretary.

Chapter 11

Analysis of Major Characters

Willy Loman

Despite his desperate searching through his past, Willy does not achieve the self-realization or self-knowledge typical of the tragic hero. The quasi-resolution that his suicide offers him represents only a partial discovery of the truth. While he achieves a professional understanding of himself and the fundamental nature of the sales profession, Willy fails to realise his personal failure and betrayal of his soul and family through the meticulously constructed artifice of his life. He cannot grasp the true personal, emotional, spiritual understanding of himself as a literal "loman" or "low man." Willy is too driven by his own "willy"-ness or perverse "willfulness" to recognize the slanted reality that his desperate mind has forged. Still, many critics, focusing on Willy's entrenchment in a quagmire of lies, delusions, and self-deceptions, ignore the significant accomplishment of his partial self-realization. Willy's failure to recognize the anguished love offered to him by his family is crucial to the climax of his torturous day, and the play presents this incapacity as the real tragedy. Despite this failure, Willy makes the most extreme sacrifice in his attempt to leave an inheritance that will allow Biff to fulfill the American Dream.

Ben's Final Mantra

"The jungle is dark, but full of diamonds"—turns Willy's suicide into a metaphorical moral struggle, a final skewed ambition to realise his full commercial and material capacity. His final act, according to Ben, is "not like an appointment at all" but like a "diamond rough and hard to the touch." In the absence of any real degree of self-knowledge or truth, Willy is able to achieve a tangible result. In some respect, Willy does experience a sort of revelation, as he finally comes to understand that the product he sells is himself. Through the imaginary advice of Ben, Willy ends up fully believing his earlier assertion to Charley that "after all the highways, and the trains, and the appointments, and the years, you end up worth more dead than alive."

Biff Loman

Unlike Willy and Happy, Biff feels compelled to seek the truth about himself. While his father and brother are unable to accept the miserable reality of their respective lives, Biff acknowledges his failure and eventually manages to confront it. Even the difference between his name and theirs reflects this polarity: whereas Willy and Happy willfully and happily delude themselves, Biff bristles stiffly at self-deception. Biff's discovery that Willy has a mistress strips him of his faith in Willy and Willy's ambitions for him. Consequently, Willy sees Biff as an underachiever, while Biff sees himself as trapped in Willy's grandiose fantasies. After his epiphany in Bill Oliver's office, Biff determines to break through the lies surrounding the Loman family in order to come to realistic terms with his own life. Intent on revealing the simple and humble truth behind Willy's fantasy, Biff longs for the territory (the symbolically free West) obscured by his father's blind faith in a skewed, materialist version of the American Dream. Biff's identity crisis is a function of his and his father's disillusionment, which, in order to reclaim his identity, he must expose.

Happy Loman

Happy shares none of the poetry that erupts from Biff and that is buried in Willy—he is the stunted incarnation of Willy's worst traits and the embodiment of the lie of the happy American Dream. As such, Happy is a difficult character with whom to empathize. He is one-dimensional and static throughout the play. His empty vow to avenge Willy's death by finally "beat[ing] this racket" provides evidence of his critical condition: for Happy, who has lived in the shadow of the inflated expectations of his brother, there is no escape from the Dream's indoctrinated lies. Happy's diseased condition is irreparable—he lacks even the tiniest spark of self-knowledge or capacity for self-analysis. He does share Willy's capacity for self-delusion, trumpeting himself as the assistant buyer at his store, when, in reality, he is only an assistant to the assistant buyer. He does not possess a hint of the latent thirst for knowledge that proves Biff's salvation. Happy is a doomed, utterly duped figure, destined to be swallowed up by the force of blind ambition that fuels his insatiable sex drive.

Linda Loman and Charley

Linda and Charley serve as forces of reason throughout the play. Linda is probably the most enigmatic and complex character in Death of a Salesman, or even in all of Miller's work. Linda views freedom as an escape from debt, the reward of total ownership of the material goods that symbolize success and stability. Willy's prolonged obsession with the American Dream seems, over the long years of his marriage, to have left Linda internally conflicted. Nevertheless, Linda, by far the toughest, most realistic, and most levelheaded character in the play, appears to have kept her emotional life intact. As such, she represents the emotional core of the drama.

If Linda is a sort of emotional prophet, overcome by the inevitable end that she foresees with startling clarity, then Charley functions as a sort of poetic prophet or sage. Miller portrays Charley as ambiguously gendered or effeminate, much like Tiresias, the mythological seer in Sophocles' Oedipus plays. Whereas Linda's lucid diagnosis of Willy's rapid decline is made possible by her emotional sanity, Charley's prognosis of the situation is logical, grounded firmly in practical reasoned analysis. He recognizes Willy's financial failure, and the job offer that he extends to Willy constitutes a commonsense solution. Though he is not terribly fond of Willy, Charley understands his plight and shields him from blame.

Chapter 12

Plot Overview

Act 1, Part 1

A flute plays softly as the light rises on a house surrounded by tall, angular buildings. The sparsely decorated kitchen is visible with a dark drape at the back leading into the living room. To the left and up a little is a second story bedroom with only a brass bed and a straight chair. Above the unseen living room is another bedroom with two beds; a stairway at the left curves up to the room from the kitchen. The empty stage between the house and the audience is the back yard, the scene of Willy's imaginings, as well as the city scenes. Whenever the action of the play is in the present, the characters act as if the imaginary walls are real and they enter and exit rooms only through doors. But when the action is in a memory, the characters step through the walls and onto the forestage.

Willy Loman, a sixty-year-old traveling salesman, enters his home late at night with two large sample cases. His wife, Linda, hears him coming up the stairs to their bedroom. She seems worried that something has happened, that he has wrecked the car again, or that he's ill, but Willy assures her that he is fine, just tired. Sitting on the bed with her, he explains that he came home because he was having trouble staying on the road while he drove, and he is unsure of what caused his distraction. It could've been the coffee he had at a roadside diner or the way he opened the windshield of the car and the scenery and sunshine just washed over him. Whatever it was, it kept taking his mind of the road, and he'd veer onto the shoulder before he knew what was happening. He was so spooked that he drove ten miles an hour all the way home, and now he's tired and grumpy because he's going to miss his morning meeting in Portland, Rhode Island. Linda urges him to talk to his boss about working in the New York area so that he doesn't have to travel anymore, but he says to her, "They don't need me in New York. I'm the New England man. I'm vital in New England." Act 1, Part 1, pg. 4. After more discussion of all the reasons why he should be working in New York, Linda suggests again that he go speak with his boss, Howard Wagner. Willy finally agrees to do it, emphasizing that if Wagner's father were still in charge of the company, Willy would have already had a New York job. Wagner doesn't appreciate Willy the way his father did. Linda offers to make Willy a sandwich to calm him down, but he changes the subject to their sons, Biff and Happy, who are asleep in their shared room. Willy mentions the fight he and Biff had that morning, and Linda gently chides him for criticizing Biff just when he got home. Willy says, "I simply asked him if he was making any money. Is that a criticism?" They argue over Biff, Linda saying that he just has to find himself and Willy claiming that at thirty-four, he'll never find himself if he keeps working as a farmhand. Willy says he's lazy, but then he says he can't understand how such an attractive and hard-working man as Biff could be lost in America, the greatest country in the world. He gets caught up in remembering how Biff was so popular in high school, but Linda brings him back to the present. Willy starts to complain about the way their house is surrounded by apartment buildings now. He goes on a tirade about the increase in the population that has caused so many people to move in around them, and his voice wakes Biff and Happy in their room. Linda hushes Willy and sends him downstairs, but before he goes, his confrontational mood subsides and he assures Linda that if Biff wants to return to Texas, he won't stop him. He says that he believes Biff will get it together soon enough. As he's walking out the bedroom door to go downstairs to the kitchen, Linda suggests that over the weekend they all go for a picnic; they can open the car's windshield like Willy did earlier. The flute music plays again, and Willy hears it as he corrects Linda about opening the windshield. He remembers that the Studebaker's windshield doesn't open. He'd spent the entire day thinking that he was driving the Chevy he owned when his sons were in high school. The flute music that only Willy can hear startles him, and Linda plays off the discrepancy. Willy goes downstairs to make a sandwich, mumbling to himself about the old days with the Chevy. The boys are awake in their room over the invisible living room, and they overhear the end of their parents' conversation and Willy's muttering.

Act 1, Part 2

Light rises in the boys' upstairs bedroom, and Biff gets out of bed and walks downstage as if standing near the door of their room and listening down the stairs to Willy's mumbling. Hap tells Biff how Willy has been acting strangely lately, mumbling to himself as if he's talking to Biff, and how he's been having trouble driving. Biff plays it off as nothing, and they reminisce about their younger days in that house and then talk about where their lives are now. Biff, walking around restlessly, admits that he has gone through job after job, but he hasn't been able to find one that sticks, one that seems worthwhile to him. He was happy ranching in Texas until spring came and he felt compelled to head home. He tells Happy, "I've always made a point of not wasting my life, and every time I come back here I know that all I've done is to waste my life."

Hap talks about the frustration of working for executives he can physically outmatch, and about having to work his way up. He explains that even though he has his own apartment, car, and plenty of women, he's still dissatisfied. Biff suggests that he and Happy buy a ranch and work it together. Hap thinks it's a great idea, but then his interest shifts back to showing the executives for whom he works that he can beat them at their own game. He wants the kind of respect that his merchandise manager, who makes $52,000 a year, gets when he walks in the store. Hap's already on his way, he swears, because he gets any woman he wants, including the fiancees of the top executives of the company for which he works. But even this is losing its charm for him. Hap also tells Biff that in much the same way that he can't help dallying with women engaged to his superiors, he also can't seem to refuse bribes at work. Biff admits that he doesn't run around chasing women anymore because he's looking for someone steady, like his mother, but he takes very little notice of Hap's confession of taking bribes. It doesn't even make a dent with Biff.

While Hap talks, Biff decides to meet with Bill Oliver, a former employer who once told Biff to come to him for help if he ever needed it. Biff believes that Oliver will loan him enough money to buy a ranch, and Hap encourages Biff to ask for it because Oliver liked Biff; Willy had taught them that being well liked is the key to success in business. Biff worries that Oliver might still believe that he stole a carton of basketballs, which is why he quit working for Oliver. He had to leave before Oliver could fire him for stealing.

As Biff and Hap are discussing Oliver, Willy starts talking downstairs like he's having a conversation. Biff gets mad at his father because he knows that Linda can hear him talking like a lunatic downstairs, and Hap asks Biff not to leave again because he doesn't know how to handle Willy anymore. The boys, disturbed by their father's behaviour, get back in bed and try to go back to sleep. The light on their room fades.

Act 1, Part 3

As Willy roots around in the kitchen, he is dimly lit while the apartments in the background fade away and the whole house is covered with leaves. Flute music plays softly and sweetly. Sitting at the kitchen table with a glass of milk, Willy's mumbling grows louder until it's directed at a specific point off-stage and he's looking through the invisible kitchen wall. He's no longer mumbling. His voice is loud like he's conversing with someone. He warns Biff about making promises to girls because he is too young to be serious about girls; he seems impressed that Biff is so popular that the girls pay for the dates. Willy tells Biff and Hap that they did a good job polishing the Chevy. Young Biff and Hap walk onstage from the direction Willy was looking, and they ask for the surprise Willy had promised, which turns out to be a punching bag so they could improve their timing. Happy keeps asking if Willy has noticed that he's lost weight. Willy dismisses him with an inattentive comment and continues talking to Biff. Biff shows Willy the new football he "borrowed" from the locker room to work on passing, and Willy laughingly tells him to return it. But when Hap suggests that Willy should be unhappy that Biff stole the ball, Willy justifies Biff's action by saying that the coach would "probably congratulate [Biff] on [his] initiative" instead of being angry about the theft because the coach likes Biff. They talk about Willy's trip and Willy tells them that he will have his own business someday that will be bigger than Charley's, their neighbour, because Willy is well liked whereas Charley is not.

Willy tells the boys that he met the mayor of Providence while he was away on his last trip. He promises to take the boys along with him in the summer so they can see New England, the place where Willy is well known and well liked. As Biff practices passing the football, he and Willy talk about how important Biff is socially since he was made captain of the football team. Willy is proud that his son is well liked. Biff, taking Willy's hand, promises to make a touchdown for Willy at the next game. As they are talking about it, Bernard, Charley's nerdy son, enters the front of the stage and comes over to remind Biff that they are supposed to study together that day; Biff is close to flunking math.

Willy makes fun of Bernard when he suggests that Biff might not graduate because of his grades. Willy doesn't believe that anyone would fail a kid who has scholarships to three universities. When Bernard leaves, Willy tells the boys that because Bernard is not well liked, he will never make it in the business world despite his good grades. He says, "the man who makes an appearance in the business world, the man who creates a personal interest, is the man who gets ahead. Be liked and you will never want." He brags more about how well known he is until a youthful Linda appears. She asks Willy if the Chevy drives well and he claims it is the greatest car ever built. The boys take the laundry from their mother to hang it up for her, and then Biff walks through the wall-line of the kitchen to the doorway at the back, and orders the friends he has waiting in the basement to sweep out the furnace room. Willy and Linda are both impressed by the way Biff's friends obey him. Linda asks Willy how much he sold on his trip and he tells her first that he sold $1200; she figures out that his commission from the sale would be $212.

He hesitates at the figure, and then says that he sold $200, making his commission only $70. While Linda adds up the total of their monthly payments, they move through the wall-line and into the kitchen. She realizes that they owe $120 in payments on their appliances and for the Chevy's new carburetor. Willy insists that he shouldn't have to pay for the carburetor because Chevy automobiles are such pieces of junk, that manufacturing them should be prohibited.

Pressured by how much money he owes, Willy worries that business won't pick up. While Linda is in the kitchen darning stockings, he moves to the edge of the stage. He tells her that he'll go to Hartford the next week because, he says, "I'm very well liked in Hartford. You know, the trouble is, Linda, people don't seem to take to me." Act 1, Part 3, pg. 23 Willy feels like people are either laughing at him or ignoring him. He thinks that maybe it's because he's fat — he'd overheard some man call him a walrus and smacked him in the face for it. Linda assures him that he is a handsome man, the handsomest man in the world to her. Through her words of reassurance, Willy hears the sound of another woman's laughter, but he keeps talking to Linda. Music plays softly and seemingly far away as he tells Linda that he worries about not providing a life for her and the boys. As he talks, the other woman is dimly seen to the left of the house and she is dressing.

Act 1, Part 4

The area to the left of the house gets brighter and Willy walks into it. The woman redresses while she talks to Willy.

She tells him that she enjoys their times together because Willy has a great sense of humour. She promises they will get together when he comes back to town in a few weeks and she'll put him right through to the buyers at the company where she's a secretary. She thanks him for the silk stockings he bought her and leaves. She's laughing as she goes, and her laughter blends into Linda's as the light on the woman goes dark and the kitchen table brightens around Linda, who is darning a pair of silk stockings.

Act 1, Part 5

As the light brightens over the kitchen table, Willy moves to the kitchen and notices Linda darning her silk stockings. He tells her to throw them away. His guilt at giving the secretary silk stockings while his wife had to mend her own makes him angry. Then Bernard runs onto the stage looking for Biff, so that they can study for the state exam. Willy moves to the forestage in agitation and tells Bernard to give Biff the answers, but Bernard refuses because it is a state exam and he doesn't want to get in trouble. Willy, still angry, threatens to whip Bernard. Linda says that Biff needs to return the football to the locker room and that he is so rough with the girls that all the mothers are afraid of him. Bernard says that Biff is driving the car without a license. Willy, overwhelmed by Linda and Bernard as well as the sound of the woman's laughter, yells at them to shut up. Bernard leaves the stage, but warns on his way out that Biff will flunk math if he doesn't study. As Linda agrees that Biff needs to shape up, Willy explodes at her and says that Biff is doing nothing wrong, that he's just spirited and has personality, unlike Bernard. As Linda goes into the living room almost in tears, Willy is alone again in the kitchen and the apartment buildings are visible behind the house. In the darkness of night, Willy wonders aloud what he ever told Biff that made him steal things.

Act 1, Part 6

Happy comes downstairs and Willy snaps back into the present. Hap tries to calm his dad and take him upstairs to bed, but Willy rambles on about how Linda shouldn't have waxed the floor because it might hurt her back. Hap asks him why he came back from his trip, and Willy says that he almost ran over someone in Yonkers, and it scared him. He wonders aloud why he didn't go to Alaska with his brother, Ben, when he had the chance. Ben was rich by the age of twenty-one because he had a diamond mine.

Hap tells Willy that he's going to retire him for life, and Willy ridicules him because he only makes $70 a week, and that won't retire him, and now Willy can't even drive past Yonkers anymore. Amid Willy's frantic tirade, Charley comes in the kitchen to find out what the noise is all about because he can hear through the thin walls. Hap goes up to bed while Willy sits down at the kitchen table with Charley to play cards. Willy insults Charley with his condescension, but Charley ignores it. Charley offers him a job so that he won't have to travel; Willy is offended, but Charley only means well.

Willy tells him that Biff is going back to Texas to be a farmhand, and Charley tells him not to worry about it, to forget Biff. Willy says if he does that, he'll have nothing to remember. He then changes the subject to the ceiling he put up. Charley tries to go along with the conversation, to seem interested, but Willy insults him more.

As the men talk, Ben enters the forestage from the right corner of the house and his music plays. Willy calls Charley by Ben's name while Ben stands on the forestage looking around and then glances at his watch insisting that he only has a few minutes. Charley and Willy continue their card game as Willy explains that a couple of weeks ago, they got a letter from Ben's wife telling them he was dead.

That was the only time they'd heard of him since he came to their home briefly on his way back to Africa. Ben asks Willy questions, and as Willy answers, Charley tries to follow the conversation that Willy seems to be having with himself. In the confusion of past and present colliding in Willy's head, he accuses Charley of cheating at their card game and Charley storms out. Willy walks through the wall-line of the kitchen to where Ben stands.

Act 1, Part 7

Ben and Willy meet for the first time since Willy was almost four years old. Willy wants him to divulge the secret of his success, to tell him what happened after he left to follow their father to Alaska. Ben tells him that instead of going to Alaska, he ended up in Africa. Ben says, "when I was seventeen I walked into the jungle, and when I was twenty-one I walked out. And by God I was rich." Act 1, Part 7, pg. 33 After Ben tells his story, he tries to leave, but Willy calls young Biff and Hap onstage and asks Ben to tell them about their grandfather - anything else to make him stay longer. Ben seems to be in a hurry to leave. Ben tells the boys about how their grandfather made and sold flutes. He would load his family into their wagon and travel westward from Boston to sell the flutes he made. Ben points out that their grandfather was such a great inventor and salesman, that he could make more in a week than a man like Willy could make in a lifetime.

Willy insists that he's bringing his boys up to be well rounded and well liked, and he makes Biff box with his uncle to prove it. As they spar, Ben trips Biff and stands over him with the point of his umbrella near Biff's eye. He tells Biff, "Never fight fair with a stranger, boy. You'll never get out of the jungle that way."

Act 1, Part 7, pg. 34 Youthful Linda, spooked by the whole display, repeatedly asks why Biff has to fight with his uncle, but Willy doesn't see anything bizarre in it, because he is too busy trying to impress Ben. In an attempt to prove that he has the pioneer spirit and the ingenuity of his father, Willy sends the boys to a nearby construction site to steal sand so they can rebuild their stoop immediately. Charley walks over and warns Willy that the cops are watching out for the boys because they've already stolen lumber. Willy bragged about their theft, although he gave the boys a mock lecture for stealing. Ben seems as proud as Willy that the boys are fearless. When Bernard reports that the watchman is chasing Biff, Willy insists that Biff wasn't stealing anything — he was doing nothing wrong. Linda, worried, leaves to look for Biff. Charley complains about business in New England and Willy insists that he has no problems selling in New England because he has the right contacts. Charley sarcastically congratulates Willy and then leaves. Ben begins to leave again, but Willy asks him to stay and talk about their father because Willy was a baby when he left; not having a chance to talk with his dad left him feeling "kind of temporary about [him]self." Act 1, Part 7, pg. 36 Ben promises to visit on his way back to Africa, and he assures Willy that he's teaching his sons the right things. Ben caps it all off with his words of wisdom about how he went into the jungle at twenty-one and came out rich, and then Ben walks around the right corner of the house and disappears.

Act 1, Part 8

Linda comes downstairs in her nightgown and robe and sees Willy out in the yard talking to himself through the door, so she goes out to check on him. In his mumbling, he asks her what happened to the diamond watch Ben gave him, and she reminds him that he pawned it almost thirteen years before to pay for Biff's radio correspondence course. Despite Linda's urging him to come inside, Willy wants to go for a walk, so he disappears around the left corner of the house in his slippers, muttering the whole way.

Biff comes downstairs into the kitchen and asks Linda how long Willy's been this way. Happy comes down the stairs not far behind him, and Linda gives them both a verbal lashing about the way they treat their father — they don't write or visit often enough, and they don't care enough about him to ask how things are going with him. Biff, touching her hair, notices that it's gray, that she's looking older, and she tells him that he can't keep coming home just to see her. Every time he comes home, he and Willy fight, and she doesn't know what's come between them, but she doesn't want Biff around if he's going to treat his father poorly.

She tells him that she won't allow him to make Willy feel bad anymore. He's either got to pay him the respect a father deserves or not come back again. Biff can't understand why she's so quick to protect Willy when he's always wiped the floor with her, and Hap pipes up to defend his father. Biff insists that Willy has no character, that he's weak, and Linda again defends her husband. "I don't say he's a great man. Willy Loman never made a lot of money. His name was never in the paper. He's not the finest character that ever lived. But he's a human being, and a terrible thing is happening to him. So attention must be paid. He's not to be allowed to fall into his grave like an old dog. Attention, attention must be finally paid to such a person."

She tells the boys that Willy is no longer a salaried salesman, but has been demoted to earning only commission, just like a beginner. He drives seven hundred miles to Boston and back, and he makes no money on the trips because all the contacts he once had are retired or dead. No one knows him any more, and he has to borrow $50 a week from Charley to pretend it's his salary so that Linda won't know he's been demoted. He's spent his entire life working for the benefit of his children, and now they are both immoral failures. Biff, out of a sense of obligation to his father, agrees to live at home and find a job in the city, but Linda insists that he can't stay if he's going to be hateful to Willy.

She wants to know what turned him against his father; he used to admire him so much and do anything to make him proud. Biff says that Willy threw him out because Biff knew he was a fake, but Biff won't explain any further. He agrees to stay and pitch in half of his paycheck, but before he can go upstairs to bed, Linda has one more confession to make to the boys. She tells them that Willy's been trying to kill himself. She says that the insurance inspector has evidence that all the times that he's smashed up the car over the last year haven't been accidents.

Linda reveals that there's some woman (this gets Biff's attention but he won't explain why) who saw Willy deliberately smash the car into the railing of a bridge. He wasn't driving fast, and he didn't skid before he crashed. The only thing that saved him was that the water was shallow. Biff tries to chalk it up to falling asleep behind the wheel, but Linda tells them that she found a short length of rubber piping in the basement with an attachment that fixes on to the rubber nipple on the gas valve of the water heater. She accidentally came across it and every day she takes it out of the basement, but puts it back before he comes home because she can't bear to insult him by confronting him about it. She blames his suicide attempts on the fact that he's put his whole life into the boys, and now they've turned their backs on him. They ignore him the way everyone else does now that his contacts are gone. Sobbing, she tells Biff that Willy's life is in his hands.

This accusation makes Biff feel bad for fighting with his dad, and he promises her that he'll behave better. Although he hates the business world, he'll go and be successful at it. Happy tells him that his problem in business was that he never tried to please people, that he did crazy things like whistling in the elevator. Biff and Hap begin arguing about whistling in the elevator and taking a day off in the summer to be outside. Hap insists that if you're going to play hooky, you've got to cover yourself so that your boss can't pin you for lying. Hap says that some people in the business world think Biff's crazy, and Biff says that he doesn't care. He says that the business world has laughed at Willy for years, too, because they don't belong in the city; they should be out in the country working with their hands and whistling when they want to. Willy walks into the house in time to hear the end of the argument. He says that Biff never grew up, and that Bernard doesn't whistle in the elevator.

The argument flares again as Willy disputes Biff's claim that people in the business world consider Willy Loman crazy. He insists that his name still carries great weight in New England stores. As he's heading up the stairs to bed, Hap tells him that Biff is going to see Bill Oliver the next day to convince him to stake Biff's business. Willy suggests selling sporting goods, and Biff, still tentative about the plan, tries to explain that he hasn't met with Oliver yet. Willy is sarcastic and Biff gets angry; he walks toward the stairs to go to bed and Willy keeps jabbing at him. Hap tries to end the argument by telling Biff his idea for going into the sporting goods business together as the Loman Brothers; they would sell their products by traveling and having sporting exhibitions where they could form teams and play against each other using the products they're selling. That way they'd be able to play ball, be the executives, work together, and make money. The American Dream — doing what they love, being their own boss, and getting rich off of it. Willy thinks it's a great idea and he gives Biff instructions on how to approach Oliver about the money — wear a suit, don't make jokes, don't talk too much, but tell his good stories and laugh because "personality always wins the day." As he's talking, Linda keeps chiming in and Willy keeps snapping at her about interrupting. Biff tells him not to yell at her, and he and Willy start arguing again just when everything seemed peaceful. In the middle of the yelling, Willy just stops arguing and walks away from them and into the living room, but he doesn't leave in a rage.

He seems to be giving in for now, feeling guilty and beaten. Linda asks Biff why he picked another fight with Willy just when he was being nice and things were sounding hopeful. She asks the boys to tell him goodnight so that he doesn't go to bed angry, and they agree before she leaves the kitchen to go upstairs. On their way upstairs, planning for the next morning's meeting with Oliver, Biff begins to talk confidently to Hap, and things start looking up. Meanwhile, Willy is in the bathroom upstairs putting on his pajamas and telling Linda how bumming around was the best thing for Biff because it's given him caliber for success. Biff overhears him as he and Hap come into Willy and Linda's room to say goodnight. Willy keeps giving him more advice for the meeting, like how he shouldn't pick up anything that might fall off the desk because that's a job for an office boy, not Biff.

Willy tells him to lie about his work out West — say it was business, not farm work. Throughout all this advice, he interrupts Linda and snaps at her some more, and Biff nears his breaking point again. He leaves the room before he picks another fight, and Willy tells him that he'll do well tomorrow because he's destined for greatness. Hap sticks his head in his parents' room to tell his mom that he's going to get married. She just dismisses him like Willy does, and he leaves. As they're drifting off to sleep, Willy reminds Linda of the championship football game when Biff waved to him from the field in front of everyone while the fans were chanting Biff's name. He knows Biff will be great because, "a star like that, magnificent, can never really fade away!" Act 1, Part 8, pg. 51. He ignores Linda when she asks what Biff has against him, but promises to talk to Howard, his boss, in the morning about working in New York. The light on Willy fades to darkness. Biff goes back downstairs and onto the forestage to smoke a cigarette. Through the kitchen wall, the water heater's gas flame begins to glow while Willy talks to Linda upstairs. Biff walks in the kitchen and goes down into the basement to find the piping Linda told them about. He takes it upstairs with him and the curtain falls.

Act 2, Part 1

Happy music plays and then fades as the curtain rises. Willy sits at the kitchen table with his coffee. He is cheerful and optimistic as Linda tells him that Biff and Hap were bright and hopeful as well before they left. Things are looking up for the Loman family. Willy builds his bright dreams of how life is going to change after today — they are going to go into business together and Willy and Linda will move out to the country and build two guesthouses so the boys can bring their families for the weekend. While Willy is dreaming out loud, Linda reminds him to ask Wagner, his boss, for an advance to pay Willy's insurance premium. While she ticks off the list of expenses, they have had recently that put them a little behind financially, Willy gripes about the quality of appliances and automobiles, and how everything breaks just when it's paid for. He goes on a tirade about the refrigerator.

He says that they should have bought one that was well advertised because Charley bought a General Electric refrigerator and has never had a problem with it. He interrupts Linda before she can remind him that the Hastings refrigerator they bought had the biggest ads in the paper. Linda reminds him that they have one more payment to make before their house is paid for, and Willy points out the irony that when it's paid for, there will be only the two of them to live in it.

He's gathering his coat and getting ready to go meet Wagner about a New York job and an advance, when Linda tells him that Biff and Hap want him to meet them for dinner at Frank's Chop House. He's so excited that his sons want to treat him to dinner that his enthusiasm for the day is boosted and life looks full of promise. He can't help but be successful today, so he goes to meet Wagner. He comes back in one last time because he forgot a handkerchief and he notices Linda mending her silk stockings. He tells her to quit mending those while he's in the house because it makes him nervous, so she hides them as he leaves. As Willy disappears offstage, Biff calls to make sure his mother told Willy about their dinner plans.

She is excited to tell him that Willy must have moved the rubber piping, but Biff tells her that he took it the night before. She seems disappointed because she thought that if Willy had moved it himself, that meant that the danger had passed. Because Biff moved it, she's still a little uneasy about Willy's state of mind. Yet Willy was in such good spirits that morning, she thinks things are changing and that life is getting better for all of them. Biff tells her he's waiting to see Bill Oliver, and before they get off the phone, she tells him to be good to his father at dinner because it will save his life. In the middle of Linda's speech, Wagner rolls a small typewriter table with a wire-recording machine on it onto the left forefront of the stage and plugs it in. Light fades from Linda and rises on Wagner as he threads the machine.

Act 2, Part 2

Willy comes into Wagner's office in an almost timid way while Wagner is threading a wire-recording machine. Willy keeps trying to talk to Wagner, but Wagner interrupts him time after time to show him the miracles of the recording machine and play back the voices of his son and daughter as they whistle songs and recite state capitals into the machine. When Willy finally finds a way to lead the conversation about the recording machine into a discussion of how he no longer wants to be on the road, Wagner realizes that Willy is supposed to be in Boston that day. He asks if Willy "didn't crack up again"

Act 2, Part 2, pg. 59 because that's happened several times before. Willy, ignoring the question, asks for a New York job, reminding Wagner that he told Willy at Christmas that he'd look for a local space for him. Wagner can't help him. Willy pushes harder, bringing up Wagner's father at every opportunity, as if claiming some great friendship with the man will guilt Wagner into finding a place for him. Willy gets angry as Wagner keeps refusing him, and Willy tries to explain to Wagner why he chose to be a salesman. Wagner hardly listens as Willy tells a story about Dave Singleman, the 84-year-old salesman who traveled from city to city making his sales from his hotel room because so many people knew and liked him. Buyers and salesman from all over New England attended his funeral, and that was Willy's aspiration when he went into sales. That's why he didn't go to Alaska with his brother, Ben. He stuck with sales because, "[in those days there was personality in it There was respect, and comradeship, and gratitude in it. Today, it's all cut and dried, and there's no chance for bringing friendship to bear — or personality They don't know [Willy] any more."

Act 2, Part 2, pg. 61. He asks Wagner again to find him a salaried position in New York, but Wagner can't do it. Willy explodes, yelling at Wagner that he's put thirty-four years into the company and now he can't even pay his insurance. Willy insists that "[you can't eat the orange and throw the peel away — a man is not a piece of fruit!" Act 2, Part 2, pg. 61-2 After the outburst and a final refusal, Wagner leaves Willy in the office to pull himself together, and Willy realizes that he has just snapped. In his efforts to recover from the emotional tumult, he bumps the recorder machine and it comes on spouting the recorded voice of Wagner's son listing the state capitals. The noise scares Willy and he calls out to Wagner who comes in and unplugs the machine.

Willy, wilted in defeat, tells Wagner that he'll go to Boston tomorrow. Wagner, however, tells him that he doesn't want Willy representing the company anymore. He fires Willy and tells him to let his sons, his fine boys, take care of him for a while so he can get some rest. Wagner leaves the office again pushing the recording machine off stage left. Willy stares into space and Ben's music begins playing again as Ben enters from the right.

Act 2, Part 3

Ben, as he keeps looking at his watch, urges Willy to leave the city and go to Alaska where a fortune is waiting to be made, and Willy's delighted at the prospect for a moment. Linda says she doesn't understand why everybody has to conquer the world. She says that Willy's life is good enough — he's well liked and his boys loved him, and he is building a relationship with his boss and the firm he works for. Ben responds by saying that if he can't lay his hand on what he's building, then he's not building anything. But Willy, remembering Dave Singleman, believes that he can match Ben's success with his own on the basis of just being liked. He believes that contacts and personality and popularity will make him rich, and the same things will make Biff a success as well.

Young Biff and Hap walk in, with Happy carrying Biff's football uniform. Ben leaves that day telling Willy that Alaska could make him rich, and Willy assures Ben that he'll make it rich from Brooklyn. Ben and his music fade into the happy music of Young Biff and Hap as Bernard rushes on stage looking for Biff and afraid that the Lomans had left for the game without him. Willy and Linda are getting ready to go to the game, and Willy walks through the wall-line of the kitchen and to the door at the back that leads into the living room, while Bernard and Happy argue over who gets to carry Biff's helmet and shoulder pads. The happy music fades away. Biff is standing in the yard when Willy walks back out through the wall-line of the kitchen to talk to him.

Willy is so proud of Biff, and Biff reminds him to watch for the moment when he takes his helmet off so Willy will know the touchdown is for him. Charley comes onto the stage. He jokes about the game and Willy gets mad at him because he isn't taking the biggest day of Biff's life seriously. Willy's temper flares and he wants to fight Charley, but Charley only tells him to grow up and walks away around the left corner of the stage. The music swells to a frenzied pitch, as Willy follows him around the house yelling after him.

Act 2, Part 4

Light rises on the right forefront of the stage where Bernard, all grown up, sits whistling to himself in the waiting room of Charley's office. Willy's voice precedes him as he comes into the office still yelling. Charley's secretary asks Bernard to handle Willy because it always upsets his father whenever Willy comes into the office. So when Willy walks in, still talking football, Bernard makes small talk with him. Bernard tells Willy he's got a case in Washington and he has stopped by his dad's office to say goodbye before he leaves. Willy notices the tennis racquets by Bernard's bag, and Bernard tells him that the friend he's staying with has his own courts. Bernard's wife just had their second son.

Willy is impressed and feels compelled to lie about Biff's success. He tells Bernard that Biff was working out West when Bill Oliver called him in because he wanted Biff to work for him very badly. Bernard just changes the subject and asks Willy if he's still working for the same firm and Willy gets choked up.

Then he asks Bernard to explain the secret of success. He wants Bernard to tell him why Biff is a failure, why it worked out that "his life ended after that Ebbets Field game" because "[from the age of seventeen nothing good ever happened to him." Act 2, Part 4, pg. 71 Bernard answers that he never trained himself for anything. He points out that although Biff flunked math and didn't graduate, he could've taken summer school, but for some reason he just gave up. Bernard remembers that Biff went to see Willy in Boston after he found out he flunked math. He was going to take summer school, but after he came back from visiting Willy in Boston, he threw his University of Virginia sneakers into the furnace because he didn't want to go anymore.

Bernard says, "I've often thought of how strange it was that I knew he'd given up his life." Act 2, Part 4, pg. 72 He asks Willy what happened in Boston, but Willy is defensive and argumentative. Charley comes out of his office before things get out of hand and tells Willy that Bernard is off to Washington to try a case before the Supreme Court. Willy is shocked, but happy for him. Bernard leaves the stage. When Bernard leaves, Charley gives Willy $50, but Willy tells him that he needs more to make his insurance payment. Charley has offered him a job before, but Willy won't take it, and now Charley is offended that Willy will take his money, but he won't work for him. The men argue and Willy admits that he was fired today and is outraged that Wagner could fire him after Willy was so close to Wagner's father when he had been in charge. Willy claims he had even named Wagner; he'd named him Howard, and the man still fired him. Charley says:

"Willy, when're you gonna realise that them things don't mean anything. You named him Howard, but you can't sell that. The only thing you got in this world is what you can sell. And the funny thing is that you're a salesman, and you don't know that." Act 2, Part 4, pg. 75

Charley tells him that being well liked doesn't mean anything; it doesn't make you rich. A lot of successful people weren't well liked, but they were successful. Again he offers Willy a job, but Willy won't take it; Charley gives him the money for the insurance payment, and Willy says, "After all the highways, and the trains, and the appointments, and the years, you end up worth more dead than alive." Act 2, Part 4, pg. 76 Charley gets a little worried, and then Willy apologizes for arguing with Bernard, assuring himself that one day he, Biff, and Hap will all be successful. Near tears, Willy says that Charley's the only friend he's got, and then he leaves. All the light blacks out before rowdy music plays and a red glow comes up behind the screen at right.

Act 2, Part 5

Happy and a waiter set up a table in the private part of Frank's Chop House, where he, Biff, and Willy are planning to meet for dinner. Hap tells the waiter that his brother, a big cattleman from out West, is in town, so bring out lobster and champagne. While Hap waits for Biff and Willy to arrive, a pretty woman walks in and Hap hits on her until Biff gets there. To get the girl interested in Biff, Hap tells her that Biff's the quarterback for the Giants and lies that he (Hap) went to West Point. Once he has her attention, he tells her to cancel her plans and find a friend so the four of them can go out together, and she goes to make some phone calls. While she's gone, Biff explains that he waited six hours to see Oliver and then the man didn't even remember him.

Biff realized while he waited for him that he'd never been a salesman for Oliver — he'd been a shipping clerk. Meeting with Oliver made him realise that his whole life has been a lie; he, Willy, and Hap had made themselves seem more important than they ever really were. He tells Hap, "We've been talking in a dream for fifteen years." Act 2, Part 5, pg. 81 Biff was so mad at Oliver's dismissal and so upset about his realization that, without meaning to, he stole Oliver's gold fountain pen and ran away. He asks Hap to help him tell Willy what happened. Biff wants to explain that he's not a failure, just to spite Willy. It's not intentional — he just can't help being a flop.

Hap tells Biff to just lie and pretend that he's got a lunch meeting with Oliver tomorrow. After tomorrow, just pretend that Oliver is thinking it over for a few weeks, and then just let it fade away. Before they can discuss it further, Willy comes in. Biff, feeling guilty and nervous, grabs Willy's hand and begins to tell him what he's figured out today. His breathing is interrupting his speech and he's running on the fumes of several drinks as he tells Willy that he was never a salesman for Oliver, but only a shipping clerk. Willy tries to insist that Biff was "practically" Act 2, Part 5, pg. 83 a salesman, but Biff interrupts and insists that they look at the facts.

Willy gets mad at Biff for lecturing him and tells the boys that he was fired today, so he's looking for some good news to give Linda. As the rapid-fire conversation continues, Biff tries to find out why Willy was fired, and Willy tries to find out what happened with Oliver, and Hap just tells Willy exactly what he wants to hear. In answer to Willy's questions, Biff tries to tell the truth, but Willy keeps interrupting. Biff gets frustrated and Willy gets angry because he thinks Biff didn't see Oliver, but he won't let Biff get more than a few words out before he interrupts him again.

As Biff tries to explain what honestly happened at Oliver's office, Willy hears a single trumpet note and apart from the stage where Willy, Biff, and Hap sit, the house is painted with a green, leafy light. As Biff's voice fades, Young Bernard enters and knocks at the door of the Loman house where youthful Linda appears. Bernard tells her that Biff failed math and left for Boston to find his dad. The light on the house goes dark, and Biff's voice is audible again as Willy mentions math over and over. Biff and Hap are trying to figure out what he's talking about, when he explodes at Biff and tells him that he'd be set by now if he hadn't flunked math. Willy sees the gold pen in Biff's hand and realizes that he stole it from Oliver. He's missed the entire explanation of what happened with Oliver, and as Biff tries to explain the pen, Willy can hear the sound of an operator's voice ringing his hotel room.

Willy keeps yelling at the operator that he's not in his room. Biff and Hap have no idea what Willy's talking about, and Biff gets down on his knees in front of Willy promising that he'll make good, he'll be successful. Willy tells him that he's good for nothing and then Willy tries to stand up, but Biff holds him down in his chair. Biff and Hap don't know what's happening because Willy is talking crazy. Biff tries to soothe him by lying and telling him that Oliver will give him the money, but he's supposed to meet Oliver and his partner for lunch tomorrow to discuss it. Biff continues with the lie, telling Willy that he can't meet them at lunch tomorrow, though, because he stole the pen.

Willy insists that Biff just tell Oliver the pen was an oversight, but Biff tells him that stealing the pen in combination with stealing the carton of basketballs when he worked for Oliver before would just be too much. He tells Willy he'll find the money somewhere else. As Willy yells at Biff for being a failure, he can hear the hotel's page calling to him and his mistress laughing. He tells Biff that he's a failure and orders Biff to go to the lunch appointment. Biff, trying to find some way out of it, opts for the truth a second time and tells Willy that he doesn't have an appointment. Willy hits him, and the girls come into the room as Hap is separating Willy and Biff. Willy's mistress says that there's someone at the door and then laughs again offstage left.

The girls sit down with them and Biff urges Willy to sit down, too. While the girls talk to Hap and Biff, Willy is about to sit down, when his mistress tells him to get up and answer the door, so he starts walking to stage right. When Biff asks where he's going, Willy says he's going to the washroom and exits stage left. While Willy's gone, the girls admit that they don't believe that Willy is Biff and Hap's dad, but Biff says, "You've just seen a prince walk by. A fine, troubled prince. A hard-working, unappreciated prince. A pal, you understand? A good companion. Always for his boys." Act 2, Part 5, pg. 90 Hap just ignores the situation with Willy, and starts planning where they're going to go after the restaurant. Biff gets mad at Hap for not helping Willy. Biff puts the rubber piping, Willy's suicide plan, on the table and tells Hap that if he cared at all for Willy, he wouldn't let something like that go on. Biff, almost in tears, runs out of the restaurant and Hap and the girls follow him, leaving Willy alone in the restroom. When one of the girls asks Hap if they're going to just leave their father, he says that Willy's not his dad, he's just some guy. They all leave the stage.

Act 2, Part 6

Knocking is heard off stage left and the Woman, who is still laughing, enters with Willy behind her. Sensuous music accompanies their entrance. Willy talks to his mistress as they dress and someone knocks on the door. Willy won't answer the door, and he starts worrying because the person at the door won't go away. He sends the Woman into the bathroom to hide while he gets rid of whoever it is at the door. He takes a few steps away from her and she disappears into the wing while he opens the door. The music stops as young Biff stands there, distraught over failing math. Biff suggests that Willy can go talk to his math teacher and convince him to give Biff the four points he needs to graduate. Biff is sure that if his teacher sees what kind of man Willy is, he'll give Biff the points to graduate. Biff explains that the teacher didn't like him because one day Biff was making fun of him before class and the teacher caught him. Willy is proud of Biff because the other kids thought his imitation was funny, and Biff shows Willy the impression he did, talking with a lisp, and the Woman offstage laughs loud enough for Biff to hear her. Willy tries to play it off like it came from next door, but the Woman enters, still laughing. Willy makes up a story about her room being painted so she had to shower in his room, and he tries to push her offstage, but she won't leave until Willy gives her the stockings he promised her. After she leaves, Willy tries to convince Biff that the story about her room being painted is true, but Biff doesn't buy it. He cries because Willy gave her the stockings that Linda was supposed to have. Willy keeps trying to downplay it and to change the subject. He promises to see Biff's teacher the next day, but Biff has changed his mind. Biff says that he won't go to the University of Virginia and his teacher wouldn't listen to Willy anyway because Willy is a fake. Biff leaves crying and Willy is left alone.

Act 2, Part 7

Willy was yelling when the waiter came in and told him that the boys left with the girls they found. Willy, sad and dejected, offers the waiter some money, but the waiter puts it back in Willy's jacket pocket. Willy heads to a hardware store to get seeds for planting a garden. The light fades. After a long pause, the sound of a flute plays softly as the light rises on the empty kitchen. Biff and Hap appear at the door of the house. Hap has roses for his mom, and he goes into the kitchen to find her, and then looks into the living room where she's sitting with Willy's jacket in her lap. Hap freezes in the doorway and as she walks toward him; he backs into the kitchen and seems afraid. He keeps backing to the right as she silently appears in the living room doorway and asks where they were. He says they met some girls and they got her some flowers, but she's so mad at the boys for deserting their father that she throws the roses at Biff's feet as he stands inside the kitchen doorway. Hap tries to play off her anger, but both she and Biff tell him to shut up. Linda orders the boys to leave and not come back. Biff, looking into the living room and his parents' bedroom, insists on talking to Willy before he goes. Hap, after being yelled at again, goes upstairs, and Biff and Linda are left in the kitchen. Linda won't tell Biff where his father is, but when Biff hears hammering outside, she tells him that Willy's making a garden, even though it's the middle of the night. Biff goes outside, and Linda follows him as the light fades on them and comes up on Willy in the centre of the front of the stage. Willy has a flashlight, hoe, and some seed packets and is measuring off the distance with his foot as he reads the planting directions on the packets. Willy stops his measuring when Ben appears at right, moving towards him. He tells his brother that Linda has suffered so much and that a man's life has to add up to something, so he's come up with a plan to make his life worth a guaranteed $20,000. Ben warns Willy that the insurance company might not honour the policy and that what's he's thinking of is a cowardly thing to do. But Willy insists that being nothing the rest of his life would be worse than what he has in mind. Ben agrees. Willy thinks that his plan is perfect because Biff will realise that he was wrong about his dad.

"Ben, that funeral will be massive! They'll come from Maine, Massachusetts, Vermont, New Hampshire! All the old-timers with the strange license plates — that boy will be thunderstruck, Ben, because he never realized — I am known! Rhode Island, New York, New Jersey — I am known, Ben, and he'll see it with his eyes once and for all." Ben warns that Biff might consider Willy a coward and a fool for what he's going to do, and that bothers Willy because he just wants to give Biff something without having Biff hate him.

While Willy is talking about his plan, Ben goes off upstage and disappears. Biff comes down from the left and Willy looks up at him in confusion. Biff reminds Willy that people can see him out in the yard rooting around in the dark to make a garden, but Willy doesn't care. He tells Biff to go away and leave him alone and Biff tells him that he's leaving for good and that it doesn't matter whose fault it is that he's a failure. Willy goes inside and Biff follows him to tell Linda that he's leaving. Biff says he won't write so that they don't have to think about him and they can start being happy again. Biff is ready to go, but Willy won't shake his hand. They start arguing again, Willy yells at him and Biff tries to explain what's happened and why he has to go.

Biff wants to leave peaceably, but Willy won't let him. When Biff asks what Willy wants from him, Willy tells him that he wants Biff to know that he wasted his life because of spite. "Spite, spite, is the word of your undoing!" Act 2, Part 7, pg. 103 Willy tells Biff that he can't blame his failure on him, and Biff argues that he's not trying to. Willy keeps going on about it and Biff finally gets angry and the arguing is loud enough to bring Hap downstairs. Biff gets so mad that he pulls the rubber piping from his pocket and puts it in front of Willy, telling him that suicide won't make him a hero or win him any sympathy in Biff's eyes.

Happy and Linda are shocked that Biff would do such a thing, but Biff won't let them take it off the table. Willy denies knowing what the rubber piping is for. Willy keeps insisting repeatedly that Biff is spiteful, and Biff, sick of lying and pretending to be who he isn't, wants to tell Willy who they really are because Biff thinks Willy doesn't know the truth. He says, "we never told the truth for ten minutes in this house." Act 2, Part 7, pg. 104 Happy tries to argue with him, but Biff points out the lie that Happy is living, pretending that he's the assistant buyer when he's really only one of two assistants to the assistant buyer. Biff tells Willy that he didn't have an address for three months because he was in jail for stealing a suit. He tells Willy that stealing has cost him every decent job he's had since he got out of high school. Willy asks Biff if he's blaming him for that, and Biff says that Willy made him think he was such a big shot that he couldn't stand taking orders from anyone, so he couldn't hold down a job. But Biff figured everything out when he was running from Oliver's office. He thought:

"Why am I trying to become what I don't want to be? What am I doing in an office, making a contemptuous, begging fool of myself, when all I want is out there, waiting for me the minute I say I know who I am!" Act 2, Part 7, pg. 105

Willy refuses Biff's assertion that they are simply common men. Biff starts toward Willy, furious and ready to fight, but Hap holds him off. Biff says that Willy was a guy who tried hard but failed like so many other guys have done, and that Biff himself is just an ordinary guy and that Willy has to realise that he's not special anymore. Willy calls him vengeful and spiteful again, and Biff breaks away from Happy. Willy starts up the stairs away from Biff, but Biff grabs him and yells that it's not anyone's fault that Biff is nothing, that's just the way it is. Then, exhausted from trying to explain and furious that Willy won't listen, Biff breaks down into sobs. He holds onto Willy and Willy fumbles for Biff's face. Crying but breaking away from Willy, Biff tells Linda that he'll leave in the morning and he goes upstairs to bed.

When Biff leaves the stage, Willy is suddenly happy because Biff cried and that means that he loves his dad. Willy says that Biff is going to be magnificent, and he hears Ben's voice say that Biff will be more magnificent when he has $20,000 to back him. Ben's music plays hauntingly in the background. Linda senses that Willy's mind has moved on to something dangerous and urges him to go to bed. Happy, still vying for attention, tells his parents that he's going to get married, but Linda dismisses him up to bed. Willy is listening to Ben as he urges Willy to go into the jungle and get a diamond. She tries to get Willy upstairs to bed, too, but he tells her that he wants to sit by himself for a few minutes to calm down, so she fearfully goes upstairs without him.

Ben's voice keeps telling him to go into the jungle and get something that can be touched and held, something substantial. Linda, on her way up the stairs, tells Willy that this is the only way to do it, and although she's talking about Biff leaving, Willy agrees with her, but he's thinking about his plan for giving Biff something to make him magnificent. Willy talks to Ben about how happy he is that Biff loves him. He believes Biff will worship him for what he's going to do for him. Ben keeps prompting Willy to act, while Linda calls to him from their bedroom. In the middle of Willy's excited babbling, Ben looks at his watch and urges Willy to hurry so they don't miss the boat and then disappears. Willy is talking football again as he looks toward the house, but when he turns around, he realizes that Ben is gone. Willy starts to panic as Linda calls to him from upstairs.

He shushes her and moves his arms as if he's fighting off faces and voices that are swarming him. Faint, high music crescendos into a great intensity that stops him. Suddenly he rushes out of the house and around the corner. Linda calls out to him and hears no answer. Biff, still in his clothes, gets up off of his bed and Hap sits up. They're listening. Linda calls out again, very afraid.

They hear the sound of a car starting and moving away at full speed. Biff runs to the top of the stairs and calls to Willy. The music crashes loudly and then trickles down to the sound of a single cello string. Biff returns to his room where he and Hap put on their jackets. Linda walks slowly out of her room. The music is a march now and the lighting suggests day. Charley and Bernard wait at the kitchen door, while Linda walks through the draped doorway to the living room in her funeral clothes. She takes Charley's arm and they all walk through the wall-line of the kitchen toward the audience. At the edge, Linda lays the flowers down, kneeling beside the grave.

Chapter 13

Topic Failure

Failure 1

Willy's entire life is a succession of missed opportunities and misinformation, and he considers himself a failure because of it. He has failed to make the drive to his business appointment, so he's going to miss out on making a sale because of it. His failure, and the failure of either of his sons to make something extraordinary of themselves, baffles him because he believes that the keys to success are contacts and popularity. Unfortunately, in the business of sales, Willy has outlived his contacts and his popularity (if he ever had it) and is now unable to make any money. If a man's role is to earn money to support his family, then Willy is a total failure.

Failure 2

Willy considers Biff's life a failure because he's not making enough money or working in the business world. He thinks that he is slacking off working as a farmhand; he had high expectations for Biff: he'd make it big in business (based on Biff's popularity in high school), and now that he hasn't, Willy is disappointed in him and dissatisfied with everything he does.

Act 1, Part 2

Failure 3: Biff can't seem to find a job that suits him, and although things were going well for him in Texas, he panicked because the job he had as a farmhand wasn't the kind of job Willy expected him to have. Biff was supposed to be in business; the fact that he was well liked and popular in high school would ensure his success. Biff failed to fulfill Willy's expectations, and that makes him a complete failure in his father's eyes.

Act 1, Part 3

Failure 4: Willy is beginning to feel like a failure because business is slowing down and he's not providing for his family the way he used to. He's losing popularity (if he ever had it), and his whole idea of what it takes to be successful is betraying him. He feels as if he has worked hard to become well liked, but now he is ignored and laughed at. People don't take him seriously. Who wouldn't feel like a failure in that situation?

Act 1, Part 6

Failure 5: Willy laments the missed opportunity of going to Alaska with his brother, Ben (who struck it rich, but in Africa, not Alaska). When Hap tries to comfort Willy with the promise of retiring him for life, Willy criticizes him because he doesn't make enough money to do that. Willy, a traveling salesman, can't even drive himself to the sales appointments he is able to make. Hap is a failure because he can't keep his word, and Willy is a failure because he can't do his job.

Act 1, Part 7

Failure 6: Willy is a failure when compared to his father. Ben asserts that he could sell more in a week than Willy could in a lifetime. Willy, when measured against Ben, doesn't fare much better, because Ben was rich by the time he was twenty-one.

Act 1, Part 8

Failure 7: Linda tells the boys that Willy has been demoted to merely earning commission on what he sells (like a beginning salesman), and he can't make sales anymore because all his contacts are dead or retired. He has to borrow $50 a week from Charley to pretend that it's his salary so Linda won't find out he's a failure at his job. She is angry because he's tried so hard to support the boys, and now that he's failing at his job, he needs their support, and the boys are choosing to look the other way.

Act 2, Part 2

Failure 8: Willy, after getting in an argument with his boss, gets fired, which means he has no way to pay his insurance or his last payment on the house. He's a complete failure now. His final contact and claim to fame was his friendship with Wagner's late father, but even Wagner doesn't give that much consideration because it probably wasn't true. But whether Wagner's father and Willy were great friends, the fact remains that Willy hasn't been able to do his job, so he loses it. Willy has no contacts, nor is he well liked.

Act 2, Part 5

Failure 9: Willy keeps thinking about how Biff failed math, and he believes that's when Biff's life was ruined. If he hadn't failed math, he would be successful by now.

Act 2, Part 7

Failure 10: Biff tells Willy that they're both ordinary men, common, just like everyone else; this is not such a terrible thing in Biff's eyes, but for Willy, being ordinary is equivalent to failure. He wanted to be the best of salesmen, and he pretended that he was. Willy realizes that his own son knows that he's a fake, and that Biff's wish is only to confront the truth and be an ordinary man. This is the summit of his failures. Willy can think of only one way to prove that he's not a failure: suicide.

Requiem

Failure 11: Willy expected the funeral to be packed because he was so well known and well liked. His funeral would prove to Biff that his father's life was worth something, but it doesn't turn out this way. The only people at Willy's funeral were his family, Charley, and Bernard. Although Willy aspired to be like Dave Singleman (a revered salesman), it didn't work out that way, and Willy Loman died a failure by his own standards. Biff considers Willy's life a failure because he had the wrong dreams. He spent too much time convincing himself he could be a successful salesman, when what he was clear he was skilled at working with his hands. If he'd followed the right dreams, and confronted his abilities in a realistic and honest way, he may not have been a failure, and his life might not have ended this way. Even in death, Willy Loman's plans fail; no one shows at his funeral, and his life insurance policy doesn't cover suicide.

Topic Tracking: Dishonesty

Dishonesty 1: Dishonesty is common throughout Death of a Salesman. Whether the lies are intentional or delusional, Willy, Biff, and Happy seem to be spewing out untruths all the time, and Biff finally realizes that they've been lying to each other and themselves so much, that they don't even know who they really are. The dishonesty begins with Willy telling Linda that he came home because he couldn't drive anymore. The reason, he later admits, is that he almost ran over a kid in Yonkers, and it spooked him.

But he doesn't lie only about the reason for his return, he also lies about his importance to the company in New England, and how he'd already be running New York if his original employer were still alive. There's no guarantee that Willy and his former boss were good friends, and Willy hasn't been important in New England for a long time (if indeed, he ever really was). He creates a false image of a skilled salesman in demand, when in reality, he's really washed up.

Dishonesty 2: Willy is on a tirade about Biff because he thinks that Biff is wasting his life; he has become a shiftless bum, when Willy had such high expectations for him. As Willy is talking to Linda about Biff, he says that he's lazy and that's why he's a failure.

But in the next breath, Willy says that he doesn't understand why someone as hard-working as Biff isn't more successful. Willy's speech is constantly riddled with inconsistencies and contradictions. These contradictions make his convictions completely unreliable.

Act 1, Part 2

Dishonesty 3: Happy admits that he seduces the fiancées of top executives at the store, and he also takes bribes. He laughs about it like it's a game, and Biff pays it no attention. Their disregard for ethics and morality is evident; accepting bribes seems everyday and normal. It doesn't occur to either of the boys that there's something wrong with this, and the audience is left to wonder how they developed such an attitude.

Dishonesty 4: Biff quit working for Bill Oliver because he was accused of stealing a carton of basketballs (which he did), but despite that, Biff believes that Oliver will loan him $10,000 to start a ranch. Biff is creating a dishonest vision of the past (like his dad). He stole from and lied to Oliver when he worked for him, and now he's lying to himself by asserting how much Oliver liked him. His lies are convinced enough to become the truth, and he can't remember which version of the story is right.

Act 1, Part 3

Dishonesty 5: Biff stole a football from the locker room when he was in high school, and he claimed that he took it because the coach told him to work on his passing. Willy acts for a moment as if Biff should return it, but when Hap implies that Biff was wrong for taking the ball, Willy defends Biff and declares that the coach, rather than being angry with Biff for stealing, would have been proud and impressed with Biff's initiative. Willy tells Biff that it's OK that he took the ball because the coach likes him. Willy tells his son it's perfectly fine to steal from people, as long as you are well liked; they'll let you get away with it.

Dishonesty 6: Willy lies to the boys about meeting and having coffee with the mayor of Providence. He likes to make his sons believe that he's an important and great man, when in reality, he is just an average guy, like everyone else. Willy gets trapped in the false image he has created, believing the lies he has been telling himself for years. He is unable to confront reality and has the expectation that people are going to react to him as a successful and important salesman. He cannot understand why people treat him like an unknown, washed up pity-case (which he is). He's just a common, everyday guy who talks as if he's so much more (he has built up an image with his kids that he cannot fill), and when he realizes that he's a failure, and everyone knows his "success" is a fake, life is no longer worth living. Willy feels worth more dead, than alive.

Dishonesty 7: When Linda asked Willy how well he did on his trip, Willy lied about how much he sold. He admitted the truth only a few sentences later, and Linda ignores the whopper he told her, but the fact remains that Willy is a liar. He contradicts himself continuously — one minute the Chevy is the greatest car ever built, the next minute it's a hunk of scrap metal.

One minute he's making $1200 sales, and the next instant, it was only a $200 sale. That's a $1,000 lie, and no one calls him on it or makes him accountable for it, so he just goes right one lying to himself and everyone else.

Act 1, Part 4

Dishonesty 8: Willy's mistress is another example of his immorality and dishonesty. He cheats on Linda, his adoring and supportive wife, with some secretary, so that he has a contact with the buyers in Boston.

Act 1, Part 7

Dishonesty 9: Willy sent the boys to steal sand from a construction site so they could rebuild the stoop of their house. Although Charley warns that the watchman is keeping an eye out for the boys because they stole lumber earlier, Willy doesn't care. He is convinced that stealing those supplies isn't wrong, and is proud of the boys being so fearless, but he never explains why it's OK for them to steal. Even when the watchman is chasing Biff, Willy refuses to admit that they're wrong. Linda, however, seems to know that what they're doing is dishonest, and she worries about the boys getting into trouble for it.

Act 1, Part 8

Dishonesty 10: Hap tells Biff that part of the reason people in the business world think he's crazy, is because he didn't lie to cover himself when he wanted to take a day off. Hap, however, brags about his excellent ability to cover himself; he can leave if he wants and the boss will never be able to pin him down for playing hooky. Dishonesty 11: Willy tells Biff to pretend his work out West was business related instead of farm work to impress Oliver.

Act 2, Part 1

Dishonesty 12: Willy, feeling guilty about betraying Linda with adultery, gets anxious and upset any time he sees her mending her silk stockings; stockings were the gift he always gave the Woman when they met. While Linda had to mend her stockings because they were so expensive, Willy's mistress got two pair every time she and Willy had their little fling in Boston.

Act 2, Part 4

Dishonesty 13: Willy lies to Bernard about how Bill Oliver called Biff in to work for him. He is intimidated by Bernard's success and embarrassed by how little Biff has done with his own life. Willy lies to make Biff seem important and successful (much like he does with himself).

Act 2, Part 5

Dishonesty 14: Hap lies to the girl he's hitting on so that he can get her attention. He's a natural at dishonesty, and he doesn't feel bad about it at all. Biff, however, realized in his meeting with Oliver, that he'd never been a salesman, just a shipping clerk. He realizes at that moment, his entire life has been a lie. His father and his brother are liars, too, because they all pretend to be what they aren't. Biff is tired of lying, and he plans to tell Willy the truth about his meeting with Oliver, but Hap encourages him to just lie and tell Willy what he wants to hear.

Act 2, Part 6

Dishonesty 15: Biff is destroyed by the realization that his father is a fraud. Finding out about Willy's affair made Biff realise his father's life was a charade. This is when Biff gives up on his own future.

Act 2, Part 7

Dishonesty 16: Biff finally confronts Willy about the lies they've all been living. He tells Willy that stealing has cost him every good job he's had since he was in high school, and that they all have been lying to each other about who and what they really are. He's tired of the lies and feels he must leave because he can't keep trying to be what he isn't. His father won't hear any of it.

Chapter 14

Summary and Analysis

Act I (Loman Home, Present Day)

The salesman, Willy Loman, enters his home dressed in a dark gray business suit and carrying two large sample cases. He appears very tired and confused, a sixty-year-old man with calluses on his hands. Linda Loman, his wife, puts on a robe and slippers and goes downstairs. She has been asleep. Linda is mostly jovial, but represses objections to her husband. Her struggle is to support him while still trying to guide him. She worries that he smashed the car, but he says that nothing happened. He claims that he's tired to death and couldn't make it through the rest of his trip. He got only as far as Yonkers, and doesn't remember the details of the trip. He tells Linda that he kept swerving onto the shoulder of the road, but Linda thinks that it must be faulty steering in the car. He had to drive ten miles per hour to get back home safely.

She tells him that he needs to rest his mind. Willy tells her that he was driving along looking at the scenery, and that suddenly he was going off the road. Linda says that there's no reason why he can't work in New York, but Willy says he's not needed there. Linda worries that Willy is too accommodating and that he should tell his boss that he must work in New York. Willy claims that if Frank Wagner were alive he would be in charge of New York by now, but that his son, Howard, doesn't appreciate him. Linda tells him that Happy took Biff on a double date, and that it was nice to see them shaving together. Linda reminds him not to lose his temper with Biff, but Willy claims that he simply had asked him if he was making any money. Willy says that there is an undercurrent of resentment in Biff, but Linda says that Biff admires his father. When Biff finds himself, both of them will be happier. Willy wonders how Biff can find himself as a farmhand. He remarks that it is a disgrace that a thirty-four-year-old man has not "found himself."

Willy calls Biff a lazy bum and says that he is lost, but then contradicts himself and says that he is not lazy. Willy complains that Linda got a new type of cheese, American instead of Swiss. Willy longs for the days when their neighborhood was less developed and less crowded. He shouts that the population is out of control. He wakes up his sons Biff and Happy, both of whom are in the double bunk in the boys' bedroom. Willy vows that he won't fight with Biff anymore, for some men don't get started until late in life, such as Edison or B.F. Goodrich.

Analysis

At the beginning of the play, Arthur Miller establishes Willy Loman as a troubled and misguided man, at heart a salesman and a dreamer. He emphasizes his preoccupation with success. However, Miller makes it equally apparent that Willy Loman is not a successful man. Although in his sixties, he is still a traveling salesman bereft of any stable location or occupation, and clings only to his dreams and ideals. There is a strong core of resentment in Willy Loman's character and his actions assume a more glorious past than was actually the case. Willy sentimentalizes the neighborhood as it was years ago, and is nostalgic for his time working for Frank Wagner, especially because his former boss's son, Howard Wagner, fails to appreciate Willy. Miller presents Willy as a strong and boisterous man with great bravado but little energy to support his impression of vitality. He is perpetually weary and exhibits signs of dementia, contradicting himself and displaying some memory loss.

Linda, in contrast, shows little of Willy's boisterous intensity. Rather, she is dependable and kind, perpetually attempting to smooth out conflicts that Willy might encounter.

Linda has a similar longing for an idealized past, but has learned to suppress her dreams and her dissatisfaction with her husband and sons. Miller indicates that she is a woman with deep regrets about her life; she must continually reconcile her husband with her sons, and support a man who has failed in his life's endeavor. Linda exists only in the context of her family relationships. As a mother to Biff and Happy and a husband to Willy, and must depend on them for whatever success she can grasp.

The major conflict in Death of a Salesman is between Biff Loman and his father. Even before Biff appears on stage, Linda indicates that Biff and Willy are perpetually at odds with one another because of Biff's inability to live up to his father's expectations.

As Linda says, Biff is a man who has not yet "found himself." At thirty-four years old, Biff remains to some degree an adolescent. This is best demonstrated by his inability to keep a job. He and Happy still live in their old bunk beds; despite the fact that this reminds Linda of better times, it is a clear sign that neither of the sons has matured.

A major theme of the play is the lost opportunities that each of the characters face. Linda Loman, reminiscing about the days when her sons were not yet grown and had a less contentious relationship with their father, regrets the state of disarray into which her family has fallen. Willy Loman believes that if Frank Wagner had survived, he would have been given greater respect and power within the company. Willy also regrets the opportunities that have passed by Biff, whom he believes to have the capability to be a great man.

Miller uses the first segment of the play to foreshadow later plot developments. Willy worries about having trouble driving and expresses dissatisfaction with his situation at work, and Linda speaks of conflict between Willy and his sons. Each of these will become important in driving the plot and the resolution of the play.

Act I (Loman Home, Present Day)

At thirty-four, Biff is well-built but somewhat worn and

not very self-assured. Happy, two years younger than his brother, is tall and powerfully made. He is a visibly sexual person. Both boys are somewhat lost, Happy because he has never risked defeat. The two brothers discuss their father. Happy thinks that Willy's license will be taken away, and Biff suggests that his father's eyes are going. Happy thinks that it's funny that they are sleeping at home again, and they discuss Happy's "first time" with a girl named Betsy. Happy says that he was once very bashful with women, but as he became more confident Biff became less so. Biff wonders why his father mocks him so much, but Happy says that he wants Biff to make good. Happy worries that Willy talks to himself. Biff, who fumbles with an old, deflated football, tells Happy that he has had twenty or thirty different types of jobs since he left home before the war, and everything turns out the same. He reminisces about herding cattle in Nebraska and the Dakotas, and says that there is nothing more inspiring than the sight of a mare and a new colt.

But he criticizes himself for playing around with horses for twenty-eight dollars a week at his advanced age. Happy says that Biff is a poet and an idealist, but Biff says that he's mixed up and should get married. When Biff asks Happy if he is content, Happy defiantly says that he is not. All Happy can do is wait for the merchandise manager to die, but even if that happens he wouldn't be able to enjoy a better position. He says that he has his own apartment, a car, and plenty of woman, but is still lonely. Biff suggests that Happy come out west with him to buy a ranch.

Happy claims that he dreams about ripping off his clothes in the store and boxing with his manager, for he can "outbox, outrun, and outlift anybody in that store," yet he has to take orders from them. Happy says that the women they went on a date with that night were gorgeous, but he gets disgusted with women: he keeps "knockin' them over" but it doesn't mean anything.

Happy says that he wants someone with character, like his mother. Biff says that he thinks he may work for Bill Oliver, whom he worked for earlier in life. Biff worries that Bill will remember that he stole a carton of basketballs, and remembers that he quit because Bill was going to fire him.

Analysis

Biff and Happy are both trapped in a perpetual adolescence. Both men are tall and well-built, but their emotional development does not mirror their physical appearance. Happy reminisces about his first sexual experience, while Biff handles a football, a sign of his childhood. The setting of the segment, the boys' childhood bedroom, also suggests that they are trapped in their past. Even the names of the two men, Happy and Biff, are childlike nicknames inappropriate for mature adults.

Biff, in particular, is a drifter who demonstrates little sense of maturity or responsibility. He moves from job to job without any particular plan, and is most content working jobs that use his physicality but do not offer any hope for a stable future. Biff is self-destructive, ruining every job opportunity that he might have, and realizes his own failure. He is aware that he is a disappointment and an embarrassment to his father, who holds great aspirations for his son. Biff feels that he is just a boy and must take steps to demonstrate a shift into the maturity of adulthood.

Happy, in contrast, is less self-aware than his brother, yet is equally confused and is similarly immature. Happy has the ostensible characteristics of adulthood including a steady profession, yet his attitude is that of a teenager. He is a manipulative womanizer who manifests little respect for the women he seduces; his euphemism for seduction, "knockin' them over," suggests at best an impersonal connection and at worst a violent subtext. Happy clearly demonstrates aspects of a Madonna-whore complex; he cannot respect women with whom he has sex, believing them to be inauthentic, and instead wishes to have as a partner a person who has "character" such as his mother. This suggests that Happy cannot respect a woman whom he successfully seduces.

Happy's immaturity is perhaps even more apparent in this segment of the play, for his adolescent qualities starkly contrast with his adult lifestyle. Although he has a respectable job, Happy compares himself to his co-workers in terms of physical accomplishment; he believes he should not have to take orders from men over whom he is athletically superior. He thus approaches the workplace with a school-yard mentality, believing that physical strength is more important than intellectual development.

Miller contrasts the ideas that the two men have with regards to success, the major thematic concern of the play. Biff believes himself to be a failure because he does not display the trappings of adulthood such as a steady occupation and a stable home life and because he has made mistakes in his life. Happy, in contrast, believes himself to be a failure because, although he is ostensibly successful, still feels empty and unfulfilled. Happy's achievements are not success as such, but rather a lack of overt failure.

Act I (Loman Home, Past)

This segment of the act takes place in the kitchen years before. Willy reminds Biff not to make promises to a girl, because girls will always believe what you tell them and Biff is too young to be talking seriously to girls. Happy polishes the new car. Willy tells the boys that he found a hammock in Albany that he will hang between the elm trees in the yard. Young Biff carries a football and wears a sweater with a large "S" on it, while Happy wears an old sweatshirt. Willy surprises the boys with a new punching bag, and as Happy exercises he brags about how he is losing weight. Biff shows Willy a football he took from the locker room, but Willy tells him to return it. Biff tells Willy that he missed him when he was away on business. Willy says that someday he'll have his own business like Uncle Charley. Willy says that he'll be bigger than Charley, because Charley is liked, but not well liked.

Willy tells the boys that he went to Providence and met the Mayor, and that he also went to Waterbury and Boston. Willy promises to take his boys on business and show them all of the towns in New England and introduce them to the finest people. As Happy and Biff toss the football around,

Bernard enters, wearing a brown sweater and corduroy pants. Bernard is worried because Biff has a state exam (Regents) the following week and has yet to study for them. Bernard heard that Mr. Birnbaum will fail Biff in his math class if he does not study, and reminds Biff that just because Willy has been accepted to UVA the high school does not have to graduate him. Willy tells Bernard not to be a pest, and Bernard leaves. Biff says that Bernard is "liked, but not well liked." Willy says that Bernard may get the best grades in school, but when he gets out in the business world people like Biff and Happy will be five times ahead of him. He thanks goodness that his sons are built like Adonises, because the man who makes an appearance in the world gets ahead.

Linda enters, and after the boys leave she and Willy discuss the troubles that Willy has been having in his business. Willy worries that others laugh at him, but Linda reassures him, saying that he is successful because he is making seventy to a hundred dollars per week. Willy also worries that people respect Uncle Charley, who is a man of few words. Linda tells him that few men are as idolized by their children as Willy is.

Analysis

Arthur Miller employs a disjointed time structure in Death of a Salesman, in which the play shifts settings and time within the act. The "present" time of the aged Willy Loman and his grown sons gives way to the time when Biff and Happy were teenagers. These scenes are explanatory: the actions and conversations of teenage Biff and Happy clarify the behaviour of the characters in their early thirties. The tone of these scenes is idyllic; the tension that is later apparent between Biff and Willy is nonexistent, while both characters demonstrate a confidence and contentment that has disappeared decades later. The segment demonstrates the inherent causes of the Loman sons' immaturity.

Willy has instilled in his sons a belief that appearances are more important than actual achievement or talent, contrasting his athletic and handsome sons with the hardworking yet uncharismatic Bernard. Willy values intangible characteristics such as personality over any actual barometer of achievement, which he dismisses as unimportant in the business world. The contrast that Willy makes is between men who are "liked" and men who are "well-liked," believing that to be "well-liked," as defined by charisma and physical appearance, is the major criterion for success. This causes his sons, particularly Biff, to eschew their studies in favor of athletic achievement. Happy continually brags that he is losing weight, while Biff, ready to go to college on an athletic scholarship, shows enough disregard for his studies to fail math. This segment also foreshadows Biff's later troubles; he steals from the locker room as a teenager just as he later steals from Bill Oliver. Although Willy does not speak directly to Happy about how he should treat girls, Miller indicates that it is from his father that Happy gained his unhealthy attitude toward women.

Miller defines several major themes of Death of a Salesman in this flashback. Most importantly, he develops the theme of success and the various characters' definitions of it. Miller presents Charley and his son Bernard as unqualified exemplars of success; Bernard is an exemplary student, while Charley owns his own business. However, Willy cannot accept the success of these two characters, believing that it is his personality that will make Willy a greater success than Charley and his sons more successful than Bernard.

Yet there is an unmistakable degree of delusion in Willy's boasting; he fails to realise the limits of charm and charisma when it masks superficiality. Even Willy's claims of his own success at this point seem invalid; he brags about meeting important and powerful men, yet can only specifically describe briefly meeting the mayor of Providence. Furthermore, he worries that others do not respect him as they do Charley and that he is not making enough money. Even in the prime of his life, Willy Loman is an inauthentic man whose dreams exceed his limited grasp.

Act I (Hotel Room, Past)

Willy crosses from one part of the stage to another, where

a woman is standing, putting on her scarf. Willy says that he gets so lonely, and gets the feeling that he'll never make a living for her or a business for the boys. The woman claims that she picked Willy for his sense of humour. Willy tells her that he will be back in about two weeks and that he will see her the next time he is in Boston.

Analysis

Miller readily switches from location to location during Death of a Salesman, as the flashback to Willy at home switches to a flashback of Willy in a hotel room in Boston. This serves as an ironic counterpoint to Linda's comment that Willy is idolized by his children; the fact that he is having an affair shows that Willy is not a man worthy of such fervent admiration. He displays the same callous disregard for women that Happy demonstrates as an adult, yet where Happy disregards women with whom he has insubstantial relationships, Willy is unfaithful to the devoted Linda. The flashback also demonstrates that Willy is not a man respected by others; the woman with whom he has an affair selected Willy for his sense of humour rather than for any substantial qualities.

Act I (Loman Home, Past)

Willy is back in the kitchen with Linda, who reassures him that he is a handsome man. Linda mends her stocking, but Willy tells her that he does not want her to do such menial tasks. Willy returns to the porch, where he tells Bernard to give Biff the answers to the Regents exam. Bernard says that he normally gives Biff the answers, but Regents is a State exam and he could be arrested. Willy calls for Biff, and Linda says that Biff is too rough with the girls. Bernard says that Biff is driving the car without a license and will flunk math. Willy also hears the woman's voice (from the hotel) room, and screams for it to shut up. Willy explodes at Linda, saying that there's nothing the matter with Biff. He asks her if she wants Biff to be a worm like Bernard. Linda, almost in tears, exits into the living room.

Analysis

This segment of the chapter, also a flashback, returns to the Loman household, which is the setting for most of the play. Miller contrasts Willy's life on the road in which he behaves like a callous womanizer with his behaviour as a husband at home. A great deal of Willy's dedication to Linda stems from his own sense of pride; he does not want her to mend stockings because it shows that he cannot provide her with the financial resources to buy new stockings. Miller further establishes the contrast between Biff and Bernard; Bernard is more concerned with Biff's studies than either Biff or Willy, while Biff is reckless and abusive.

Willy Loman deals with each of these problems through denial. He tells Linda that there is absolutely nothing wrong with Biff, particularly in comparison to Bernard. However, Willy feels the strain of his indiscretions, as is shown when he hears the voice of the woman with whom he has had an affair. The problems that Willy has during his later years are to a great extent self-inflicted, the product of long-standing guilt for his actions.

Act I (Loman Home, Present Day)

Willy tells Happy that he nearly hit a kid in Yonkers. Willy wonders why he didn't go to Alaska with his brother Ben, because the man was a genius: success incarnate. Ben ended up with diamond mines: he walked into a jungle and came out rich at the age of twenty-one. Happy tells Willy that he should retire. Charley, a large laconic man, enters. Happy tells Willy to go to bed, but Charley signals to Happy to go. Charley wears a robe over pajamas and claims that he has heartburn and can't sleep. Willy tells Charley that he needs to take vitamins to build up his bones, but Charley says there's no bones in a heartburn. As Willy and Charley play cards, Charley offers Willy a job, which insults him. Willy asks Charley why Biff is going back to Texas, but Charley tells him to let Biff go. Willy talks about the ceiling he put up in the living room, but refuses to give any details. When Charley wonders how he could put up a ceiling, Willy shouts at him that a man who can't handle tools is not a man, and calls Charley disgusting. Uncle Ben enters, a stolid man in his sixties with a mustache and an authoritative air. Willy tells Ben that he is getting awfully tired, but since Charley cannot see Ben, Willy tells him that for a second Charley reminded him of his brother Ben, who died several weeks ago in Africa. Ben asks Willy if their mother is living with him, but Willy said that she died a long time ago. Charley, who cannot see Ben, wonders what Willy is talking about. Finally Charley becomes unnerved and leaves.

Analysis:

If Charley and Bernard are the symbols of tangible material success in Death of a Salesman, Willy's older brother Ben symbolizes the broadest reaches of success, which are intangible and practically imaginary. Whether Ben is a Horatio Alger figure, a character whose history is to be taken literally, is disputable; some aspects of his biography are so romanticized and absurdly grandiose that it is likely that the information that Miller gives concerning Ben is filtered through Willy Loman's imagination. When Ben appears in the play, it is only as a representation of Willy's imagination. For Willy, Ben represents fantastic success gained through intangible luck rather than through the boredom of steady dedication and hard work; Ben has gained what Willy always wanted but never could achieve.

The encounter between Charley and Willy illustrates that Willy feels some jealousy toward his friend for his success. Willy offers advice to Charley at every opportunity in an attempt to assert some dominance over him. He interprets a man as a person who can handle tools well, returning to a physical definition of manhood in comparison to monetary or status-based definitions that would assert Charley's superiority.

Likewise, Charley seems to realise Willy's envy, and behaves tentatively toward his friend. Although he does injure Willy's pride by offering him a job, Charley does so tentatively, for he has great pity for Willy that he knows he must mask. Charley does, however, give the most sound advice to Willy, advising him to let Biff do what he pleases and leave for Texas.

Act I (Loman Home, Past)

While Willy talks with Ben, Linda (as a younger woman) enters. Willy asks Ben where his father is, but Ben says that he didn't find his father in Alaska, for he never made it there. Ben claims he had a very faulty view of geography and ended up in Africa instead of Alaska. Willy was only three years, eleven months old when Ben left. Young Biff and Happy enter, and Willy introduces them to Uncle Ben, a "great man." Ben boasts that their father was a very great man, an inventor who could make more money in a week than another man could make in a lifetime. Willy shows Biff to Ben, and says that he's bringing up Biff to be like their father. Biff and Ben start to spar; Ben trips Biff, then tells him never to fight fair with a stranger, because he will never get out of the jungle that way. Ben leaves, wishing Willy good luck on whatever he does. Willy claims that he can hunt snakes and rabbits in Brooklyn. Young Happy brags about how he lost weight.

Charley returns, wearing knickers, and reprimands Willy for letting his kids steal lumber from the nearby building that is being refurbished. Willy says that he reprimanded them, but that he has a "couple of fearless characters" as his children. Charley tells him that the jails are full of fearless characters, but Ben says that so is the stock exchange. Bernard enters and says that the watchman is chasing Biff, but Willy says that he is not stealing anything. Willy says that he will stop by on his way back to Africa, but Willy begs him to stay and talk. Willy worries that he's not teaching his sons the right kind of knowledge. Ben repeats that when he walked into the jungle he was seventeen, and when he walked out he was twenty-one and fantastically rich.

Analysis

Once again, Miller shifts the setting of the play to previous years in a seemingly imaginary scene that contrasts Willy's failed aspirations with the supposedly great accomplishments of his brother Ben. Willy deals almost entirely in superlatives. Ben is a legendary man who, out of pure luck, ended up the owner of a diamond mine. Ben, who exists as an extension of

Willy's imagination, speaks of their father in similar terms, as a "great man" and an inventor. These boasts are exaggerations meant to emphasize Willy's feelings of inadequacy in comparison to his brother and father. Willy even pathetically attempts to justify life in Brooklyn as a life comparable to that in the outdoors. This familial history provides a neat complement to Willy's relationship with Biff; just as Biff feels himself a failure in his father's eyes, Willy perceives himself to be inadequate in comparison to his father and brother.

The second appearance of Young Biff and Young Happy reinforces the values that Willy has instilled in his sons. Happy once again brags about losing weight, showing his focus on physical appearance and athleticism, while Biff steals from the nearby construction site. For Willy, stealing is merely an extension of a capitalist mindset; he makes no distinction between the fearless character in jail and the fearless character in the stock exchange.

This demonstrates the insufficiencies of Willy's views on success: he attributes success to luck or immorality and cannot see the virtues of hard work and discipline as shown by Charley and Bernard. Willy can conceive of success as a mantra by Ben or the result of fearless daring, but he cannot imagine that hard work and dedication are critical to the formula. Willy's business values inform his instructions to his sons, while their instruction by Willy inform their behaviour in the business world.

Act I (Loman Home, Present Day)

Ben leaves, but Willy still speaks to him as Linda enters. Willy wonders what happened to the diamond watch fob that Ben gave to him when he came from Africa. Linda reminds him that he pawned it to pay for Biff's radio correspondence course. Biff and Happy come downstairs in their pajamas, and ask Linda how long Willy has been talking to himself. Linda says that this has been going on for years. Linda says that she would have told Biff, if he had an address where he could be reached. She also says that Willy is at his worst when Biff comes home, and asks Biff why they are so hateful to one another. Biff claims that he is trying to change.] Linda tells Biff that a man is not a bird to come and go with the springtime. Biff tells his mother to dye her hair again, because he doesn't want her looking old. Linda says that someday Biff will leave for a year, come back and find his parents are gone. Biff says that she is not even sixty, but Linda asks if he thinks about Willy. She says that if Biff has no feelings for his father, then he has no feeling for her either. Linda says that Willy is the dearest man in the world to her, and she won't have anyone making him feel unwanted. Willy re-enters, but Linda tells Biff not to go near him.

Biff tells her to stop making excuses for Willy because he never had an ounce of respect for her. Happy tells Biff not to call their father crazy. Biff says that Willy has no character, and that Charley would never act this way, to which Linda replies "then make Charley your father." She tells him that Willy never made a lot of money, and that he is not the finest character, but he is a human being and "attention must be paid" to him. Linda recounts the indignities that Willy has suffered, such as having to borrow money from Charley, and she calls Happy a philanderer.

Biff wants to stay with his parents and promises not to fight with Willy. Biff says that Willy threw him out before because his father is a fake who does not like anybody who knows the truth about him. Linda says that Willy is dying and that he's been trying to kill himself. When Willy had his car accident in February, a woman saw that he deliberately smashed into the bridge railing to drive his car into the river, and it was only the shallowness of the water that saved him. Willy has also tried to use the gas line to kill himself. Biff apologizes to Linda and promises to stay and try to become a success. Happy tells Biff that he never tries to please people in business, and that he whistles in the elevator.

Willy enters and tells Biff that he never grew up, and that Bernard does not whistle in the elevator. Biff says that Willy does whistle, however. Biff tells Willy that he's going to see Bill Oliver tomorrow to talk about the sporting good business. Happy says that the beauty of the plan is that it would be like they were playing ball again. Willy reminds Biff to wear a business suit, not to crack any jokes, and not to say "gee." Willy says that it is personality that wins the day. Willy reprimands Linda for interrupting, Biff tells him not to yell at her, and the two start fighting once again. After the boys leave, Linda worries that Oliver won't remember Biff. Willy says that if Biff had stayed with Oliver he'd be on top now. Willy reminisces about Biff's ball game at Ebbets Field.

Analysis

Miller, who returns to the present reality of the play in this segment, definitively establishes that the "flashbacks" occur in the context of Willy Loman's imagination and are a symptom of a larger dementia. Linda attributes her husband's hallucinations to Biff's presence, likely a sign that Biff reminds Willy of his failures as a father and as a businessman. However, the aspect of Willy's dementia that Miller focuses on during this segment of the play is the effect which it has on Linda. She has been the one to deal with Willy's erratic behaviour alone, and doing so has made her age considerably. She is her husband's only defender, even when this role threatens to further exacerbate the conflicts that her family faces.

Miller deals with the indignities that Willy has suffered largely in terms of their effect on Linda. Since her existence and identity depend entirely on her husband, she staunchly defends him even when she realizes that he does not deserve to be defended. When she tells Biff that he cannot love her if he does not love Willy, Linda essentially chooses her husband over her children.

She does this largely out of a strong feeling of duty toward Willy, for she knows that she is the only person who shows any concern for whether he lives or dies. Significantly, she centers her defence of Willy on his status as a human being and not his role as a father or husband. In these respects, Linda thus admits Willy's failures but still maintains that "attention must be paid" to him. This declaration is significant in its construction; Linda declares that someone must regard Willy, but does not specify anybody in particular, thus avoiding a particular accusation of her sons. She condemns society in general for the ill treatment of her husband. As shown by Linda's condemnation of Happy's philandering and Biff's immaturity, Linda has few qualms about confronting her sons, yet when she demands attention for her husband she does not lay the blame only on them.

However, as Miller ennobles Linda as the long-suffering and devoted wife, he nevertheless shows Willy Loman to be undeserving of the respect and admiration Linda accords him. Biff emphasizes the fact that Willy has no sense of character and no respect for Linda, while hints about her physical appearance emphasize that Linda has aged considerably because of her demanding husband.

The final segment of the first act serves as a turning point for Biff, who realizes that he must "apply himself" as his parents have demanded of him. This revelation comes when Linda reveals that Willy has attempted suicide, finally focusing on the severity of his plight. Willy's suicide attempts are the mark of a failed man, but, more importantly, show the disparity between his aspirations and his actual achievements.

Biff's idea of a sporting goods business with his brother demonstrates the various character flaws of Biff and his father. It continues the family emphasis on appearance and personality over substance and achievement. Biff places his aspirations for success on Bill Oliver just as his father depended on Frank Wagner; Linda rightly worries about this, thinking that Bill Oliver may not remember Biff. Finally, the idea of the sporting goods business emphasizes the immaturity of Biff and Happy; both men want to work in sporting goods as an attempt to relive their youth and high school athletic glory. Even Willy himself sees this as an opportunity for himself and his sons to regain what they had lost decades before.

Act II (Loman Home, Present Day)

Willy sits at the kitchen table the next morning. He claims that he slept well for the first time in months. Linda says that it was thrilling to see the boys leaving together, and says that Biff had a new, hopeful attitude. Willy dreams about buying a little place in the country. Linda asks Willy if he will talk to Howard today, and he says that he will tell Howard to take him off the road. Linda tells Willy that the refrigerator is broken, and he complains that she didn't buy a well-advertised brand. Linda tells him that he is supposed to meet the boys for dinner at Frank's Chop House. As soon as Willy leaves, Linda gets a phone call from Biff. She tells him that the pipe that Willy connected to the gas heater is gone; Willy must have taken it away himself.

Analysis

The second act begins with a dramatic shift in tone from the previous act, as Willy now appears cheerful and optimistic. Most importantly, the pipe connected to the gas heater with which Willy tried to commit suicide is now gone; Linda automatically assumes that Willy took it away himself, although this will come into question later in the play.

If a sense of optimism dominates this act of the play, it is nevertheless somewhat unfounded. Willy has gone from suicidal to confident and cheerful in the matter of one night, despite the fact that nothing concrete has been resolved. His plans depend almost entirely upon the success of Biff's meeting with Bill Oliver, an eventuality that seems tenuous at best.

Act II (Wagner's Office, Present Day)

Willy enters the office of his boss, Howard Wagner, a thirty-six year old man sitting at a typewriter table with a wire-recording machine. Howard is ecstatic about his new machine, and shows Willy recordings of Howard's daughter and son. Willy tries to tell Howard what he wants, but Howard insists on playing a recording of his wife. Willy tells Howard that he would prefer not to travel anymore, but Howard insists that Willy is a road man. Willy says that he never asked a favor of any man, but that he was in the firm when Howard's father used to carry him as a boy.

Howard insists that he does not have a spot. Willy talks about how being a salesman used to be a position that had personality in it and demanded comradeship and respect, but today there is no room for friendship or personality. Willy keeps asking for lower and lower salaries, moving from sixty-five to fifty to forty dollars per week. Willy insists that Howard's father made promises to Willy. Howard tells him to pull himself together, and then leaves. Willy leans on the desk and turns on the wire recorder. Willy leaps away with fright and shouts for Howard. Howard returns and fires Willy, telling him that he needs a good, long rest. Howard tells him that this is no time for false pride and he should rely on his sons.

Analysis

In this segment of the second act, Arthur Miller uses Howard Wagner as a symbol of progress and innovation in contrast with Willy Loman's outdated notions of business tactics. Most of the details in Howard's office emphasize technological innovation and novelty, from his well-appointed, modern office to the recording machine that fascinates Howard. This shows that Howard is more interested in the future than the past, as he ignores Willy to consider his new machine. In contrast, Willy speaks not of his future with the company but with his history and past promises. That Willy is frightened by the recorder is a symbol of Willy's obsolescence within a modern business world; he cannot deal with innovation. Even his values, as he notes, belong to a different time. Willy speaks of a past time when being a salesman demanded respect and friendship, a time that has clearly passed, if it ever existed at all.

Willy once again falls prey to his idea that personality and personal relationships are critical factors in the business world. He cites the memory of Howard's father bringing Howard as a newborn to the office and his own role in helping to name the boy. While personally relevant, in terms of the business world this fact bears little weight.

Act Two (Loman Home, Past)

Howard exits and Ben enters, carrying his valise and umbrella. Willy asks him if he has secured the Alaska deal.

The younger version of Linda enters, and she tells Ben that Willy has a great job in New York. She tells him not to go to Alaska. She wonders why everybody must conquer the world, and tells Willy that he's well-liked, and that Old Man Wagner promised that Willy would be a member of the firm someday. Young Biff enters with Young Happy. Willy insists that it is "who you know" that counts, but Ben leaves. Young Bernard arrives, and begs Biff to let him carry his helmet, but Happy wants to carry it. Willy prepares to escort them to the championship game. Willy tells Charley that he cannot go to Biff's baseball game because there is no room in the car. Willy is insulted when he thinks that Charley forgot about the game. Willy prepares to fight Charley.

Analysis

Miller once again shifts the setting of the play to an earlier date in order to contrast Willy's present experiences with those of his idealized past. The reappearance of Ben is symbolic of those dreams that Willy Loman has sacrificed in favor of a more mundane existence. This segment gives some indication that Linda has, in some respects, limited her husband by forcing him to take a more stable path. She claims that not every man has to conquer the world, perhaps assuming that Willy Loman is not a man capable of doing so.

However, Miller reemphasizes Willy's belief in personal connections as the critical factor in business. By this point in the play, Willy's claim that it is not "who you know" that counts has been thoroughly disproved, for Willy was fired by a man whom he has known since his birth. Bernard and Charley's reappearance in this segment foreshadow their later roles in the play. This segment reestablishes the contentious relationship between Charley and Willy, who is shocked to think that Charley may not be in total awe of Biff's athletic achievements. It also reiterates the way in which Bernard remained in Charley's shadow. This dynamic among the characters has obviously shifted, and Miller's insertion of a flashback at this point foreshadows a later development of the dynamic between the Lomans, Bernard, and Charley.

Act II (Charley's Office, Present Day)

Bernard, now mature, sits in Charley's office. Jenny, his father's secretary, enters and asks Bernard to go out into the hall because Willy is shouting to himself. Willy talks to Bernard, who tells him that he's going to go to leave for Washington soon. Bernard's wife just had a son, their second. Willy tells Bernard about the deal with Bill Oliver, and asks Bernard what his secret is. Willy wonders why Biff's life ended after the Ebbets Field game, and from seventeen onward nothing good ever happened to him.

Bernard asks why Willy did not tell Biff to go to summer school so that he could pass math. Around that time, Biff disappeared for a month to see his father in New England, and when he came back he burned his UVA sneakers. Bernard wonders what happened in New England. Charley enters and tells Willy that Bernard is going to argue a case in front of the Supreme Court.

Charley gives Willy some money, and asks what's going wrong with him. Charley says that he offered Willy a job, and wonders why he refused. Willy complains about Howard firing him, but Charley says that things like naming a child do not matter: the only thing that matters is what you can sell. Charley offers him a job again, even though he admits that he does not like Willy and Willy does not like him. Willy refuses once more, and Charley realizes that the sticking point is jealousy. Charley gives him money for insurance, and Willy remarks that a person is worth more dead than alive. Willy tells Charley to apologize to Bernard for him, and, on the verge of tears, tells Charley that he is his only friend.

Analysis

Miller juxtaposes the unsuccessful Willy Loman with the great successes of Bernard and Charley in this segment. Miller continues to develop Willy Loman as a pathetic and deranged character who hallucinates and shouts to himself as he walks through the hallway of an office building. Bernard, in contrast, is a successful man, esteemed in his profession and content with his private life.

The portrayal of Bernard that Miller offers in this segment is ironic, considering Willy's previous comparisons of Bernard to his sons. While Willy believed that Bernard's more serious behaviour and lack of "personality" would hobble him once he entered the business world, the opposite seems to be the case. While Happy is at best moderately successful and unhappy and Biff is an outright failure, Bernard, whom Willy believed to have skills not applicable to the business world, is an obvious success.

Bernard himself even seems to realise that Willy's expectations for his sons have been thwarted, and holds back from telling Willy the reason why he is going to Washington in order to avoid embarrassing him. Bernard also serves to elucidate the development of the relationship between Willy and Biff Loman. Bernard can pinpoint a turning point in their relationship, citing a specific time after which Biff's attitude toward his father changed. Bernard seems to attribute this occurrence to Biff's current failure, claiming that Biff never wanted to go to summer school or graduate high school after visiting his father in New England. Miller makes it clear that Willy is directly responsible for Biff's failures. According to Bernard's interpretation of the event, Biff is nearly self-destructive, ruining his chances for a stable future in order to spite his father.

Charley also represents a degree of success and serenity that Willy is unable to achieve. It is Charley who best identifies the problem with Willy's philosophy of business: Willy wrongly believes that it is personality and intangible factors that are critical to success, while Charley knows that it is in fact more concrete factors such as sales that determine whether a man is successful. Charley also realizes the degree to which Willy is jealous of him and his son; he believes that this is the reason that Willy will not accept a job from him.

The relationship between Charley and Willy is not based on affection, but rather on custom and a developed sense of obligation. Charley admits that he does not like Willy and Willy dislikes him in return, but Charley is in fact Willy's only friend. This declaration is one of the few moments in the play in which Willy seems to realise and acknowledge his own pathetic state. This is accompanied by Willy's claim that a person is worth more dead than alive, which emphasizes Willy's suicidal state and foreshadows events to come.

Act II (Restaurant, Present Day)

At the restaurant, Stanley the waiter seats Happy in a table in the back, where there is more privacy. Happy tells Stanley that Biff has returned and is trying to set up a family business. A lavishly dressed girl enters and sits at the next table, and Happy tells Stanley to bring her champagne. Happy tells the girl that she ought to be on a magazine cover, and the girl says that she has been. Biff enters as Happy flirts with the girl, who is named Miss Forsythe.

Happy tells Miss Forsythe that Biff is a quarterback with the New York Giants. Happy asks the girl out, and asks her if she can find a friend for Biff. The girl exits, and Happy remarks that girls like that are why he can't get married. Biff tells Happy that he did a terrible thing. Bill Oliver did not remember Biff, and walked away when Biff approached him. Biff stole his fountain pen, though. Biff insists that they tell their father tonight to prove that Biff is not lying about his failures just to spite Willy.

Happy tells him to say that he has a lunch date with Oliver tomorrow and to prolong the charade, because Willy is never so happy as when he is looking forward to something. Willy arrives, and tells his sons that he was fired. Although Biff tries to lie to Willy about his meeting with Oliver, Biff and Willy fight when Willy thinks that Biff insulted Bill Oliver. Biff finally gives up, and tells Happy that he cannot talk to Willy. As Biff tries to explain, Willy imagines himself arguing with Young Biff and Young Bernard about Biff failing math, and imagines Bernard telling Linda that Biff went to Boston to see Willy. Biff continues to explain what happened while Willy imagines the woman in the hotel room. Miss Forsythe returns with another woman and Willy leaves. Biff and Happy argue over who should do something about their dad. Happy denies to the women that Willy is their father.

Analysis

While Biff's failures and flaws have been a major preoccupation throughout the play, this segment demonstrates how detrimental Happy's character flaws can be. A compulsive womanizer, Happy tells blatant lies to the women that he meets, claiming that Biff is a professional athlete, then gets rid of his father in favor of seducing Miss Forsythe. In the final, most cruel move that Happy makes, he denies that Willy is his father, thus repudiating his father even more callously than Biff has done.

Biff, in contrast, merely continues his pattern of foolish mistakes in this segment. While Biff may have started to fail in order to spite his father, by this point his self-destructive behaviour is ingrained. His plan to ask Bill Oliver for money was dubious at best, but Biff made it even more unlikely by psuedo-accidentally pocketing his fountain pen. In contrast to Happy, Biff does show some concern for his father's feelings; he worries that Willy will think that Biff intentionally botched the meeting with Bill Oliver.

The Loman sons' insistence on framing Biff's meeting with Bill Oliver in the best possible terms shows that their true interest in the sporting goods business is not for personal gain, but rather to please their father. Biff believes that he cannot tell Willy the truth about his meeting with Bill Oliver, because Willy will think that Biff purposely sabotaged the meeting as an affront to him. Biff's concern is primarily what his father thinks of him and what effect this will have on him; his failure during the meeting, with the exception of his embarrassment over taking the fountain pen, is barely a consideration unless it involves how his father will react to the event. Miller demonstrates that in spite of his weakness, Willy still dominates his sons, whose actions are based on how their father will react to them.

Willy's hallucination about Young Biff failing math and visiting him in Boston gives a greater indication of the reason why Biff garnered such animosity toward his father. Willy ties Biff's visit to Boston with his affair in the same city; the likely confrontation between Willy's life at home as a father and his life on the road as a salesman seems to provide the motivation for Biff's spiteful, self-destructive behaviour.

Act II (Hotel Room, Past)

Willy follows the Woman as he buttons his shirt. Someone knocks on the door, but Willy says he is not expecting anybody. The Woman claims that Willy ruined her and that whenever he comes to the office she will make sure that he goes right through the buyers and never waits at her desk. Finally, Willy tells the Woman to stay in the bathroom and he opens the door. It is Biff, who tells Willy that he flunked math. Biff begs Willy to talk to Mr. Birnbaum, his teacher, to convince him to pass Biff. Biff says that Birnbaum hates him because Biff made fun of his lisp. Biff hears the woman laugh, and she enters from the bathroom. Willy tells Biff that the woman is staying in the next room, which is being painted, so he let her take a shower in his room. Willy throws the woman out, as she claims Willy promised to buy her a pair of stockings. Willy tries to explain that the woman is a buyer, but Biff tells him never mind and starts to cry. Willy admits that he had a relationship with the woman, but claims that it means nothing to him, and that he was lonely.

Analysis

Once again returning to the Loman family's past, Miller finally gives a full explanation for Biff's refusal to take a summer school course, the critical event that determined his chain of failures. It is Willy's infidelity that prompted the change in Biff, as he learned that his father was having an affair with the woman in Boston. Yet the revelation of this reason for Biff's bitterness is not the only example in this segment of how Willy has carelessly ruined the lives of those around him. Willy has ruined the reputation of the Woman, but can offer nothing to her in return. Despite the promises that he has made to her, he denies and discards her. This parallels Willy's earlier insistence that Linda should not mend stockings. Stockings serve as a symbol of what Willy can provide and as a measure of his success.

Act II (Restaurant, Present Day)

At the restaurant, Stanley stands in front of Willy as Willy shouts at the waiter, thinking that he is Biff. Stanley tells Willy that his boys left with the two women and said that they will see him at home. Stanley tries to help him. Willy asks if there is a seed store in the neighborhood, because he has to buy some seeds to plant. Willy leaves for the seed store.

Analysis:

Yet another humiliation for Willy Loman occurs in this segment: his sons have abandoned him at the restaurant, leaving him alone with the waiter while they go out with the two superficial women. Willy's preoccupation with seeds is symbolic of his realization that he has created nothing permanent or worthwhile in his life. As a salesman, he is merely a liaison for what others create, while the family that he made himself has abandoned him at the restaurant. Seeds symbolize something more permanent and tangible even than his family. This new theme also relates back to Willy's seeming embarrassment at Ben's notion that he cannot hunt or fish in Brooklyn; Willy worries that, as a salesman, he is not close enough to nature. His wish to plant seeds is a way to compensate for this deficiency.

Act II (Loman Home, Present Day)

Happy and Biff return home to find their mother there. Happy gives her flowers, and tells Linda that he and Biff met two girls. Linda knocks the flowers to the floor at Biff's feet and stares at him silently. She asks whether or not they care if their father lives or dies. She says that they wouldn't even abandon a stranger at the restaurant as they did their father. Linda asks Happy if he had to go to his "lousy rotten whores" tonight, but Happy insists that all they did was follow Biff around trying to cheer him up. Linda throws them out, calling them a pair of animals. Linda says that Willy didn't have to say anything to her because he was so humiliated that he nearly limped when he entered the house. Biff insists that he talk to Willy, but Linda refuses to let him. They hear a noise outside; it is Willy planting his seeds in the garden.

They find Willy outside, carrying a flashlight, a hoe and a handful of seed packets. Willy imagines that he talks to Ben about his own funeral. He says that people will come from miles around, because he is well-known and well-liked, but Ben says that he is a coward. Biff tells Willy that he is not coming back anymore and that he has no appointment with Oliver. Willy does not believe Biff, and tells him that he cut down his life for spite. Willy refuses to take the blame for Biff's failure. Biff takes the rubber tube out of his pocket and puts it on the table. Biff asks if it is supposed to make him feel sorry for his father. Biff tells his father that the reason that he and Linda couldn't find him for months was that he was in jail in Kansas City for stealing a suit, and that he has stolen something at every good job since high school. Biff says that he is a dime a dozen, and so is Willy, but Willy insists that neither of them are unimportant. Crying, Biff asks Willy to give up his phony dream. Willy remarks that Biff likes him, and Linda says that he loves him. Willy is amazed that Biff cries for him. Happy tells Linda that he will get married and change everything. Everybody goes to sleep but Willy, who remains in the kitchen talking to Ben. Linda calls from her bedroom for Willy to come to bed, but Willy runs out of the house and speeds away in his car. Biff and Happy don jackets, while Linda walks out in mourning clothes and places flowers down on Willy's grave.

Analysis

The final sequence of the second act parallels the end of the first act in structure and emotional resolution. Linda once again acts as the conscience and voice of reason in the household, berating Biff and Happy for their lack of concern for their father. Biff and Happy, in turn, resolve to do improve themselves: Happy decides to settle down, while Biff breaks down emotionally and cries for his father. Biff admits that he was unavailable for months not because he did not care to contact his parents, but rather because he was in jail. This contradicts earlier indications that he did not care for his parents.

The final confrontation between Biff and Willy seems aligned along different concerns for each man. While Biff focuses on Willy's false dreams for himself and for his sons, Willy seems concerned only with what his sons think of him. Willy still retains a belief that Biff and Happy are important people capable of great success, while Biff takes the more realistic view that they are common people incapable of achieving their unrealistic dreams. This returns to the theme of Willy's boundless aspirations, which guarantee that he will never be satisfied with any degree of success in his real life. It is this inability to fully achieve success that drives Willy Loman to suicide.

Willy Loman's suicide can be interpreted as a noble sacrifice, driven by the belief that Biff may go into business with the insurance money he gained from his death. Paradoxically, Willy's suicide may be related to his reconciliation with his elder son; having realized how much Biff cares for him and convinced that Biff does not behave out of spite, Willy can now sacrifice himself for his son.

Requiem

Charley tells Linda that it is getting dark as she stares at Willy's grave. Deeply angered, Happy tells Linda that Willy had no right to commit suicide. Linda wonders where all of the people that Willy knew are. Linda says it is the first time in thirty-five years that she and Willy were nearly free and clear financially, because Willy only needed a little salary. Biff says that Willy had the wrong dreams and that he never knew who he was. Charley says that "nobody dast blame this man," for Willy was a salesman, and for a salesman there is no rock bottom to the life. A salesman has to dream. Biff asks Happy to leave the city with him, but Happy says that he's going to stay in the city and beat the racket, and show that Willy did not die in vain. Charley, Happy and Biff leave, while Linda remains at the grave. She asks why Willy did what he did, and says that she has just made the last payment on the house today, and that they are free and clear.

Analysis

Willy Loman's funeral is a cruel and pathetic end to the

salesman's life. Only his family and Charley attend, while none of his other customers, friends, or colleagues bother to pay their respects. However, the funeral rests primarily on Willy's status as a salesman: it is the character of a salesman that determined Willy's course of action, according to Miller. For a salesman, there are only dreams and hope for future sales. Happy and Biff interpret Willy's suicide in terms of these business dreams: Happy wishes to stay in the city and succeed where his father failed, while Biff rejects the business ethos that destroyed his father and plans to leave New York. Both Happy and Charley frame Willy Loman as a martyr figure, blameless for his suicide and noble in his aspirations, repudiating the humiliations that Willy suffered during the course of the play.

The play ends on an ironic note, as Linda claims that she has made the final payment on their house, creating a sense of financial security for the Lomans for the first time. Willy Loman worked for thirty-five years in order to build this sense of security and stability, yet committed suicide before he could enjoy the results of his labour.

Chapter 15

Study Questions

Q. Do you agree that Biff was an irresponsible son in Death of a Salesman?

Or

Q. Would you like to recommend this kind of life to everyone?

Have you ever felt as if you do not know what to do with your life? Everyone does sometimes, but certain people are like that their whole life. These people are irresponsible and depend on others to survive. In "Death of a Salesman", Biff is one of these people. He is irresponsible because he depends on Happy, depends on Willy, and does not know what to do for a living. Biff looks up on Happy as an example of good life. It seems to him that Happy's life is stable and successful. Even though this is not true, Biff lets it bother him. He wants Happy to get him a job in New York so they could work together. This shows some of his dependency and irresponsibility. Biff does not seem as if he could live on his own successfully. This disappoints both Happy and Willy. But this is not the only problem Biff has. Biff also depends on Willy to get him through life. Willy's low morals cause Biff to think it's all right to concentrate on football when he was in high school. Biff does not think he has to work in school. When he flunks math, he does not know what to do and once again turns to Willy. Now Biff cannot go to college and since he has been concentrating on football, he has little or no skills at anything else. He depends on Willy's support to help him. But since Willy's expectations of Biff are not met, Biff does not receive the help he needs and moves off on his own. This leaves Biff to find a goal in life and reach it. Finally, Biff does not know what to do for a living. He is constantly moving around, unsure of what to do next. This may be because of his uncertainty of a future. Biff has never held a steady job. Because of this, he has never held a steady home. This shows a lot of irresponsibility. Until he knows what he wants to do, Biff cannot settle down and become an adult. This inconsis-tency in employment makes Biff irresponsible. So far in Biff's life, he has not accomplished anything.

He depends on Happy and Willy, and does not know what to do for a living. He realizes that he has wasted his life and has to find something besides football to succeed in. With Happy becoming tired of his antics and Willy on the verge of a breakdown, Biff is now on his own and has to become responsible. Maybe next time you don't know what to do with your life, you'll think a little harder.

Q. Discuss the American Dream in Arthur Miller's Death of a Salesman.

Or

Q. What impact does this American Dream had on others life?

Death of a Salesman is centered around one man trying to reach the American dream and taking his family along for the ride. The Loman's lives from beginning to end is a troubling story based on trying to become successful, or at least happy. Throughout their lives they encounter many problems and the end result is a tragic death caused by stupidity and the need to succeed. During his life Willy Loman caused his wife great pain by living a life not realizing what he could and couldn't do. Linda lived sad and pathetic days supporting Willy's unreachable goals. Being brought up in this world caused his children to lose their identity and put their futures in jeopardy.

Willy lived everyday of his life trying to become successful, well-off salesman. His self-image that he portrayed to others was a lie and he was even able to deceive himself with it. He traveled around the country selling his merchandise and maybe when he was younger, he was able to sell a lot and everyone like him, but Willy was still stuck with this image in his head and it was the image he let everyone else know about. In truth, Willy was a senile salesman who was no longer able to work doing what he's done for a lifetime. When he reaches the point where he can no longer handle working, he doesn't realise it, he puts his life in danger as well as others just because he's pig-headed and doesn't understand that he has to give up on his dream. He complains about a lot of things that occur in everyday life, and usually he's the cause of the problems. When he has to pay for the repair bills on the fridge, he bitches a lot and bad mouths Charley for buying the one he should of bought. The car having to be repaired is only because he crashes it because he doesn't pay attention and/or is trying to commit suicide. Willy should have settled with what he had and made the best of things. He shouldn't have tied to compete with everyone and just made the best decision for him using intelligence and practicality. Many of Willy's problems were self-inflicted, the reason they were self-inflicted was because he wanted to live the American dream. If he had changed his standards or just have been content with his life, his life problems would have been limited in amount and proportion.

Willy's problems in life were usually caused of his chase towards the American dream. Every problem he had and every upsetting or hostile moment he experienced was also inflicted upon Linda, his wife. The hell she went through everyday was because she was his wife. Linda took each day one at a time and each day was filled with stressful worrying about Willy. Imagine how she felt when she found out about Willy's suicidal tendencies, she must have tried extremely hard, as not to take it personally. Linda tried as best she could to try and help Willy, but it wasn't her fault she was not able to get through to him. Willy did not respect Linda or give her the treatment and recognition she deserved. She spent the days mending her silk stockings getting gray hair and worrying about her husbands welfare. Meanwhile Willy found companionship with numerous mistresses and gave away Linda's well-deserved stockings. Linda agrees with everything

Willy says and stays content throughout the whole play. The one time she explodes is when the boys came home from the restaurant after leaving Willy alone. She shows emotion and with a little anger and hostility her true feelings.

Biff and Happy's futures when they were small all depended on the way they were brought up. Willy was the only one with any say in the way the kids were brought up. Linda went along with whatever Willy said. Willy taught them that if they were handsome and successful, opportunity will come to you. Happy learned nothing from Willy's demise but insists that his father had "the only dream you can have- to come out number-one man". Biff and Happy idolized their father when they were young. The stories they were told made them picture their father as a popular, successful, well-known salesman. As Biff grew up, he found himself being told things about his father like "A salesman has to dream, it comes with the territory." At the end of the story when Linda says they we free, Biff is free to realise his dream of owning a ranch out West where he can live close to the natural world. Biff also realizes that his father had the wrong dreams and didn't know who he was. Biff is sure he won't make the same mistakes his father did. Meanwhile, Happy is more like his dad, determined to stay in town and prove himself to everyone. Having Biff acknowledge the dishonesty of his own life, insists on the end of their phony dream.

Although the Loman's lives were full of many problems, the problems were not all caused by Willy striving for the American dream. Willy's problems, (that usually affected the whole family) were caused by little decisions made throughout his lives. He had a choice of whether or not to do something, he just made the wrong decision most of the time because he wanted to live the American dream. The majority of problems Willy encountered were decide upon with the idea of the American dream in mind, although the end result of the problems were not purposely meant to turn out as bad as they usually did. Willy Loman put his family through endless torture because of his search for a successful life. He should have settled with what he had and been happy. One dream is not worth all the pain and problems his caused, he should have learned to be content and, as harsh as it may be to believe, he should have realized what he could have accomplished and given up on his dream.

Q. Describe the funeral scene in the play ?

Or

Q. What was the situation in the Loman House after the funeral?

They all return to the house. The fully paid for house. The sight of it brings back a slight sob to Linda's throat, when she reaches the cement stoop her sobbing once again becomes full. Charley looks to her but is at a loss for words. Happy puts his arms around his mother and holds her. Biff only looks on at it all. For a brief second he sees the Willy's fate in Happy's eyes as he holds Linda. Willy's death has brought Biff to know what he is more than ever. He's not a salesman and neither is Happy but Happy is just like is father and Biff fears nothing can be done to change the course of life Happy has chosen upon Willy's death. The small grieving party enters the house and each takes a seat in the living room. Linda has gained control over herself again. No one dares to say a word they each sit by themselves accompanied by their own thoughts. Biff's mind is racing now. Thoughts of how his life will not end like Willy's. Biff has no master plan for his life he just wishes to begin his life. His real life. "Construction" Biff accidentally says allowed. Everyone looks at him. What about construction. Happy says to Biff.

Tomorrow I'll look for a job in construction is Biff's reply. I'll start at the bottom and I'll gradually raise my position. Someday maybe architecture or engineering. By god I'm gonna do something with my life weather it's to my families approval or not. Charley looks at Biff and says. Biff I don't know if this is the right time for this. It's sounds like a good idea to me but I honestly don't think this is the time to talk about it. I'm sorry Charley you're right I'm going to bed now I'll see you all tomorrow. Biff stands up stretches his arms and back and goes off to bed. Biff wakes up early the next morning. No one else has woken yet and Charley had gone home the night before. Despite the death of his father hanging over him like a dark, dreary cloud Biff is in an unexplainably great mood. He felt as if his life was just beginning on this day. He is wearing his blue suit, makes himself some eggs and toast, and has a cup of coffee. Then he was off to find an honest job. Biff wanted to make a sort of amends with the old construction company him and Happy used to steal from. This was Biff's first choice. He arrived at the company building straitened himself out and went in. As he entered the lobby a young receptionist met him. Biff stated his business and asked if any job were open. The receptionist handed him an application to fill out. Biff took a seat by a window and started on the application. the first question he encountered was that of experience. Biff began to make up false places of employment for himself. When he noticed this was exactly what his father and happy would be doing he threw out the application and asked for another. If he didn't get the job honestly he didn't want the job at all. Biff put applications out for a few hours most places followed the basic routine as the first. Then he returned home. Happy and Linda were in the kitchen eating lunch when he came in. Linda and happy ignored him so he made himself some lunch and sat down at the table with them.

What's with the "cold shoulder" you guys are giving me. Biff asked.

We aren't giving you a "cold shoulder" we simply don't have anything to say to you was Linda's reply.

Well would you like to hear about my day?

The phone rang just as he finished his question. Linda got up to answer it.

It's for you Biff. It's the Altec construction agency.

Biff took the phone and said thanks mom. Linda reproached Biff's thanks with an uh-huh and she sat down to her meal again.

Biff hung the phone and told Linda and Biff that they wanted him to come in for an interview right away. I just put the application in this morning and they want to interview me already. Isn't that great guys!

That's good was Linda's only reply.

You know what Mom, Happy I really don't care how you feel about me but I'm not going to let you two financially fade away just because you dislike me. If I get this job you are getting a portion of my paycheck whatever you need to keep yourselves afloat. I'll move out if that's what you want. The only thing you'll ever see from me is my money!

With all that said Biff left the house not waiting for a reply he didn't expect.

Biff arrived at the Altec company building still in his blue suit before he entered he looked at the suit and wished he hadn't worn it. the suit went along with his father's belief of image being foremost important. Biff no longer wanted a job simply for his image. Biff entered the building walked straight to the receptionist and stated his name. The receptionist told him that Mr. Lansing, the personnel manager was expecting him and she pointed towards the office door Labeled Personell Manager, Mr. Lansing. Biff thanked the receptionist and he walked over to the door. Before Biff knocked however he took the suit coat off and set it on a chair then he knocked on Mr. Lansing's office door. A man dressed in a suit very similar to Biff's opened the door and said hello my name is Mr. Lansing please come in and take a seat. Biff followed Mr. Lansings instruction and sat down in a comfortable leather chair in front of Mr. lansing's fine Cherry desk. By the look of the personnel manager's office Biff thought to himself that this company must be quite successful and he was assured that he wasn't making a mistake with this business venture.

Okay Mr. Loman lets get started. Mr. lansing asked Biff a few simple questions. Then he asked Biff when the soonest he could start.

I could start today if you want me to Biff told him.

Great Biff you see a few of our workers have recently left the company to begin their own and we are in desperate need right now. I don't want to rush you into it. So we won't start you today but how's tomorrow sound around 12:00am at the Westmore Voice recording construction site on Philips street.

That would be great Mr. Lansing. The sooner I can make some money the better. Please call me Charles I try and keep good relations with our employees and I want you to know that if you ever have any problems or comments to come to me with them. Okay.

Sure thing Mr.... Charles.

All right then you will be met by Bryan Acker tomorrow at the construction site. He's a fellow worker and he'll provide you with any training you need. Have a good day and good luck Biff.

Q. Discuss how the American Dream in Death of a Salesman misguides the protagonist?

Or

Q. Discuss how the dreams and hopes go wrong in the play?

Death of a Salesman deals with hopes and dreams gone wrong. This does not necessarily have to be the "American" dream as such, because all people share the same hopes and dreams, regardless of nationality. The underlying factor, and the inevitable truth is that we all have to dream, dreams are important for human existence. It is evident to the reader that for Willy, his ultimate dream was to follow in the footsteps of Uncle Ben and become a successful salesman. Unfortunately for Willy, most of his dreams are illusions, yet he is unable to come face to face with this fact. At the plays conclusion, Biff is susceptible to succumb to the fact that his father, Willy, did in fact have "all the wrong dreams", and the reader will agree that this is ultimately what lead to Willy's downfall.

Willy's false hopes and dreams are evident in the fact that he wants to be a mirror image of his brother Ben. "The man knew what he wanted and went out and got it!" Willy believes that Ben has the "ultimate life", and strives to follow in the dream of being a successful salesman. This brings forth the notion of Willy kidding himself, and not knowing any different. "The jungle is dark but full of diamonds." The jungle metaphor is continually bought to the reader's attention throughout the novel. Like Ben, Willy hopes to strike it rich in the business world of New England. Yet Willy never finds the diamonds (success), and he leaves life without fortune or fame. In many ways, the jungle also represents the American

Dream ideal that Miller often criticized. It is the opinion of Willy that the job of a salesman is the most enjoyable of all jobs. "...And the smile on your face" gives the reader the notion that Willy is happy in his job, which Willy himself leads himself to believe. Evidently, this only turns out to be another illusion that Willy has created for himself. Nearing the novels conclusion, it is evident to the reader that Willy is unable to maintain this smile, and he is no longer happy in his job. Willy's illusions throughout the novel are also evident to the educated audience.

When explaining why they can't leave the crowded city to live in New York, Willy tells his wife, "I'm the New England man. I'm vital in New England." Unfortunately for Willy, this is just one of his many illusions evident to us. Like his brother Ben who conquered the wilderness, Willy feels that he must live on the frontier, building a house and planting a garden for his family if he wants to properly care for them. He tells Linda, "Before it's all over we're gonna get a little place out in the country, and I'll raise some vegetables, a couple of chickens..." Unfortunately, times have changed and his dream is no longer possible. In essence, the illusions that Willy experiences come directly from him having the "wrong dreams" and ideas about life.

Biff rightly informs us that Willy had "all the wrong dreams", and he, as Willy's son, is evidently one of the first characters to realise this fault about Willy. "Take that phony dream and burn it..." is what Biff yells at Willy in between tears and emotion. "I am not a leader of men...and neither are you." Willy is continually expecting great things of his son throughout the novel as is evident to the reader. Biff, in this particular scene nearing the plays conclusion, tries to 'drive it into' Willy that he is not a huge success, and to stop having such high expectations. While Biff realizes that their father "had the wrong dreams," Happy defends Willy's aspirations, saying, "I'm gonna show you and everybody else that Willy Loman did not die in vain. He had a good dream. It's the only dream you can have-to come out number-one man. He fought it out here, and this is where I'm gonna win it for him."

As an objective reader, we must appreciate the fact that not all of Willy's dreams and aspirations were morally wrong. As his son Happy informs us, his ultimate dream was to come out "number-one man." Although not achieved by Willy himself, it is evident to all readers that this is a strong dream to hold onto.

So ultimately, at the novels conclusion, it is unfortunate that Willy had to lose his own life just to provide for his family's future. Yet it becomes evident to the reader that this is perhaps one of Willy's dreams come true. Willy has achieved the "American dream" at the cost of his own life, yet at the same time, he has given new life to both of his sons and his wife through funding. As a man, he has a countless number of hopes and dreams. Unfortunately, most of these are illusions, which Willy can not seem to comprehend. Yet the audience is still able to display compassion and sorrow toward his overall situation, because after all, "he's only a little boat looking for a harbour."

Q. Discuss the main cause of Willy Loman's Depression in Death of a Salesman?

Or

Q. Do you agree that the old age of Willy causes major depression and death?

Arthur Miller's, "Death of a Salesman," shows the development and structure that leads up to the suicide of a tragic hero, Willy Loman. The author describes how an American dreamer can lose his self-worth by many negative situations that occur throughout his life. The structure and complications are essential because it describes how a man can lose his way when depression takes over.

The first comlication which occurs in Act I, is when the reader acknowledges that Willy put his whole life into his sons, Biff and Happy, and they turned their backs on him. Willy always believed that biff would be this great, successful businessman and it turned out that Biff is still searching to find himself, which disappoints Willy in the worst way. The conflicts between Willy and Biff are rooted very deep. It all started when Biff was younger and he had failed his math class.

He traveled to Boston to visit Willy, who was on a business trip. He had told that he had let Willy down and comes to find out that Willy is with another woman. Biff leaves and never takes that math class over. Willy felt guilty about this and believes that deep inside that he is responsible for Biff's choices in life and his failure to be successful. This conflict makes Willy weak and tremendously guilty, which stays with him as a reminder.

The second complication that destroys Willy is his aging. By getting older he can't do the things he used to do. His aging affects his work because he is not the salesman he once was. He is not making enough money to support his wife, Linda, and himself. Being 60, Willy is getting too old for the traveling he does for his work. Willy asks his boss, Howard, for a raise and Howard fires him. Willy is really worn out and Howard knows this. This situation in end destroys Willy's pride and he could never ask his sons for money.

The last complication at the end of Act II, is the conflict between Willy and Biff. Biff finally wants to get everything straight and clear with his father. Biff shows Willy the rubber tube that Willy wants to kill himself with. An argument erupts from this and Biff tries to explain that he was never what Willy wanted him to be. Willy realizes that Biff loves him, even if he isn't the best person. This last situation has totally broken Willy down to a very tired man and he believes that his life is totally finished.

The play concludes in a tragic end when Willy leaves the house and crashes his car to end his life. With all the failing attempts, this time it had been successful. The structure of complications lead to the destruction of an American dreamer and the dreams of his sons. Willy wanted a dream that seemed materialistic and unimportant compared to the cost of his own life.

Teacher's Comments

I think you are right on when it comes to Willy's depression. He just seems to wallow in self-pity the whole play, never forgiving himself for the things that have gone wrong in his life. I want to shake him and say, "get over it!" His depression not only affects him, but his entire family.

In the first paragraph, at first, I felt that the depression would have been the subject that would be developed based on how you worded it in the sentence; I was not exactly clear as to what your thesis statement was. Also, I noticed that your tenses were not consistent (i.e. He was this....He is this).

Q. Discuss the Impact of Isolation in Death of a Salesman?

Or

Q. "Loneliness was the major reason for Willy's suicide" Explain.

Arthur Miller's play Death of a Salesman is the story of a man, Willy Loman, gone deaf to the outside world. Though many try to help him, he shuts them out and creates his own reality in which he is successful and loved by everyone. In Death of a Salesman, Willy has many influences both good and bad attempting to direct his life; it is his refusal to choose the helpful advice that will ultimately lead to his downfall.

One negative influence in Willy's life is the inability of his friends to confront him about his problems. It is Willy's wife that causes him the most harm. In her vain attempt to protect Willy, she actually allows his eventual death. The first sign of her negligence comes in one of Willy's flashbacks. Willy brags, "I did five hundred gross in Providence and seven hundred gross in Boston". But as Linda begins calculating his commission, the value rapidly diminishes to "roughly two hundred gross on the whole trip". Linda sees what is going on but does not confront him. A very similar situation occurs later in their life when she finds out that Willy is no longer on salary, but borrows money every week from Charley. Again she will not confront him. By not confronting Willy in either of these instances, Linda allows him to sink further into his false reality. But Linda makes an even worse mistake that allows for Willy's suicide.

She acknowledges his suicidal tendencies when she says, "He's been trying to kill himself". She tells the boys that she has found the rubber hose in the basement, but she still will not confront Willy. Another character who is unable to be straight with Willy is Willy's boss Howard Wagner. Howard allows Willy to keep his job, but does not pay him. If he had just fired him right out it would of forced Willy to find a new job. By stringing him along, Howard allows Willy to maintain his fantasy world unchallenged. These are examples of the most negative influences in Willy's life simply because they have the ability to help but choose not to.

It seems that the only people who want to help Willy, are those who he least listens to. In fact the two best influences on Willy come from the same family. Bernard grew up with Biff and Happy but chose a much different path. At a key time in Biff's life, Bernard warns "I he doesn't buckle down he'll flunk". In this scene Bernard is trying to tell Willy that he is instilling the wrong values in his sons who are destined for failure. Willy however does not want to listen to Bernard because he has the most popular and athletic son in town. But even later when Willy sees Bernard's success he will not listen. Bernard sees that Willy is still holding on to a job that is not working for him and tells him "sometimes, Willy, it's just better for a man to walk away". Willy can only respond by asking "But if you can't walk away?". Charley, Bernard's father, even takes trying to help Willy a step farther. Charley sees early on that Willy's job is not working out and begins offering him a job. Charley continues to offer this job until the end. And even though Willy refuses to take a job from Charley, Charley continues to loan Willy the money he needs every week knowing he will never get paid back. In this play Charley and Bernard are the only characters from the beginning to the end that truly do everything they can to help Willy; yet still Willy refuses to listen to them.

Because Willy does not want to listen to the outside world, he is forced to create his own sources of guidance. This guidance comes in the form of Ben his brother and Dave Singleman. Ben appears to the audience in the form of Willy's flashbacks. He excites Willy with tales of self-made fortune. Willy uses Ben as a scapegoat in order to explain his own failures. He makes himself believe that if he had gone with Ben, he too would be rich. By doing this he avoids facing his own failures as a salesman. Though we never see Dave Singleman, he is the single most powerful influence on Willy. He is Willy's personification of the perfect salesman. Willy hopes to gain the respect and success that Dave Singleman had. But in reality Dave represents the superficiality, which Willy bases his life on. All of the good qualities that Dave Singleman possessed were superficial. Nothing is said about his family life or character. Willy needs to realise that it is the inner qualities that count. By creating a mold of the ideal man in his head, Willy sets himself up for disappointment. When he is unable to be the ideal man he wants to be, he looses his will to live and deems himself as a failure. But because he has shut himself off from those around him, no one is able to reach him before it is too late.

Q. Discuss the Powerful Conclusion of Death of a Salesman?

Or

Q. Briefly describe the dual concept of successful and unsuccessful life of Willy?

The play "Death of a Salesman" shows the final demise of Willy Loman, a sixty-year-old salesman in the America of the 1940's, who has deluded himself all his life about being a big success in the business world. It also portrays his wife Linda, who "plays along" nicely with his lies and tells him what he wants to hear, out of compassion. The book describes the last day of his life, but there are frequent "flashbacks" in which Willy relives key events of the past, often confusing them with what is happening in the present. His two sons, Biff and Happy, who are in their 30's, have become failures like himself. Both of them have gone from idolizing their father in their youth to despising him in the present. On the last few pages of the play, Willy finally decides to take his own life. Not only out of desperation because he just lost his job, with which he was hardly earning enough to pay ordinary expenses at the end. He does it primarily because he thinks that the life insurance payout will allow Biff to come to something, so that at least one of the Lomans will fulfill his unrealistic dream of great wealth and success. But even here in one of his last moments, while having a conversation with a ghost from the past, he continues to lie to himself by saying that his funeral will be a big event, and that there will be guests from all over his former working territory in attendance. Yet as was to be expected, this is not what happens, none of the people he sold to come. Although perhaps this wrong foretelling could be attributed to senility, rather than his typical self-deception. Maybe he has forgotten that the "old buyers" have already died of old age.

His imagined dialogue partner tells him that Biff will consider the impending act one of cowardice. This obviously indicates that he himself also thinks that it's very probable that Biff will hate him even more for doing it, as the presence of "Ben", a man whom he greatly admires for being a successful businessman, is a product of his own mind.

But he ignores this knowledge which he carries in himself, and goes on with his plan. After this scene, Biff, who has decided to totally sever the ties with his parents, has an "abrupt conversation" with Willy. Linda and Biff are in attendance. He doesn't want to leave with another fight, he wants to make peace with his father and tell him goodbye in a friendly manner. He has realized, that all his life, he has tried to become something that he doesn't really want to be, and that becoming this something (a prosperous businessman) was a (for him) unreachable goal which was only put into his mind by his father. He doesn't want a desk, but the exact opposite: To work outside, in the open air, with his hands.

But he's willing to forgive Willy for making this grave mistake while Biff was in his youth. He simply wants to end their relationship in a dignified way. Willy is very angered by this plan of Biff's, because it means that he is definitely not going to take the 20000 dollars and make a fortune out of it. Happy, who has become very much like his father, self-deceiving and never facing reality, is shocked by what Biff says. He is visibly not used to hearing the naked truth being spoken in his family. He objects by telling another lie, "We always told the truth!" This only serves to enrage Biff further, after Willy has already denied shaking his hand, which would have been a gesture of great symbolic meaning. For Willy, it would have meant admitting to everybody that he was wrong, and it would show acceptance of his son's true nature. But Willy goes on to say that Biff is doing all of this out of spite, and not because it is what he really wants. Spite, because the teenage Biff had once caught him cheating on Linda, and that was the turning point from being admired, to being hated by Biff. So now, instead of generously forgiving, Biff becomes just as angry and aggressive.

They almost get into a physical fight, but he suddenly lapses intro utter sadness and desperation, and cries, holding on to Willy. After he has left, Willy is deeply moved, because he realizes that Biff actually liked him. But even this realisation does not make him understand Biff, and he proclaims again that Biff "will be magnificent!". And his mental voice, in the form of Ben, adds that this will certainly be the case, especially "with twenty thousand behind him". He is freshly motivated to proceed with his old plan by his gross misinterpretation of Biff's startling behaviour. He is simply unable to realise, that money is not what Biff wants or needs. Although he does realise, that Biff, despite everything, loves him, and perhaps this is to him another incentive to give him the money.

At the funeral, Happy is unchanged, his old self. He says that "[they] would've helped him", even though he himself had been extremely cruel to Willy by abandoning him at a restaurant just before the big quarrel, and certainly this wasn't the only incident where he had shown no regard at all for Willy. Happy has obviously not learned a thing from the entire tragedy, which is why Biff gives him a "hopeless" glance near the end of the Requiem. Biff speaks of the "nice days" that they had had together, which all involve handyman's work Willy had done on the day.

Charley adds to this that "he was a happy man with a batch of cement". This adds a new dimension to the tragedy, because it all indicates that Willy was, just like Biff, a man who enjoys physical work. If this was the case, then Willy could simply never admit to himself, like Biff finally did, that he WASN'T going to make big money. Linda voices her regret over not being able to cry, alone at Willy's grave. An explanation of this would be, that she simply cannot understand and forgive him these last acts. First, the not letting Biff go, and then committing suicide, despite the fact that Biff had made his intentions so clear. Also, she might interpret into his self-inflicted death, which leaves her behind alone, that he did not love her. This conclusion of the tragedy fits the rest of the play well. The dramatic character development is quite unpredictable, neither are the specific events, which makes it a compelling read.

Q. Discuss the Delusion of Willy Loman?

Or

Q. How the dream of vacation in America of Willy Loman shatters?

Or

Q. "The jagged edges of a shattered dream." Do you find that the play leaves you with such an impression?

Death of a Salesman tells the story of a man confronting failure in the success-driven society of America and shows the tragic trajectory which eventually leads to his suicide. Willy Loman is a symbolic icon of the failing America; he represents those that have striven for success but, in struggling to do so, have instead achieved failure in its most bitter form. Arthur Miller's tragic drama is a probing portrait of the typical American psyche portraying an extreme craving for success and superior status in a world otherwise fruitless. To some extent, therefore, Death of Salesman is concerned with the 'jagged edges of a shattered dream' but on another more tragic and bitter level, it also evokes the decline of a man into lunacy and the subsequent effect this has on those around him, particularly his family.

Miller amalgamates the archetypal tragic hero with the mundane American citizen. The result is the anti-hero, Willy Loman. He is a simple salesman who constantly aspires to become 'great'. Nevertheless, Willy has a waning career as a salesman and is an aging man who considers himself to be a failure but is incapable of consciously admitting it. As a result, the drama of the play lies not so much in its events, but in

Willy's deluded perception and recollection of them as the audience gradually witness the tragic demise of a helpless man.

In creating Willy Loman, Miller presents the audience with a tragic figure of human proportions. Miller characterises the ordinary man (the 'low man') and ennobles his achievements. Willy's son, Biff, calls his father a 'prince', evoking a possible comparison with Shakespeare's Hamlet, prince of Denmark.. Thus, the play appeals greatly to the audience because it elevates an ordinary American to heroic status. Death of a Salesman seems to conform to the 'tragic' tradition that there is an anti-hero whose state of hamartia causes him to suffer. The audience is compelled to genuinely sympathise with Willy's demise largely because he is an ordinary man who is subject to the same temptations as the rest of us.

Miller uses many characters to contrast the difference between success and failure in the American system. Willy Loman is a deluded salesman whose vivid imagination is far greater than his sales ability. Linda, Willy's wife, honorably stands by her husband even in the absence of fundamental realism. To some extent she acknowledges Willy's aspirations but, naively, she also accepts them. Consequently, Linda is not part of the solution but rather part of the problem with this dysfunctional family and their inability to face reality. In restraining Willy from his quest for wealth in the Alaska, the 'New Continent', ironically the only realm where the "dream" can be fulfilled, Linda destroys any hope the family has of achieving 'greatness'. Even so, Linda symbolically embodies the play's ultimate value: love. In her innocent love of Willy, Linda accepts her husband's falsehood, his dream, but, in her admiration of his dream, she is lethal. Linda encourages Willy and, in doing so, allows her sons, Biff and Happy, to follow their father's fallacious direction in life.

Willy's close friend Charlie on the other hand, despite his seemingly ordinary lifestyle, enjoys far better success compared to the Lomans. Charlie differs to his friend considerably: he is financially secure whereas Willy can barely afford to pay the next gas bill. Similarly, Charlie never indoctrinated his son, Bernard, with the same enthusiasm as Willy. Subsequently, Charlie stands for different beliefs to Willy and, ironically, ends up far more successful. He is a voice of reason for his friend but is only useful if Willy follows his advice. Instead, Willy's proud and stubborn nature ensures that he will never accept Charlie's many generous job proposals. The Dream, as Willy perceives it, is still within grasp of the Lomans thus an ordinary job would not fulfil the true expectations Willy holds of either himself or Biff. Ironically, these job proposals are the one gate left open to Willy and his hopes of becoming 'great'.

According to Biff, his friend, the 'anemic' Bernard, is not 'well liked'. However not 'well liked' he may be, Bernard, through constant persistence, has grown up to be an eminent lawyer. He appears to be proof enough of the "system's" effectiveness and affirms the proposition that success is achieved through persistent application of one's talents.

Whilst everyone around Willy experiences success and wealth, the Loman's themselves struggle financially. The play romanticises the pioneering dream but never makes it genuinely available to Willy and his family. Willy reveres success. He wants to be successful, to be "great", but his dream is never fulfilled. Indeed, he feels the only way he can actually fulfill his dream is to commit suicide so that his family may subsequently live off his life insurance.

It seems Willy's dead brother, Ben, is the only member of the Loman family who has ever achieved something "great" when he proclaims, 'when I was seventeen I walked into the jungle, and when I was twenty-one I walked out. And by God I was rich.' Ben is idealised by Willy since he fulfilled the genuine American Dream: to start out with nothing and eventually become rich through effort and hard work. Ironically, this wealth is achieved outside America suggesting that there is little left available for the ordinary individual within the country's own boundaries. Instead, one must look elsewhere for true "greatness", underlining the fact that, for the majority, the much sought after American Dream' is a myth. The play is ambiguous in its attitude toward the business-success dream, but certainly does not rebuke it openly. Nevertheless, when Charlie declares, 'Nobody does blame this man', Miller hints at the responsibility of the state influenced 'Everyone should have a dream' campaign behind Willy's death, suggesting that the salesman was driven too far, pressurizing himself into suicide. Miller also seems to judge America in hinting that there is far greater success to be found outside of its land. Indeed, it seems there is a lot of room for failure (and ruin) as well as 'greatness' in America. Hence, Willy is a foolish and ineffectual man for whom we feel pity.

Willy detaches himself from reality, living in a life of idealism and dreams that never materialise. One example of Willy's deluded perception of reality lies in his constant disgruntlement with the American car industry. In truth, Willy has always scorned his cars. Even in the 1930s when, according to Willy, the Chevy was at its prime, the Chevy is still insulted by its owner! These, and other such instances in the play, evoke a prime flaw in Willy's character: he is never, fully content with what he possesses at present.

Instead, he lives in a deluded world where imagination and past experiences collude and, frequently, appear as far more desirable eras. As a result, Willy continually finds aspects of his life 'remarkable' but never actually realises that as a salesman and a father, he is a failure. This lack of understanding eventually leads to his tragic death; a death he could not escape for he brought it on himself. In killing himself, Willy finally becomes a man of purpose and reason. He had been trying to make a gift that would crown all those striving years; in this instant, all those lies he told, all those dreams and vivid exaggerations would now be given form and point. In American Society the only option open to Willy as such was to be a salesman. Tragically, he eventually feels he must, symbolically, trade his own life for his family's wellbeing whereby they will hopefully experience a life of greatness without, ironically, himself present.

Death of a Salesman has a form that allows for the simultaneity of past and present, enabling the events in Willy's life to proceed from the fragmented logic of his own experiences. Thus, while Miller ensures that the audience experience Willy's perception of reality, it also recognises it as objectively real. Indeed, Miller's juxtaposition of incidents from Willy's internal and external experience brings the audience to sympathise with Willy. Consequently, the audience is able to share the nightmare experience of the protagonist and eventually deduce their own opinions of the death of a salesman.

Miller said of Death of a Salesman that it was 'a slippery play to categorize because nobody in it stops to make a speech objectively stating the great issues which I believe it embodies'. Subsequently, no single character acts as Miller's mouthpiece, nor does any one speech offer a direct reflection of his opinions. And, although there are no genuine soliloquies in the play, Miller's juxtaposition of events from the anti-hero's past and present enable the playwright to illustrate Willy's insanity with similar effectiveness. Consequently, this expressionistic device allows the audience to genuinely symphathise with Willy's jaded state of mind and allow them to eventually deduce their own opinion of Willy's character.

Death of a Salesman may also be interpreted as an allegorical representation of America. Willy's garden can be perceived as a microcosm of American society as tower blocks continued to be raised around him. This suggests that, for the 'ordinary' person, the literally 'Lo-man' in comparison to the skyscrapers, life has become overshadowed at the cost of capitalism. The audience is left with the image of the garden that will never grow; the ordinary person has been left behind and even rejected by wealthy capitalists.

With everyone succeeding except Willy, Miller also suggests that there is far more success outside America. Indeed, there are nothing but fruitless hopes and 'shattered dreams' to be found within the nation. And, in one last vain effort, Willy attempts to 'grow' something for his family in his buying of seeds to plant in the garden. Nevertheless, even Willy has come to realise that his life is a failure when he declares, Oh, I'd better hurry-Nothing's planted. I don't have a thing in the ground.'

Nevertheless, it seems that Miller's intention in writing about the death of a salesman, a seemingly mundane occurrence in twentieth-century society, was to express the playwright's own vision of American Society and the nature of individuality. Death of a Salesman may be interpreted as being solely a play about the failing America and the 'jagged edges of a shattered dream' but it does, nevertheless, engage Miller's belief that 'the common man is as apt a subject for tragedy as kings are'.

Chapter 16

Critical Essays

Critical analysis of Four Characters

The play "Death Of A Salesman", the brainchild of Arthur Miller was transformed and fitted to the movie screen in the year 1986. The play itself is set in the house of Willy Loman, and tells the melancholy story of a salesman whom is in deep financial trouble, and the only remedy for the situation is to commit suicide. In the stage production of this tale, the specific lighting, set, and musical designs really give the story a strong undertow of depression. And logically the screen and stage productions both differ greatly in regards to the mood they set. Moreover the movie production can do many things that just cannot be done on stage, with reference to the setting of course. To generalize, the play gives us a good hard look at the great American Dream failing miserably. However the combination of both the stage and screen productions accurately depict the shortcomings of the capitalist society.

Death of a Salesman specifically focuses on four characters, the first being the main character Willy Loman, his wife Linda, and their two sons Hap and Biff Loman. As mentioned, the focal point of this play is Willy Loman, a salesman in his early sixties. Throughout the story we are told the hard life, emotions and triumphs of Willy the salesman. Early in the play we learn that he has recently been demoted to working for commission, which later in the play,(on par with his luck) translates into Willy getting fired. As the plot unfolds we discover that Willy had a rich brother who recently died named Ben, whom Willy looked upon with great admiration for becoming extremely wealthy and the ripe old age of 21. However Willy also becomes very depressed when Ben leaves, the fact being that he re-realizes the meagerness of his own life, and that he is still making payments on all of his possessions. Willy then comprehends that bye the time his worldly possessions are paid for...they shall no longer be of any use. For example, the Loman house has become virtually unnecessary now that the two sons have moved out. It isn't until after Willy's death that the final mortgage payment is made....for a house with no one inside it. The one example of this statement is given by Linda during the final paragraph of the play,

"I made the last payment on the house today. Today, dear. And there will be nobody home. We're free and clear..........we're free.......we're free............we're free"

As the plot thickens, Willy the salesman plummets deeper and deeper into depression until his most likely route of action, which of course is suicide. However the reasoning behind this course of action, we find, is his genuine love for his family, along with Willy's deep longing to supply his family with as much money as he can possibly get his hands on. As we learn more about Willy's trials and tribulations, the age old expression "like father like son" appears out of nowhere like a beacon. Like his father, Willy's son Biff also has some problems of his own, the main one being that Biff cannot seem to find his niche in life. Furthermore, we are told that Biff at one point did in fact have his future all planned out. It turns out that Biff was a shoe-in for a position on the University Of Virginia State football team. However, that chance was all but lost when Biff did not qualify to pass his final mathematics course. Now as you can imagine the fact that Biff had to explain this to his father was quite a large problem in itself. But to add insult to injury, when Biff made the trip to Boston to explain his mathematical dilemma, he is horrified to find that his father has been with another women. And this one incident would leave Biff being an entirely different person altogether. He didn't even make an attempt to finish his math in summer school. After Boston, Biff couldn't have cared less what happened to his own life. However, as is in life, out of something horrible comes something worthy. And Biff finally comes to the realization that he in fact wants to make his future. And that future entails working in the outdoors on a farm. The other reasoning behind this life decision is of course, is to go against the wishes and values that his father has tried to instill in Biff his entire life. Biff pours his heart to his brother Hap one quarter through act I.

....."To devote your whole life to keeping stock, or making phone calls, or selling or buying. To suffer fifty weeks a year for the sake of a two week vacation, when all you really desire is to be outdoors, with your shirt off.."

Fortunately for Biff, he determines his future by the play's conclusion. He comes to the understanding that he and Willy were never meat to be business men. Including that they were intended to be working on a farm with their hands. And after vexing to procure Hap to come with him (which is to no avail), he escapes from his home to continue on with the rest of his life. Which for Biff seems to be the soundest choice, the decision that Willy just couldn't make. Hap on the other hand stays with his father, and at play's end decides to follow in Willy's footsteps. That of course is to succeed at business at all costs.

Both the stage and screen rendition utilize a mélange of distinct effects to set the tone and to enact the specific place where the action transpires. For example, the stage interpretation utilizes a unique convention that involves walking through the set to delineate circumstances in the past, or episodes going on inside the mind of Willy. This illusion can be easily created with specific cross fades and musical underlay, and of course willing suspension of disbelief. Divergently, in the screen production the set is obviously utilized in a completely different manner.

On that account the movie uses a distinct fading and brightening lighting technique, that still stays true to the conventions set forth by the playwright. The one device that the screen production contains that the stage does not, is the ability to display the past events of Willy's life in a completely accurately set manner. Meaning when there is a flashback to a previous happening, the setting travels back in time as well. Which, from a certain perspective, better illustrates the past recollections of Willy and his family. As mentioned the stage production successfully employs music to delineate certain characters or the tone of that particular instant.

There is in fact music used in the movie, however it is only a small aspect of the screen medium whereas it is an integral component of the stage version. Although you cannot fully comprehend the importance of the music by simply reading the play, it must be performed right in front of you.. While the movie gives you a generally decent feel for the musical intonation. In its entirety the music does an excellent job of setting the mood that Willy is in.

The play is set inside the house of Willy Loman. Surrounding his house are some tall building that are quite visible on the edges of the set. The house itself contains two bedrooms, a living room and a kitchen. This is also, where the majority of the action of the play takes place. All other action happens outside the house lines. This for a stage audience requires them to suspend their disbelief even further. Whereas in a movie the viewer isn't required to stretch any of his or her imaginations. Although this particular screen production utilized an uncommon convention that allowed the viewer to actually see through the set.

One other interesting convention used by the designer was that there was no roof on the house at certain times during the performance. And in place of the roof were huge buildings and skyscrapers. These buildings were used to divulge a over-powering feeling of gloom. This tool is much more effectual in the movie, due to its original and abstract nature. This was also was very helpful during Willy's dreams, on account of the house would exude an aura of peace an tranquility. Together with the prevalent set in the movie, (where there is a roof and normal fencing), the idea is very well perceived.

In spite of the fact that this play has been described as a modern tragedy, there has been some controversy to that description. The reason being that it does not accompany the standard protocol of tragedy. Traditionally speaking, a tragedy usually begins with the main character in the midst of a prominent position of piety. And over the course of the play becomes transformed and that character flips to a lower level of status. A tragedy is also reputed to acquaint its audience with regard to life. The audience should leave a tragedy feeling virtuous about themselves, even though the tragedy concludes on a note of melancholy. This is why scholars say they cannot include this play in the definition of tragedy.

This famous tale of a salesman contains a singular main character; Willy (The Salesman)Loman, his two strapping young lads Happy and Biff, and of course his adoring wife Linda. Willy struggles to climb his way up the American capitalist hierarchy, but its seems his ship will not come in. In spite of the fact that Willy would much rather be laboring with his hands, he is set in the mindset that his real love could never make enough money.

Disappointment after disappointment Willy decides that his only way to provide for his family would be to commit suicide. The number one son of the salesman, Biff, is paving his way for a discouraging life. Symbolically speaking, the character of Biff represents Willy at a younger age, for they both carry the same characteristics. However Biff is given the same chance to do something with his life, and surprisingly enough he takes it. As for Willy's other son, Happy decides that he will take the same long, hard road as his father, only he thinks that he'll make it.

The Character of Willy Loman seem to be the consummate model to illustrate the dissension of the American capitalist ideals. For example he is a salesman who dons an aged suit that is ceaselessly creased during the course of the screen production, moreover in the script is directed to appear dilapidated. He drive an archaic, run down vehicle on the brink of extinction. While on the contrary, a proper salesman must appear presentable and attractive to market his goods. And Willy definitely does not harmonize with the ideals of being a salesman, divergently he pains to match it. Moreover that is the reason why he doesn't belong inside the world of business. As exemplified in the passage made by Biff in the requiem. "When he'd come from a trip; or on Sundays, making the stoop.... You know something Charley, there's more of him in that front stoop than in all the sales he ever made."

This story seems to epitomize the frivolity of agonizing to achieve something as insignificant as money and power. It definitely makes one question the social values of the American capitalist system, and why certain individual continue to pursue the ideals of that system on a daily basis. For the downside to the capitalist dream is hopelessness. And that downside is more that apparent in the Loman family.

Tragedy and the Common Man

Three Works Cited/ "If the exaltation of tragic action were truly a property of the high-bred character alone, it is inconceivable that the mass of mankind should cherish tragedy above all other forms" (Dwyer). It makes little sense that tragedy should only pertain to those in high ranks. As explained in his essay "Tragedy and the Common Man," Arthur Miller sets out the pattern for his own idea of a tragedy and the tragic hero. This pattern supports the idea that a tragedy can occur in characters of common men as well as those in high places. In his paper, he demonstrates that it should be possible for everyone to be able to identify with the tragic hero. Miller redefines tragedy as more common occurrence than what might happen in such tragedies as portrayed by Shakespeare and Euripides, thus defining Death of a Salesman as a tragedy.

Willy Loman is a tragic hero. His fear is that he wants to be viewed as a good, decent human being. He wants to believe that he's a well liked, decent person who doesn't make mistakes. The truth is that he makes mistakes, many that haunt him, and that he is human. Willy does not consider this normal and severely regrets such failures such as raising his children poorly, as he sees it, not doing well in business, though he wishes he was, and cheating on Linda, showing her to be a commodity of which he takes advantage. "The quality in such plays that does shake us... derives from the underlying fear of being displaced, the disaster inherent in being torn away from our chosen image of what and who we are in the world" (Miller, "Tragedy..."). Willy's "underlying fear of being displaced" is the real tragedy. He wants to do things right, but the fact is he has many incidences that haunt him. Consistently throughout the play, Willy drifts in and out of a dream. He is constantly haunted by memories of his dead brother Ben who struck it rich the jungle.

He also has flashbacks of incidents that haunt him in other areas. For example, the sequence in which Biff catches Willy with a woman other than Linda. This haunts Willy because he sees it as part of why Biff does not love him. "Tragedy then is the consequence of a man's total compulsion to evaluate himself justly" (Miller, "Tragedy..."). This is Willy's flaw. The circumstances in his life and the identity he has created for himself are being affronting by his inner reality to "evaluate himself justly." This flaw is "...his inherent unwillingness to remain passive in the face of what he conceives to be a challenge to his dignity, his image or his rightful status" (Miller, "Tragedy..."). Indeed this is the case with Willy.

He decides to take action rather than complacently become outdated. Willy continually argues with those around him in order to try to keep his personal dignity. These include his argument with Howard that he can still sell, his arguments with Charley over the card game and the job, and his argument with Biff about not being "a dime a dozen." "I am not a dime a dozen! I am Willy Loman and you are Biff Loman"! Willy, in addition to meeting Miller's definition of a tragic hero, in a way connects with the traditional requirements. Willy, after he receives an assurance that Biff loves him, offers the only thing he knows to somehow make recompense; he takes his own life. He does this so Biff will attain the insurance money.

Here we can see that Willy's sincere desire is directed at something greater than himself, his image, or his success. He is motivated by his love for his son. Therefore, since his primary focus is beyond himself, it consequently elevates him. "He taps into and is accordingly clothed with the grandeur tragedy" (Dwyer). Willy, like traditional tragic heroes, has a tragic flaw. "The possibility of victory must be there in tragedy" (Miller, "Tragedy..."). Setting aside Willy's "tragic flaw," there is a certain amount of hope that Willy will change. If there is something to bring the element of hope into the play, there also comes the conceivable possibility of change. "Change is the compelling force, without which, there would be no hope". And with change, comes the conceivable possibility of victory. The entire play, Willy lives by the credo "be well liked." "Someday I'll have my own business, and I'll never have to leave home any more... bigger that Uncle Charley! Because Charley is not liked. He's liked, but he's not well liked"! He finds this untrue as he increasingly makes less and less money on business trips.

"Howard, and now I can't even pay my insurance! You can't eat the orange and throw away the peel! A man is not a piece of fruit"! He, however, refuses to change his view of the world and continues his struggle upstream. What makes this tragic, though, is that he does not change. It is his "tragic flaw" that brings this failure about him. His unwillingness to submit passively to the established order and values takes him down. He has a set idea in his mind about how he wants to be and the way he wants his children to be. He is a salesman and refuses to be anything else. "I thought I'd go out with my older brother and try to locate him, and maybe settle in the North with the old man. And I almost decided to go, when I met a salesman in the Parker House... and he was eighty-four years old, and he drummed out merchandise in thirty-one states... he'd pick up the phone and call the buyers, and without even leaving his room, at the age of eight-four, he made his living". Willy, even at an early age, had a chance to change and become like his brother Ben, but chose not to.

He saw the life of a salesman and refused to do anything else. He had decided what he wanted to be. In the end, because of his unwillingness to change and submit passively to the established world, Willy dies at the hands of his tragic flaws. The common man, indeed, can relate to Willy Loman. His stubborn refusal of character change along with his fear of being denied his identity by the world and his attempts to believe that existence can be justly evaluated brings upon him the death of a tragic hero. This death locks him into place both as a hero by Miller's standards and by traditional standards. "Did Arthur Miller provide us with this essay as a response or defence of Death of a Salesman? Is he trying to justify his work by remolding the definition of tragedy to justify and elevate this play? Whatever the case it is clear that Death of a Salesman fits the model set forth by Miller in 'Tragedy and the Common Man'"

The Importance of Bernard in Death of a Salesman

All of the characters in the performance Death of a Salesman have special traits that are indicative of their personality and literary purpose in the piece. Each serves a particular purpose and symbolizes distinct goals, functions, or qualities. The author places every character in a specific location to contrast, or emphasize another character's shortcomings, mistakes, or areas of strength. For this purpose, Bernard, a character in Death of a Salesman, is placed next to Biff, the protagonist's son. Biff, is lost in a world created by his dazed father, who instills in him a set of false values, and eventually becomes a failure in his early age. In spite of the fact that Bernard admires Biff and believes he is able to help him prosper, Biff is unable to listen. Bernard also interacts with the protagonist himself, again showing the same traits that are indicative of his character. Bernard, who is a successful student and later a successful attorney, is opposite the characteristics Biff is taught makes a man great.

Our first example of Bernard's character is his interaction with Biff is in Act I, when the reader infers Bernard is tutoring Biff: "Biff, Listen Biff, I heard Mr.Birnbaum say that if you don't start studyin' math he's gonna flunk you and you won't graduate. I heard him!" These initial statements, spoken by Bernard, are indicative to the reader of how helpful he tries to be to Biff. He is among the only characters with a sense of reality; the only character that tries to help Biff take concrete, analytical steps to helping him succeed. He understands the consequences of Biff's actions, and tries to dissuade his directionless ambition towards a more solid goal. "He's gotta study Uncle Willy. He's got regents next week." "Just because he printed University of Virginia on his sneakers doesn't mean they've got to graduate him, Uncle Willy." Once again, this illustrates Bernard is the one of the only characters in tune with reality. He cares for Biff and wants to see him graduate. This is why he is constantly pushing Biff to complete his work.

As Bernard matures, he continues his modest, responsible attitude towards life. The protagonist himself is confronted with Bernard's character, and comes to terms with the sudden insight his son is no where near as well off as Bernard, even though they were initially given the same opportunities. Now, the reader infers Bernard is an attorney: "Oh, just a case I've got there, [Washington] Willy." When Bernard describes his Supreme Court case as "just a case", the reader sees how admirably modest he is.

He has become a great man, as inferred from his lines, without being well liked or extremely handsome. He is a developed gentleman, which the protagonists admires, and confides in Bernard asking him where did his son miscarry. "But sometimes, Willy, it's better for a man just to walk away." In this last line of advice, given by an adult Bernard to Willy, the protagonist, the reader sees his basic foundation of caring for another person is not destroyed: he still means for the best in what he does and says. He is concerned for the needs of both the protagonist and his son, and proves this by telling Willy to continue with his life and let his son find his own path.

In conclusion, the character traits of the players in Death of a Salesman are evident. It is also apparent that they are placed juxtapositionally with each other to highlight the other's features. The characters' indicative qualities are what makes animates the plot, and makes for a vibrant literary piece.

Death of a Salesman Essay: Isn't That Remarkable

"Isn't that remarkable." This single, brief statement may appear to be a trite cliché, yet in Death of a Salesman this favourite exclamation of Willy Loman takes on a much broader meaning. In the early part of the play, however, when Willy makes this remark, the reason is not particularly remarkable, or, if so, only in Willy's terms. Yet, during the course of the action the line develops into a comment on Willy's prosaic and confused mind. To start with, the remarkable aspect of the quote is that Willy Loman utters it when he is faced with an epiphany, a sudden realization. To demonstrate, this line takes on significance in the scene where Willy goes to borrow money from Charley. Willy always thought of Charley as the epitome of what Willie thought he detested. Yet, when Willy realizes that this man whom he had disparaged over the years was, indeed, his only friend, he says in utter amazement, "Isn't that a remarkable thing."

As with other utterances, the realization is not remarkable, except that Willy had never been able to see reality long enough to recognize Charley's importance. This single line, then, demonstrates how Willy may finally begin to realise, too late, just how much he is liked. Another realization occurs between Willy and his son, Biff. After an emotional scene in which Biff breaks down on his father's shoulder, trying to make him understand their lives, Willy responds by saying, "Isn't that-isn't that remarkable. Biff, he likes me." This is suddenly a remarkable realization for Willy, who had believed that Biff was destroying his own life just to spite his him. Willy and Biff had just experienced two emotional scenes where Willy doubted Biff's affections. The impact of the realization that Biff loves him has Willy confide this "new information" to his imagined brother Ben. Again, he uses the single, brief statement, "Isn't that a remarkable thing." Thus this simple statement leads Willie to do a remarkable thing for his family-he commits suicide.

To finalize, a line used early on as a cliché, during the course of the play becomes a commentary on the state of Willy Loman's life and how far from reality he truly was. Yet, though Willy did find some events in his life "remarkable," he could not realise that as a salesman and a father, he was a failure. Unfortunately, this lack of understanding leads to his death, a death he could not escape for he brought it on himself. Isn't that remarkable?

Realism in Arthur Miller's Death of a Salesman

Realism may be defined as an attempt to reproduce the surface appearance of the life of normal people in everyday situations. Basically realism is a situation that normal people can relate to based on their own experiences. Realism is extremely prevalent in the play Death of a Salesman. The characters in the play have real world problems. Lack of money is one of the problems, which is a problem for many people. There are also many conflicts within the family; related to each characters definition of success.

Willy Loman also wants his children to have a better than he has and tries to do everything he can so they will have a better life, including ending his own. One realistic situation that many people can relate to is money problems. Money is one of the main problems that Willy Loman had throughout the play. The Loman family had many purchases on payments. Linda even states "for the vacuum cleaner there's three and a half due on the fifteenth" (Miller 1650).

The Loman family was living from week to week. Every time Willy came home from a fairly successful day selling, he would think he was finally getting ahead. Willy would tell Linda how much he had made, but she would then point out how much they owed on everything. Willy then felt overwhelmed and said "My God, if business don't pick up I don't know what I'm gonna do!" (1650). Linda would then reassure Willy and tell him "Well, next week you'll do better" (1650). Many people in real life have this same problem. Every time they feel they are getting ahead financially, a problem occurs and they find themselves right back where they started.

Most people also have to deal with problems and conflicts within their family throughout their life. Family problems were not exempt from the characters in Death of a Salesman. Biff's idea of success was completely opposite from Willy's. Willy viewed success as achieving money and power; Biff however viewed success in life as being happy. Biff realized that "I'm just what I am, that's all" (1703). Biff realized he was "a dime a dozen" (1703), but his father could not accept this reality. This situation where parents always keep telling their children what they should do with their lives is common in many families. In truth, Biff and Hap are where they want to be in life, but Willy just cannot accept their children's contentment. Biff spent most of his life trying to please Willy, but Biff finally realized that he never could. He was what he was.

The most realistic part of the play may have been about how much Willy loved his children and how he wanted their life to be better than his own. Willy raised his children the best he could. The character Ben even seemed to appear when Willy was trying to make a decision on how to make the boys lives better. This situation with Ben makes it appear that Willy has such a hard time making a decision about what is best for the boys that he relies on his imagination for an answer.

The main reason Willy ends up killing himself is because he thinks it will help Biff start his own business with the life insurance money. Willy did everything with the best of intentions and thought his actions and decisions would benefit his children. Most parents are the same way and will do anything in their power to help their children. When reading Death of a Salesman, most people can relate to the problems of the Loman's. The similarities of the Loman's problems to the everyday problems that average people face make this a play full of realism.

Death of a Salesman: Illusions of Grandeur

Willy is at the bottom of the totem pole in a capitalistic world. He owns nothing, and he makes nothing, so he has no sense of accomplishment. Robbed of this, he develops the theory that if a person is well liked and has a great deal of personal attractiveness, then all doors will automatically be opened for him. Willy built his life around these dreams. However, for Willy to live by his ideals necessitates building or telling many lies, and these illusions replace reality in Willy's mind. He tells lies about how well liked he is in all of his towns, and how vital he is to New England. At times Willy even believes his own lies and becomes enthusiastic when he tells his family that he made more money than he actually did.

Willy then fills his sons so full of this concept of being

well liked that when Biff flunks math he goes to Boston to search for his father. He thought that since Willy is so well liked, that he will be able to convince the math teacher to change the grade. It was during this time that Biff encountered his father in the hotel room with a woman. Willy's strong desire to be well liked is what drove him to have an affair in Boston. The fact that she would go to bed with him promoted his ego after a hard day of being turned away by buyers. Therefore, the affair is more of an ego booster than a strong desire for Willy to be involved in an illicit love affair.

Biff couldn't accept that his father had committed adultery, and from that point on, he saw his father as a fake. Willy's life began to close in on him and he had nothing more to live for except his illusions and fond memories of the past. More and more, Willy's life involves his dreams and all of the dreams go back to the year before Biff made his break with Willy. Therefore Willy's entire life has been lived according to his ideas about personal attractiveness and being well-liked. He never questioned these values and never realized that he lived in a world of illusions and dreams. He tried to bring up his children in that same world but he could not keep up the false front, and Biff would not live that way after the incident in Boston.

Arthur Miller's Death of a Salesman Exposes Morals and Values of American Culture

Arthur Miller's play, "Death Of a Salesman" is a very elaborate play that tells the story of a man's dream to achieve greatness from nothing. It almost seems to make fun of American society's competitive nature, "Imagine? When the mail comes he'll be ahead of Bernard again!" Willy (1215)

The title "Death Of a Salesman" leaves nothing to the imagination of how this play ends. Indeed this is a story about the noble, cowardly death of Willy Loman, a traveling salesman. Arthur Miller used the efficient idea of using flashbacks to allow the play to take place within a few days instead of years. Willy Loman as the central character, lives with his wife, Linda and has two sons, Biff (elder) and Happy.

Willy Loman who is quite literally a "low man" has so many personality traits accurate to real life, this is no surprise since Miller based Willy's character on his uncle, Manny Newman. Miller said, "That homely, ridiculous little man had after all never ceased to struggle for a certain victory, the only kind open to him in society - selling to achieve his lost self as a man with his name and his son's name on a business of his own" Willy was defiantly in a struggle however, he was certainly not in a struggle to convince himself he was doing better than he really was, "I can park my car in any street in New England, and the cops protect it like their own." Willy (1165). Willy Loman did not want to die, he went to Ben to seek approval of what he thought would please the family"...Ben, I want you to go through the ins and outs of this thing with me.

I've got nobody to talk to, Ben, and the woman has suffered, you hear me?" Willy (1210) He also proved this with his many "near incidents" and the rubber pipe. According to "Suicide: The facts and myths" by Judi Marks, "Attempted suicides are a sorrowful form of communication, but they're also trial runs for the final event." Anyone who commits suicide actually does not want to die and reality, just wants a solution to end their problems or pains. In this case Willy's problem was he thought he was so well-liked by society, however what he wanted most was for his sons to like him, and for his wife to not have to suffer his torment anymore. His suicide could have been prevented.

John mason Brow said, "miller's play is a tragedy modern, and personal, not classic; its central figure is a little man sentenced to discover his smallness rather than a big man undone by his greatness." This Is an excellent point, Willy was so sure of himself being so well-liked and having personal attractiveness. He believes he is so successful and thinks so highly of himself. However, Willy keeps getting closer and closer to realizing he is not a great as he thought. The more he knows this the more closer to death he is. The quote uses the term "sentenced" which is a very accurate word implying Willy is being passed judgment on, he is being banished from society for life as they all leave him behind, alone and isolated. Starting with Howard taking his job away, then Biff and Happy leaving him behind in the restaurant, and finally Linda went to bed when she could have seen that Willy was going to kill himself and instead she should have stayed with him and encouraged him.

The play can be seen from 2 points of view regarding Willy. Willy could be a hero or he could be a pathetic fool with no achievements. Willy can be seen as a a pathetic fool because he could not make his success in life so he had to play make-believe as if a child. "He had the wrong dreams. All, all wrong." Biff (1216) eventually when life gets hard and he realizes what an inconvenience he really is, he kills himself. It is a quick escape from his problems. When Willy died he expected to have a huge memorial just like the Dave Singlman character he so admired.

When Willy was discussing with Ben what he should do he describes what his funeral might be as being exactly like he described Daves, "...he thinks I'm nothing, see,, and so he spites me. But the funeral—Ben, that funeral will be massive! They'll come from Maine, Massachusetts, Vermont, New Hampshire!..That boy will be thunder struck, Ben, because he never realized—I am known! Ben, and he'll see it with his own eyes once and for all. He'll see what I am,..." Willy (1210)

Willy as a hero comes in place, Happy said at Willy's funeral, "...I'm gonna show you and everybody else that Willy Loman did not die in vain. he had a good dream. It's the only dream you can have—to come out number-one man. he fought it out here..." (1216) When it is obvious that Willy only killed himself to free his family of his burden and to provide Biff a chance at business success. It was a sacrifice, he gave up his life to give freedom and hope to his family. "We're free...We're free" Linda (1217)

According to "The Family Constellation" by Alfred Alder, Happy really takes his place in the play. "A second child...tends to compete more aggressively for attention and the feeling of self-worth that goes with it. The second child often avoids areas where the first one has succeeded, and often succeeds where the first one has failed." In the end at the restaurant scene when Biff knew he could not follow Willy and his version of success, Happy took the part with no hesitations, he started lying, creating a bit of a dream world, going off with women (a parallel to Willy's adultery), he even told the women that he did not know who the rambling man was, it was his father. Unfortunately Happy is doomed to repeat his father's mistakes.

"Death of a Salesman" shows both family and society conflicts. It is most effective when looked at as exposing society. It causes you to evaluate the morals and values of this culture. It reminds us that what we prioritize and hold most important can cause irreversible damage to the ones we hold dear. The play is depressing, but a truthful reflection of our materialistic society.

Lack of Morals and Ethics in Arthur Miller's Death of a Salesman

Much of a person's personality is derived from his or her parents or the people with whom they live. One's behaviors are a reflection of his or her up bringing. All actions of others in one's environment have an impact in one's behaviors. That is especially true of parent's influence on a child. Nearly all morals and ethics are learned from parents. Sociologists have indicated that as time progresses American ethics have decayed immensely. Parents in America have become more lax with their children, and the strictly enforced code of ethics seems to have diminished. Arthur Miller's play, Death of a Salesman, portrays the consequences of the laxity of parents with regards to ethics through the relationship of Willy Loman and his two sons, Biff and Happy.

Rather than having played a positive role model for his sons Willy Loman, established a poor standard of morality. For example, when Biff was in high school he was the star of the football team. One afternoon he stole a football from the locker room. When Willy became cognizant of Biff's actions, Wily did not punish Biff. Instead, he told Biff that the coach was likely to congratulate Biff for his show of initiative.

Similarly, at another point in the play Biff and Happy stole lumber from a nearby construction site. Instead of teaching the boys a lesson in ethics Willy was proud of his sons. In fact, he bragged about the amount of construction materials the two stole. Willy allowed the boys to steal, which could be considered an immoral act, worse yet, Willy's praise for their actions prohibited Biff and Happy from knowing stealing was an immoral act. Studies have shown that at a very young age children were extremely impressionable. Teaching the difference between right and wrong would give hope for a moral future. In the play there was little hope for Biff and Happy because Willy continued to show poor standards of morality in a positive light.

In addition to stealing, being dishonest also surfaces as an unethical behaviour that was practiced and thus promoted by Willy Loman. Willy was a salesman who had a rocky past few months. Instead of admitting his failure to his wife, Linda, he lied about his income. He lead Linda to believe he earned more than he actually did. Each month his debt grew greater and greater because he had borrowed money to continue to live the lie. With the knowledge that Willy lived a lie, Biff saw no wrong in dishonesty. In turn, he too lied to Linda. He told her that he was ready to settle down with one women. His statement was only said to please Linda; it could not have been further from the truth. Dishonesty is against traditional ethics. If Willy taught it as an unethical behaviour Biff and Happy would be aware of it as well.

Moreover, Willy's poor treatment of others revealed his unethical character and also paved the path his sons would follow. An example of Willy's poor treatment of people was his affair. Although, Willy and Linda were married for many years, Willy must not have been satisfied with his marriage, because he had an ongoing affair with another woman. Linda would have been crushed to know about Willy's unfaithfulness. Willy's poor treatment of Linda lead his sons to believe that dishonesty toward others was acceptable. They too treated women as objects. For example, at one time they left their father at a restaurant so they could go rendezvous with a couple of woman. Through his dishonesty, Willy was not even competent enough to teach his sons the most important law of ethics, the golden rule. Do onto others as one would want done onto them. In a perverse way the Loman boys did practice the golden rule. They did to Willy what he did to others. In conclusion, Willy's relationship with his sons in Death of a Salesman reflected the lack of enforcement of morals and ethics in the American society. Through the character Willy Loman, Arthur Miller demonstrated that it was necessary to teach children a solid code of ethics, which should be applied to everyday life. Without an ethical background people would lead immoral lives. Perhaps, if Willy had been more strict and a more positive role model his sons would have turned out as more ethical and conscientious people. Rarely does a parent who behaves unethically raise a child who grows up to be remotely ethical.

Willy's Life in Death of a Salesman by Arthur Miller

Willy's life in Arthur Miller's Death of a Salesman can be summed up by Charley's one line, "When the hell are you going to grow up?" Willy's spends his entire life in an illusion of a great man with both popularity and successful. Meanwhile, Willy displays many childlike qualities. Many of these qualities have an impact on Willy's family. His two sons Biff and Happy pick up this behaviour from their father. Willy's idealistic and stubborn actions stem from a false sense of is importance in the world

Willy is like an impetuous youngster with high ideals and high hopes. Children always save high hopes for their future, hopes of having great jobs and being rich. Willy believes he can achieve that kind of success by being a businessman. He thinks is he "the man who makes an appearance in the business world, the man who creates personal interest is the one that gets ahead." He avoids growing up by making excuses and avoiding obstacles.

Like a little child, he wants everything his way even though other options are wiser. After recently being fired, Charley offers Willy a job. Rather than financially securing his family, he allows his arrogance to prevent him from working for his friend. He convinces himself he is at the top of his profession. Willy does not get his way and challenges Charley to a fight after Charley told him to grow up. His childlike behaviour prevents him from doing the logical thing.

Willy, like most children, he thinks that he is more than he actually is. During the story, he prides himself on how well he sells, but when Linda calculates his sales and their debts, Willy reveals that he lied about how well he sells. He also thinks he is very popular and many people will be at his funeral, but when the times comes, no one is there to pay their respects. Like a child, he believes the world revolves around him. Willy Loman is a child trapped in a man's body. He makes excuses and lies to prevent himself from doing better. The self-assurance he holds blinds him from reality, trapping him in an illusion. When he finally realizes his mistakes, like a child, he runs from his problems thru death rather than grow up and face them.

The Narcissistic Willy Loman in Arthur Miller's Death of a Salesman

Many dilemmas throughout the recent decades are repercussions of an individual's foibles. Arthur Miller represents this problem in society within the actions of Willy Loman in his modern play Death of a Salesman. In this controversial play, Willy is a despicable hero who imposes his false value system upon his family and himself because of his own rueful nature, which is akin to an everyman. This personality was described by Arthur Miller himself who "Believes that the common man is as apt a subject for a tragedy in its highest sense as kings were".

An additional segment of his common human nature is Willy's self-centeredness. Although one might say that the American Dream is imposed upon him by the society, Willy himself creates his dream. Willy supports this claim when he praises Dave Singleman's career to Howard: "And when I saw that, I realized that selling was the greatest career a man could want". His nostalgia for a non-existing future is also proven by the fact that no one else in his environment has a similar, impossible dream: "If he were not wearing the rose colored glasses of the myth of the American Dream, he would see that Charley and his son are successful because of lifelong hard work and not because of the illusions of social popularity and physical appearances". Surely, the false ego and pride predicted to come from his assured success are the bridges that prevents Willy from seeing through his fake dream, pushing him to persuade the rest of his family to worship it along with him.

Biff sadly bites the apple when he realizes his fate:

Willy! I ran down eleven flights with a pen in my hand today. And suddenly I stopped, do you hear me? And in the middle of that building and I saw—the sky. I saw the things that I love in this world. The work and the food and the time to sit and smoke. And I looked at the pen and said to myself, what the hell am I grabbing this for? Why am I trying to become what I don't want to be? What am I doing in an office, making a contemptuous, begging fool of myself, when all I want is out there, waiting for me the minute I say I know who I am! Why can't I say that, Willy?

From then on he is a changed man and tries to extricate Willy from his sea of confusion. But Willy is pushing the boat down to stay afloat instead of getting in it. When he finally realizes what the people around him are trying to do, he finally ends up drowning. Letting Biff continue living on a worthwhile life, he submits to his inner voice, which is Ben, and commits suicide. A good comparison to Willy's life is the story of Sisyphus: "The gods had condemned Sisyphus to ceaselessly rolling a rock to the top of a mountain, whence the stone would fall back of its own weight. They had thought with some reason that there is no more dreadful punishment than futile and hopeless labour". Like Sisyphus, Willy attains nothing in his life, no matter how hard he tries, but the mere happiness of controlling his own worthless fate.

He does so because of his narcissistic personality, which drives him to do everything in the play for himself. He manipulates his kids to achieve his avaricious plans with the goal to win his own battle for dignity. He lacks empathy and throughout the play, willfully avoids self-examination by creating his own universe. His schizophrenia keeps the suspense rippling the play as intended by Miller: "Tragedy, then, is the consequence of a man's total compulsion to evaluate himself justly". This suspense is Willy's fallacious hope transmitted to the audience, his struggle to evaluate himself justly. As intended originally, "Miller was going to name this play `Inside his head' ". Miller wants the spectators to experience the internal conflicts inside Willy's mind. He wants one who analyses the text to understand the motivations behind the selfish and malevolent intentions of Willy. Furthermore, he wants the reader to realise that Willy is above all a common man imbedded with the sinful nature of man.

Finally, many hermeneutics are proposed by critics about how to perceive Willy. But an evaluation must be made of the detriment he solicits to the society. Society has not to adapt to his needs, and because he can't see this fact he perishes as a human being. His failure and lack or excess of determination to succeed is his will to do harm. This misuse of will causes a break in the Loman family. "Willy Neglects to instill in his sons the moral values a parent should teach a child". Then it would follow that he would be responsible for his death and the jeopardy his loved ones are left behind with. After all, it wasn't a dream that drives the car into a brick wall. It is he. His death is an intentional suicide, a crime.

The Coward Revealed in Arthur Miller's Death of a Salesman

In the play Death of a Salesman by Arthur Miller, the main character, Willy Loman, is a struggling salesman. Willy Loman is a complex character who confuses illusion with reality. In a way, Willy has two personalities in this play. The one we see in the present action is a tired man in his sixties. The other Willy is the one we see in flashbacks. He is young and confident. In Act Two, Scene Fourteen, Willy's son Biff tells him that he loves him. Willy can tell that Biff is not just saying this out of pity because Biff is sobbing. In a flashback, Willy speaks to his dead brother Ben. Ben keeps saying "Time, William, Time", reminding him that suicide is closing in. Ben also tells Willy that he should come to the jungle. In this scene, the jungle represents opportunities for success. The reason that Ben tells Willy to come to the jungle, is that when in the jungle, Willy can get the diamonds. The diamonds represent the insurance money that the family will get from Willy's accident. Therefore, Ben is saying that the only way Willy can get twenty thousand dollars in insurance money is to kill himself, or symbolically Ben is saying that the only way to get the diamonds is to enter the jungle. Willy also talks to Ben how great Biff would do with all of that money.

Willy thinks one more time about Biff and how he was a great football player. This shows that Willy still thinks of Biff as a football hero, which is one of the reasons Willy thinks Biff is so magnificent. As Willy is finishing up his thoughts, his wife, Linda, is calling him to come up to bed. After this happens, the sound of a speeding car is heard driving off into the night. In the same scene, Willy's wife Linda has come to make a peace with their two sons, Biff and Happy. Linda also suspects that Willy may kill himself. She made a big mistake by leaving the disturbed Willy alone. The rubber tubing that Linda found on the heater foreshadows Willy's suicide. Linda doesn't want Willy to kill himself, but believes that she cannot interfere with his business.

I believe that Willy's suicide was an escape from shame. He couldn't keep living his life as a lie. Willy could not face reality. When people talked to him, he only heard what he wanted to hear. He was a very distracted and disturbed man. After losing his job, he felt he was too unsuccessful to go on living. His principles in life were based on being popular. He believed that if you were popular, you would be successful. Eventually, he faced reality and realized that he was not popular. A combination of his shame and his unpopularity is what killed Willy Loman. He felt like a failure.

From Willy's point of view, the suicide was an act of love. He believed that by killing himself, Biff would be much more successful. Willy thinks that Biff is magnificent and wants to show it to him by giving him twenty thousand dollars in insurance money. A problem could arise here because it is not even certain that Willy's suicide will be called an accident. If the insurance company sees it as a suicide, Biff will not get the money.

From the family's point of view, the suicide was very confusing. Each member of the family had a different idea of why Willy killed himself. Linda was wondering why no one had come to the funeral. This shows that Linda had always trusted Willy and had believed all of the phony dreams that Willy had told her. Linda had reason to believe that Willy killed himself because of the mortgage payments. This is very ironic because after Willy killed himself, the house was paid off and they were free and clear of any more payments. Biff comes to realise that Willy had "the wrong dreams". Biff is still going to go out west to fulfill his own dreams instead of making himself big in New York which is something he hates. Happy believes that his father was a great man. He wants to prove that Willy did not die in vain. He will justify Willy's dreams by being manager of the store. It seems that Happy is almost becoming another Willy.

I believe that Willy's suicide was a cowardly act. Since he was fired, he felt that he had no reason to live. It seemed that the only thing that mattered to Willy was success and money. When he didn't have either of those things, he did the only thing he felt he could do and that was to take his own life for sum of twenty thousand dollars. Willy did not give much thought as to how his family would feel after killing himself. He only thought about the money they would possibly get from the insurance company. I feel he took the coward's way out by killing himself instead of trying to solve his problems.

Willy Loman thought his suicide was a courageous act. He thought he was being very brave by killing himself. He felt that he took the hard way out. Willy may have thought that he was the only one to suffer. His confusion between illusion and reality was very strong at the end of the play. He thinks he is going into the jungle to get diamonds but in reality, he is killing himself to get insurance money.

Biff saw Willy's suicide as a cowardly act. He realized that all of Willy's dreams were wrong, and that Willy had the wrong perspective on life. By committing suicide, Willy took the easy way out. Biff still will miss his father but he will not let his sorrow overcome him.

In conclusion, Willy Loman was a very confused and disturbed man. He would look into the past to see where he made his mistakes. He suffered from delusions. By killing himself, he is portrayed as a coward who certainly had his priorities confused.

Arthur Miller's Death of a Salesman as Social Commentary

Arthur Miller's Death of a Salesman portrays the Loman's and all the family conflicts they faced. It's also apparent on a bigger scale that this play is a social commentary. It touches all the problems brought on by wealth and success in our culture. Death of a Salesman is more effective as a reflection of society and the problems it faces than as a depiction of family conflicts. The play showed how Willy Loman's longing to be successful controlled his life and ruined his family. Willy also represents a large piece of society.

He portrays the people in our culture that base their lives on acquiring money. Greed for success has eaten up large numbers of people in this country. It's evident in the way Willy acts that his want of money consumes him. This constantly happens in our society; people will do anything to crawl up the ladder of success, often knocking down anyone in their way. Death of a Salesman also reflected how families treat people once they are older. Willy raised Biff and Happy when they were completely dependent on him, but the boys aren't willing to help Willy out when he needs them.

This is more effective when looked at as if Willy represents all the older people in our society. It shows how the elderly are looked down upon, are thought to be crazy, and have their jobs taken away for no reason other than age. At times you feel sorry for Willy because these things are happening to him and he is powerless against them. This makes the reader stop to examine our own culture and the ways we discriminate against people who should be our equals and treated with respect. This play also represents how Willy's actions affected his entire family.

He always pushed the boys to have to be the greatest at everything they did. This made the children grow up to always feel like they could never do enough to please their father. They ended up doing things against what they truly wanted. Biff never found a sufficient occupation and was forced to do things like steal. Happy ended up lying to make things always seem better than they were. But it's how this represents society that makes it so effective.

The biggest issue this play imitates is peer pressure. Willy's pressure on the kids is like pressure from friends to do things you normally wouldn't do. Our culture thrives on peer pressure. It can sometimes be positive, like when it pushes you to give your best effort, and sometimes negative, like when it causes you to conform excessively. Either way, Death of a Salesman shows the effects of society's pressure on normal people. Willy is just a man who wanted to be well off. To him, this meant rich and successful. Many people are just like Willy; they have to be well liked because to them, that's what success is.

Death of a Salesman shows both family and society conflicts. However, it's definitely more effective when looked at as an exposing of society's conflicts. It forces you to evaluate the morals and values of this culture. It shows what kinds of things we hold most important and all the hurt that results from making those the most valued things. The play is a depressing but truthful reflection of our society.

The Destruction of Willy Loman in Arthur Miller's Death of a Salesman

Willy Loman is a traveling salesman who has worked for the Wagner firm for 34 years. He is now 61 years old and his job has been taken off salary and put on commission. He has a family and he boasts to them that he is "vital in New England," but in fact he is not vital anywhere. Willy has many strong beliefs that he strives to achieve.

He wants to own his own business and he wants to be "bigger than Uncle Charley" and especially he wants to be a great success and he tries to emulate Dave Singleman. He wishes to die the "Death of a Salesman" and have many buyers and salesmen mourn for him. He also tries to be a good father, and husband.

However Willy's aims in life have been useless as he hasn't really achieved anything. He got fired by Howard, his sons are both failures and they abandoned him in a restaurant toilet. His relationship with his wife is plagued by his guilt for committing adultery. He has to borrow $50 a week from Charley. He can't even keep his mind on one thing for a long time. He can't drive a car. Willy gets so fed up with all of these things that he want's to commit suicide and eventually, he does. This topic suggests that Willy's deterioration occurs because the principals he believes in. To a large extent this is true. After 34 years of Willy's life, he loses his job. To a normal person under normal circumstances, being retrenched is a time when you feel useless.

But for Willy, since everything else is going wrong at the same time, he feels like a useless old man. Willy thought that just because he named his boss, that he would have a secure future with the company but as Charley said "them things don't mean anything? You named him Howard, but you can't sell that." Even though Willy wasn't even getting paid a salary, Howard didn't want him to even represent the company in case Willy "cracked up" again.

Although Willy is mostly destroyed by his own ideals there are other things that destroy him as well, like Howard, Happy and Biff. Willy is emotionally destroyed when Howard fires him. Then, both of his sons disown and abandon him in Frank's Chop House. Both Happy and Biff left their father talking to himself in the bathroom while they wanted to have a good night out with the girls. That also destroyed Willy because it showed that his sons didn't really care if he lived or died.

Willy can't even drive a car though because he can't keep his mind on anything for a long period of time. In the past he has had a few car accidents because his mind keeps wandering "Where are you guys, where are you? The woods are burning! I can't drive a car!" Willy knows though that he is deteriorating and that nobody can help him except for him.

Willy Loman, is indeed a 'low man'. He has a very low self esteem and the only person that really doesn't love him is himself. Willy had great goals (ideals) in practice, but the only thing that he didn't realise is that if he didn't achieve those goals it wouldn't be the end of the world. Willy took it a step to far though, he thought that his life wasn't worth living anymore, therefore Willy Loman was definitely destroyed by his own ideals.

Theme of Success in Arthur Miller's Death of a Salesman

One of the important themes in Death of a Salesman is the nature of success. Many people believe that success is about making a lot of money. They say that with money comes happiness. However this may not always be true. In other words success is defined as the accomplishment of something that was desired. Furthermore it is about being happy, proud and secure about yourself. Although true success originates from the heart, achieving it requires hard work and determination. In Death of a Salesman, the characters that are successful are Dave Singleman, Ben and Bernard.

Dave Singleman was a successful individual. He was an eighty-four year old salesman in the Parker House. In order to make a sale all he had to do was "pick up his phone and call the buyers, and without ever leaving his room, he made his living...". This quote describes his success as a salesman. At the age of eighty four he was able to make an adequate amount of sales. Although he did not get rich from the sales that he made, he enjoyed what he was doing. As a result of his success life, he died honorably. "He died the death of a salesman, in his green velvet slippers...". This example shows that he was successful right until the end. After living the life of a successful salesman he died the death of a salesman. When he died, he was still wearing his green velvet slippers, which in a way symbolizes that his success is still with him. Another example that shows Dave had a successful life was at his funeral. "When he died, hundreds of salesmen and buyers were at his funeral. The second successful character is Willy's older brother, Ben. This man became successful by taking a risk. He "walked into the jungle, and comes out, the age of twenty-one, and he's rich.". When Ben went to Africa, he found diamonds in the mines and as a result he became rich. This incident has made Ben's life successful and ever since, Willy has been regretful. If Willy was to take the risk, he too would be successful. Not only is Willy envious but he also idolizes Ben because of his success.

Willy often asks Ben, "what's the secret?". This quote proves that Willy is aware of Ben's success. As a result Willy want's Ben to tell him the secret to success. The real reason Ben was successful was because he had determination. "He knew what he wanted and went out and got it." Although Willy changed his mind about going, it did not stop Ben from going. He knew what he wanted and in the end, his determination brought him success.

The third successful character is Bernard. In the past he was a typical nerd and nothing more than a follower. As fifteen years pass by, Bernard turns out to be a very successful individual. He has finished university and is now an important attorney.. Moreover he is "...gonna argue a case in front of the Supreme Court.". In this example one can obviously see that Bernard is successful. Being chosen to argue a case in front of the Supreme Court proves that Bernard is successful because it shows that he is at a high position in his career.

Furthermore Bernard is married and has two sons, showing that he is settled. Therefore he is not only successful career wise but he also has a family to look forward to at the end of the day. Moreover, Bernard's friends are also successful. He goes to Washington "to stay with a friend who's got a court.". As a result of his hard work along the way, Bernard has earned him friends who are on the same level as him. They respect him for who he is, and u In conclusion, the three characters from Death of a Salesman that are successful are Dave Singleman, Ben and Bernard. These characters earned their success by working hard. As a result of hard work and devotion money is usually the prize. However in some cases happiness may also be a reward of success. Although success is often related to money, status, rank and fame, we must not forget that success is also emphasis on the heart, the inner being and the seed plot for our thoughts, motives and decisions.

Impact of Charley on Willy in Death of a Salesman

Charley had a huge impact on Willy in the play Death of a Salesman. Willy is jealous of Charley's success. Repeatedly, Willy would go to Charley's to borrow money to pay the bills. Biff and Happy were failures; Willy refuses to recognize this because Bernard, Charley's son was so successful. Charley's effect on Willy has caused him to become extremely spiteful.

At the end of every week, Mr. Loman found himself at Charley's feet, begging him for money. Charley continually gave him the money to keep him quiet. This is ironic because Willy thinks that he is so much better then Charley, when in fact he was just incredibly jealous. When Willy was fired from his job, his only friend Charley offered him a job. Willy reprimanded Charley for insulting him. This made a very clear assertion of Willy's jealousy.

In Willy's eyes, his children were remarkable. They were, popular, good at sports, and intelligent. When in reality Biff and Happy were rapidly declining. Charley would try to tell Willy about his kids. Willy never listened because it pained him to see Bernard more successful then Biff and Happy.

Charley was content with his life. His son was happily married with two sons. His job was going great. Willy on the other hand was scared of life itself. He lied to his family and Charley about everything. Repeatedly he contradicted himself. He said that blue-collar workers were stupid and were not going anywhere. However, he would brag to Charley about all the work he did around the house. Willy was never happy with what he had. He always thought he could have better.

If Willy just listened to his family and his friends, then he might still be alive. Willy ignored reality. He was a jealous, selfish person. He liked to make things bigger than they were. Charley helped Willy realise this. However, it was already too late. There was no turning back, he was going to kill himself, and no one could stop him.

The Conflicted Willy Lowman in Arthur Miller's Death of a Salesman

Willy Lowman is a character that most anyone can identify with. He has two sides to his life; On one side he creates an image of being successful, well liked, and bold. On the other side he feels old, unsuccessful, defeated and disliked. He maintains the successful image to comfort his wife and friends. This veil of success becomes thinner and thinner until he lingers between fantasy and reality of the cruel world, often changing back and forth in the course of a conversation. The core of Willy's slow painful demise into nothingness is based upon his beliefs.

Willy thinks that success is not what you know, but who he knows and how well he is liked. These beliefs he instills in his sons, who find themselves adrift and meaningless just like their father. In addition Willy sees the world changing, and his own inability to change with it, will seal his fate. He misses the open land and the smell of flowers in the summer, the pollution and high rise apartments add to Willy lies dismal existence. An example of Willy's shift from fantasy to reality is during his conversation with his wife about the Chevy. He thinks the car is fantastic, the best ever built. Later he and his wife discuss some bills that were paid, and when told about the bill to get the Chevy's carburetor fixed, he says that they ought to prohibit the manufacture of the car.

Willy Loman is finding himself less and less capable. He dreams of making it big and has visions of Uncle Ben who gives him advice on how to get rich, but never the kind of advice Willy wants to hear. Willy is concerned about his image. He is a great showman who can brag and flaunt like the best of them, and as witness to the hard truth of his failure he continues to weave fairy tales and live in fantasy. Willy wants his sons to be better off and more successful than him, but he has already corrupted them, and they too claim achievements well beyond reality. Biff comes to the reality of his position in life in the opening of the play. He knows he is not cut out for the business world. Biff prefers to move back to Texas and work on a farm. Although he realizes working on the farm won^t make him successful, he knows that it's his calling in life. Happy who is fairly stable and comfortable in his work, prefers to continue with the charade, and the deception so as long as it! makes life easier for him.

Although his sons will not be successful, I think Willy Loman did the best he could. Willy is not to blame for his sons disappointments, although he has delayed their success by giving them false ideas about success. The family situation is that of the standard dysfunctional family. he mother is upset by her sons because they have no respect for Willy and show no concern for his decline. Willy loves his wife, but often mistreats her, cuts he off in mid conversation and belittles her. Biff begins to hate his father because of the constant pressure to succeed, along with his fathers adultery and abuse of his mother. However Biff still cares very deeply for his father deep down inside. Willy's favourite son is Biff; however Biff is also a continual source of disappointment for his father because of his inability to assert himself in the business world.

Happy is most like his father in the way that he much prefers fantasy over reality. Happy is willing to continue with pretending everything is all right so as long as it makes life easier. The conflict is Willy versus nature. Nature being the environment and Willy's inability to change and conform to it's dynamic and changing nature.

The characters in this play are easily understood because of their similarity to most people who find themselves washed up in this game called life. People watching the play can easily identify with these characters who represent the average working class family. Nobody wins in the end because it's real life. The father kills himself, hoping that the insurance money will send his family on their way to success; and in actuality the insurance money from his death will heal no wounds, or right any wrongs.

Death of a Salesman as Parody of the American Dream

In 1949, Arthur Miller wrote the play, Death of a Salesman. The play is a parody on the concept of the American Dream. The aim of this essay is to explain in what ways this statement can be said to be true. But at first; what is the American Dream? Well, if you are an American and if you have a family, a house and a car, a decent job with a good salary and if you consider yourself to be surrounded by people who respect you for who you are, you can be said to have reached the American Dream. The concept of the American Dream became a popular idea during the nineteenth century when millions of people immigrated to America in search of better lives. At that time, a better life could mean a cottage or perhaps a house, some cattle and a piece of land to cultivate. Even today the meaning of the American Dream is quite the same; be sure to have valuable possessions, a social life with high standard and keep up good standards.

The phrase the American Dream came into the American vocabulary starting in 1867 when writer Horatio Alger came out with his book "Dick." It was a rags-to-riches tale of a poor boy in New York City who saves his pennies, works hard and eventually becomes rich. It became the model that through honesty, hard work and determination, the American Dream was available to anyone willing to make the journey.

There are several connections to the concept of the American Dream in Death of a Salesman. One can be found on page 32 when the principal character

Willy Loman expresses his jealousy towards the successes of his brother Ben. Ben knew what he wanted, Willy says. He started with the clothes on his back, walked into the jungle and came out enormously rich at the age of twenty-one owning several diamond mines. Willy continues: "That man was a genius, that man was success incarnate!". Another example of a man's success, and therefore also of the American Dream, is found on page 38. Willy's imaginary memory of Ben describes their father as a great inventor who traveled with his whole family westwards through America. He was successful in selling his inventions and he also became rich. On page 54

Willy remembers one occasion when his son Biff was playing at Ebbets Field. There was this glow around him and people cheered his name when he came out. He was a star then and this kind of personal success is also a typical example of the American Dream. And as described on page 62, Willy himself experienced a personal success in his work. It reached its peak in 1928, when his commission average was at its highest level.

The whole story of the play is in itself a parody on the American Dream. Willy Loman is a weary 63-year-old man who wants nothing more than to reach the American Dream, but in reality he fails (has failed?) big time. He is no longer a good salesman, he does not earn enough money, he does not manage to communicate with his family, his sons' lives are a disappointment to him and he disrespects his own family by having a mistress. The parody lies in the gap between Willy's wishes and his actual accomplishments. Willy does not have a healthy ideal self, compared to his real self. The rift is too deep for two feasible reasons. Firstly, it is not possible for Willy to achieve all of his goals due to external circumstances such as a changed labour market and the free will of his sons. Secondly, it is not possible for Willy to achieve all of his goals due to internal circumstances such as a decreasing capacity to master social situations and a consciously made choice to commit adultery.

Willy Loman, in his naive world between determined hope and painful awareness, represents a parody of the American Dream. But at the same time, he represents a memorable saying by George Bernard Shaw: "You see things as they are and ask, 'Why?' I dream things as they never were and ask 'why not?'"

Irony in the Requiem of Arthur Miller's play, Death of a Salesman

Arthur Miller's play, Death of a Salesman tells a sad story of a man who was too proud to admit that he was a failure. Willy Loman created a world of illusion to help him to continue with the daily drudge of living. He spent his life trying desperately to convince himself, and others, that he was successful and "well liked" until the day he died. The requiem is the last act of Miller's play where the sad truth of Willy Loman's existence is revealed to the audience and the Loman family. The requiem serves as a place where Miller paints a picture of Willy's death as an ironic end to his tragic life.

Charley's speech during the funeral is vital to understanding Willy as a tragic character because Charley takes the blame away from Willy for his death. "Nobody dast blame this man", are the opening words to Charley's speech that depicts Willy Loman as a product of his environment and a victim of his profession. He explains that the life of a salesman is an upward struggle to sell himself, "riding on a smile and a shoeshine...when they (customers) start not smiling back - that's an earthquake...and you're finished." Here Charley is alluding to Willy's inability to separate the personal from the professional. Willy took his professional rejections personally and it was a blow to his character. Willy wanted so desperately to be liked that he convinced himself that he was liked so he would be able to continue on with his life and his career. It is important that the audience sees Willy's delusions as a coping mechanism to deal with his personal failures, and therefore takes pity on him. If the audience blames him for his death then his death is not viewed as a tragedy.

Miller continues to drive the sympathy out of the audience when Willy's oldest son, Biff, gives his analysis of his father's life. Biff comes to a realization at the end of the play that his father lived a life of illusion, "He never knew who he was." Willy spent so much time believing in the false promises of wealth and popularity that the life of a salesman could bring that he never took the time to realise that he really enjoyed working with his hands, "...there's more of him in that front stoop than in all the sales he ever made." Biff implies that his father wasted his life as an unsuccessful salesman saying that "he has all the wrong dreams". He should have spent his life in a profession that he was good at and that he could take pride in instead of wasting his life trying to reach unattainable goals as an unsuccessful salesman. The tragedy behind this is that

Willy wasted so much of his life being mentally invested in the American Dream that he was blinded to any other alternatives. There are aspects of Willy's death that are both tragic and ironic such as the attendance of Willy's funeral. Before Willy's death he had a conversation with a vision of his older brother Ben in which Willy described the motives behind his suicide. Willy wanted to prove to his son Biff once and for all how well known and respected he was. "Ben, that funeral will be massive! They'll come from ME, MA, VT, and NH...that boy will be thunderstruck, Ben, because he never realized - I am known!" Willy envisioned his final triumph where he could finally prove his worth to his family, and the only way that he could do that would be in death. Ironically, no one attends his funeral except for his family and Charley. Instead of his funeral being his final triumph it is his final humiliation. The absence of people at the funeral validates to the Loman's and the audience that Willy's entire life was an illusion. Sadly, even Willy himself did not realise the fallacy in his proclamations of fame and success.

Another ironic twist on the death of Willy Loman is the fact that he took his own life because he thought that he would be more financially beneficial to his family if he was dead. Willy foreshadows his suicide during his final conversation with Charley when he says, "After all the highways, and the trains, and the appointments, and the years, you end up worth more dead than alive." Willy truly believes that he is doing what is best for his family by taking his own life, in his eyes his twenty thousand dollar insurance policy will be worth more to his family than his own life. He envisions that the money will go to his son Biff and he will be able to become the successful man that Willy always knew that he would be, "...imagine that magnificence with twenty thousand dollars in his pocket." Ironically in the requiem the audience realizes that Willy's death was in vain because his son, Biff, not get the insurance money because suicide was not covered in his policy. His death also convinces his other son, Happy, to follow in his father's footsteps toward an unrealistic dream of unattainable goals.

Willy's wife Linda also plays a role in the irony at the requiem. Linda takes a moment alone with Willy's grave telling him, "I made the last payment on the house today. Today, dear. And there'll be nobody home." Ironically Willy kills himself just before he is "free and clear" of debt. There is also another ironic piece to Linda's final words to her husband. She says to him, "Why did you do it? I search and search and I search, and I can't understand it, Willy." This is ironic because throughout the play Linda is the only person that loves Willy unconditionally for who he is, but in reality she has no idea who he is at all.

Linda never let herself understand Willy's psychological problems, therefore the only thing she can think to blame for his suicide is their financial burden. The requiem serves as the final chapter of Willy's life where, for the first time, the harsh realities of his life are revealed. Sympathy is pulled from the audience and reasons for Willy's behaviour are given. Willy cannot be blamed for his actions because he was merely a salesman that was so far sold on the idea of the American Dream that was incapable of seeing his life for what it really was, even in his final moments. The requiem shows that Willy died just as deluded as he lived.

Biff's Changing Perception in Arthur Miller's Death of a Salesman

n Death of a Salesman, Biff's perception of society is altered through a chain of events throughout the play. His unrealistic expectations about how to succeed, learned from his father, eventually caused the destruction of his fantasies. His concept of an ideal society, where being liked is what is needed to succeed, is harshly changed to a reality where he must realise that hard work and devotion are necessary to prosper.

Through a series of events, Biff gradually comes to a realization of what is necessary for success. First, we are shown a part of his childhood where Biff is told that "the man who makes an appearance in the business world, the man who creates personal interest, is the man who gets ahead." This idea appears in direct contrast to Bernard, one of Biff's childhood friends, who works and studies hard. Biff decides that Bernard will not succeed because he is "only liked, not well-liked," and being well-liked is the cornerstone of success. Nonetheless, later in the play we see that Bernard has become very successful, underscoring one of the messages in the play, that success is not just a result of popularity. Second, we are shown a scene in Boston soon after Biff has just failed math for the year. He discovers his "heroic" father having an affair. Biff comes to the painful realization that his father's values, his views, and everything that Biff had made the foundation of his life, are all completely "fake" and "phony." Unfortunately, he has nothing with which to replace it.

Lastly, Biff decides to leave to try and find himself, but an argument develops between Biff and Willy. Biff begins to see himself as like his father, "nothing," just an average man trying to make a living, and quite possibly failing. Biff's earlier image of his father's greatness has crumbled entirely, leaving a lost young man trying to find his way. Biff realized that he now needs to find his own values in life. He has finally tasted reality and now must dive head first into the pot, without any real preparation. Thus, it is clear that in the novel Death of a Salesman, Biff's perception of society is drastically altered. He discovers that his father's values, not his own, directed his life, leaving him with few if any tools of his own to develop a value system and shape his future. Biff became disillusioned with society as he understood it, a process which resulted from a series of events depicted in the play. Each event furthered Biff's loss of his fantasies about how the world worked until, with his father's death he was left with the knowledge that the old rules did not work, but that he had no new rules with which to replace them.

Father-son Relationships and Conflicts in Arthur Miller's Death of a Salesman

In many literary works, family relationships are the key to the plot. Through a family's interaction with one another, the reader is able decipher the conflicts of the story. Within a literary family, various characters play different roles in each other's lives. These are usually people that are emotionally and physically connected in one way or another. They can be brother and sister, mother and daughter, or in this case, father and son. In the Arthur Miller's novel, Death of A Salesman, the interaction between Willy Loman and his sons, Happy and Biff, allows Miller to comment on father-son relationships and the conflicts that arise from them.

During most father-son relationships, there are certain times where the father wants to become more of a "player" in his son's life than his son believes is necessary. The reasons for this are numerous and can be demonstrated in different ways. Miller is able to give an example of this behaviour through the actions of Willy Loman. When Biff comes home to recollect himself, Willy perceives it as failure. Since Willy desperately wants his oldest son, Biff, to succeed in every way possible, he tries to take matters into his own hands. "I'll get him a job selling. He could be big in no time". The reason that Biff came home is to find out what he wants in life. Because Willy gets in the way, matters become more complicated. Partly due to Willy's persistence in Biff's life, they have conflicting ideas as to what the American dream is. Willy believes that working on the road by selling is the greatest job a man could have. Biff, however, feels the most inspiring job a man could have is working outdoors.

When their two dreams collide, it becomes frustrating to Willy because he believes that his way is the right way. If a father becomes too involved in his son's life, Miller believes friction will be the resultant factor. As unfortunate as it is, there are many instances where a father favors one son over another, which leads to social conflicts within the less-favored son. In most cases it is the oldest son that is being favored while the younger son is ignored. Usually the father doesn't even realise what is happening. He simply gets too caught up in the successes of his eldest son and he may even try to live out his life through his son's experiences. Because Willy has dreams of grandeur for Biff, Miller subtly shows how Happy is overlooked.

Throughout the novel, Willy makes references to how wonderful Biff is. "You got greatness in you, Biff. You got all kinds of greatness". Happy, however, is barely talked to. This kind of favoritism has a profound effect on a child. In order to be acknowledged by his father, Happy believes that he must become Willy's version of a success by acquiring wealth and being popular. He convinces himself that this is the only way he'll ever be truly happy. In the end though, he realizes that he is not happy. " It's what I always wanted. My own apartment, a car, and plenty of women. And still, god dammit, I'm lonely". Happy has been living his entire life in a way that he believes will bring him attention from his father, yet he becomes more miserable than if he had gone his own way. When a father chooses to look favorably upon one son over another, disharmony occurs in the father-son relationship as well as in the son's life. Within a father-son relationship, it is the responsibility of the father to provide sound values and leadership for his sons. In almost every family, the sons will look to their father as a role model and a hero. It is in the father's best interest to use this opportunity to instill qualities that will allow his sons to become responsible individuals.

Miller uses the Loman family to show how a father acts when he is more concerned with appearance than anything else. Willy is obsessed with popularity. He believes that if a person is popular, he has everything. Since Willy was never popular himself, he adores the fact that his sons, and Biff in particular, are. In a sense, Willy idolizes his children more than they idolize him. Because Willy sees that his boys have attained what he deems as important, he forgets to teach them moral values. When Biff steals the football from school, Willy rationalizes the theft, saying that it is alright because he is popular. Willy also doesn't take any stock in education. When Bernard chastises Biff for not studying, Willy tries to justify it by saying that a person doesn't need intelligence in the real world if he has good looks. "Bernard can get the best marks in school, but when he gets out into the business world you are going to be five times ahead of him. The man who makes an appearance in the business world is the man who gets ahead. Be liked and you will never want". Because Willy's sole belief is that a person should be popular, his sons never learn any genuine values. Miller attempts to show the conflicts that occur as a result of a father not teaching his sons any morals. Willy ingrains in Biff's head that a person can do anything as long as they are popular. Because of this belief, Biff develops an addiction to stealing. The reason he lost his job with Oliver was because he stole basketballs from him. He has trouble all his life because he steals.

"I stole myself out of every good job since high school". It is this reason that has caused all his problems with Willy, and Willy is to blame because he never told him differently. Happy also has a sour relationship with Willy because of the lack of values he has. Willy always tells them that being popular is the best quality to have. Happy meets some women at the restaurant where he and Biff are supposed to meet Willy. When Willy starts to fall apart on them, Happy tries to ignore him so that he won't look bad in front of the women. "No, that's not my father. He's just a guy". Willy never instills family pride in them. It is this reason that a gap exists in their relationship with him. Arthur Miller's ability to have characters interact with one another allows him to comment on father-son relationships and the conflicts involved.

A father is the most important thing a boy can have in his life. They relate to one another on a level that cannot be achieved through a mother-son relationship. It is important to have communication in the relationship because talking brings the two closer. A father, though, needs to know when to play an active role in his son's life, and when to be more of an observer. If he mixes the two up, serious repercussions may occur. A father can be the best thing in his son's life, but he needs to care for the right.

Critical Analysis of "Death of a Salesman"

A Greek tragedy is a story, which involves a character with a tragic flaw that leads to his or her downfall. In the American tragedy Death of a Salesman by Arthur Miller, Willy Loman displays many traits, which lead to his downfall. Willy

Loman displays a great deal of stubbornness and a warped sense of success as well as a lack of parenting skills. Throughout the play, Willy reveals many bizarre and uncommon characteristics that in the end contribute to his suicide. Willy's stubbornness and pride plays a major role throughout the play in major scenes.

The pride and stubbornness, which Willy possesses, hinders him throughout the play. One of the most prominent scenes in which Willy's pride gets to him is when Charley offers him a job. Willy's response to Charley's first push to get Willy to take the job is, "I – I just can't work for you, Charley." After Willy turns down the first offer, Charley again tries to get Willy to take the job and Willy responds by saying, "I can't work for you, that's all, don't ask me why." Even though Willy lost his job and cannot afford anything, he still refuses a job offer from Charley. Willy has too much pride to accept anything from anyone.

Another prominent example of Willy's excessive stubbornness is when he sees Linda mending her stockings. When Willy sees her mending stockings, he tells her to throw them out with the idea that he will just buy new ones. Willy is too stubborn to realise that he cannot afford to buy new stockings and the only way to keep the stockings in wearable condition is to mend them. Linda realizes what their economic situation is but Willy cannot swallow his pride and accept the fact that he cannot afford anything. Willy also demonstrates excessive stubbornness and pride while talking to Bernard. When Bernard asks what Biff is involved in, Willy responds by telling him he is working on something very big. Willy will not admit that Biff is not really working on any thing at all and even though he is trying to get a business set up he will most likely never amount to anything big. Willy simply has too much pride to admit that his life is anything less than perfect. In addition to Willy's excessive stubbornness and pride, he also displays a warped sense of success.

One of Willy's most prominent flaws is his warped sense of success. Willy's view of success is one that is not shared by many as seen through out the play. One of Willy's warped views of success concerns Biff's football career. Willy has so much excitement regarding Biff playing football that he completely disregards that fact that Biff is in danger of failing in school. Bernard comes to warn Biff to study for the Regents exam and Willy responds by saying, "Let's box, Bernard!" Willy shows complete disregard for the fact that his son could fail because he expects his son's athletic talents to carry him through life. Another incident occurs when Willy is talking to Biff regarding Bernard.

He tells Biff, "Be liked and you will never want." Willy believes that success revolves solely around the views that people have regarding a person. He does not realise that someone liking him will not put food on his table and money in his wallet. Willy also has a warped sense of success regarding Dave Singleman. Dave Singleman was a man who, at eighty-four, could make his living by calling clients from his room. Willy thinks that Dave Singleman is the definition of success. He does not realise that there are other ways to be successful in life. While Willy's warped sense of success plays a major role throughout the play, his poor skills as a parent and role model are the most prominent of his traits.

Willy displays poor parenting and role model skills throughout the entire play. There are many scenes early in the play, which lead the reader to recognize the flaws in Willy's parenting and role model skills. When Biff steals football from the locker room Willy first responds by saying, "I want you to return that." This is obviously the right thing to say to any child who takes something that is not rightfully theirs. However, three lines later Willy then contradicts himself by saying, "Sure, he's gotta practice with a regulation size ball, doesn't he? To Biff: Coach'll probably congratulate you on your initiative!" This is instilling the wrong moral ethics in Biff. Biff now believes that if he steals something his father will not get angry but will approve of the action. Many scenes throughout the play demonstrate Willy's inability to act as a role model to his children. One of these scenes is when Biff discovers his father's affair with "the woman". Biff until this point had always looked up to Willy and thought of his father as almost invincible. This incident changes many of Biff's views regarding Willy. It creates a dark side to Willy and questions Biff's previous views of his father. At this point in the story Willy's status as a role model to Biff is certainly lower than in previous scenes. Perhaps the biggest mistake that Willy makes as a parent and role model is his suicide. While Willy kills himself with the intentions that Biff will collect insurance money, this is not how other people will most likely see it. Willy's family is left to believe that Willy kills himself out of depression. Willy tries to kill himself several times throughout the play out of depression so it is the only logical reason. It is only at the end that his motives change slightly. Willy believes that what he is doing will benefit his family when in fact his family is only saddened by his loss. Willy's death is in part due to the array of traits he demonstrates throughout the play.

There are many character traits, which Willy Loman possesses. Willy's excessive stubbornness and pride surface many times through out the play as a major flaw in Willy. The warped sense of success Willy displays not only contributes to his failures but his children's as well. Willy demonstrates his poor parenting and role model skills in a variety of scenes. Willy Loman's story is one of tragedy and regret. It is a story of man vs. himself, in which man was not able to overcome the power which lie inside of him.

Criticism

Arthur Miller's classic American play, Death of a Salesman, exposes the relationship between gender relationships and dysfunctional family behaviors. In this play, the themes of guilt and innocence and of truth and falsehood are considered through the lens of family roles. Willy Loman, the salesman whose death culminates the play, is an anti-hero, indeed the most classic of anti-heroes. According to an article on the play in Modern World Drama, Willy is "a rounded and psychologically motivated individual" who "embodies the stupidity, immorality, self-delusion, and failure of middle-class values." While his self-delusion is his primary flaw, this characteristic is not necessarily tragic since Willy neither fights against it nor attempts to turn it toward good. Dennis Welland in his book, Miller: The Playwright summarized this view, critiquing critics who believe that "Willy Loman's sense of personal dignity was too precariously based to give him heroic stature." Although he is ordinary and his life in some ways tragic, he also chooses his fate. The article in Modern World Drama confirmed that "considerable disputation has centered on the play's qualification as genuine tragedy, as opposed to social drama."

Although Willy is dead by the end of the play, that is, not all deaths are truly tragic. The other characters respond to Willy's situation in the ways they do because they have different levels of access to knowledge about Willy and hence about themselves. An analysis of the relationships among these characters' insights and their responses will reveal the nature of their flawed family structure.

According to conventional standards, Biff, the older son of Willy and Linda, is the clearest failure. Despite the fact that he had been viewed as a gifted athlete and a boy with a potentially great future, Biff has been unable as an adult to succeed or even persevere at any professional challenge. Before the play opens, he had been living out west, drifting from one low-paying cowboy job to another, experiencing neither financial nor social stability. Back in New York, he is staying with his parents but seems particularly aimless, although he does gesture toward re-establishing some business contacts. Although one could speculate that the Loman family dynamics in general have influenced Biff toward ineffectuality, as the play progresses readers understand that one specific biographical moment (and his willingness to keep this moment secret) provides the key to his puzzling failure.

Near the end of the play, Bernard, Willy's nephew, asks Willy about this crucial incident. Although Biff had already accepted an athletic scholarship to the University of Virginia, he failed math his last semester in high school; his best option was to make the course up during summer school. Before he makes this decision, Biff visits Willy, who is in Boston on business. According to Bernard, Biff "came back after that month and took his sneakers — remember those sneakers with 'University of Virginia' printed on them? He was so proud of those, wore them every day. And he took them down in the cellar, and burned them up in the furnace. We had a fist fight. It lasted at least half an hour. Just the two of us, punching each other down the cellar, and crying right through it. I've often thought of how strange it was that I knew he'd given up his life. What happened in Boston, Willy?" Willy responds defensively: "What are you trying to do, blame it on me?"

What had happened, of course, as Willy subsequently remembers and as he has probably remembered frequently during the intervening years, was that Biff had discovered Willy in the midst of an extramarital affair. In contrast to Linda, who frequently appears with stockings that need mending, this other woman receives gifts of expensive stockings from Willy. The existence of this woman (and perhaps others like her) is one factor contributing to the financial strain of the Loman family. Biff understands this instantly, and he also understands the depth of Willy's betrayal of Linda — and the family as a whole. The trust Biff had given Willy now seems misplaced. Indeed, according to the flashbacks within the play, the young Biff and Happy had nearly idolized Willy, so this betrayal while Biff is yet an adolescent is particularly poignant. As Biff is about to make a momentous life decision, in other words, he is confronted with duplicity from the man he had looked to as a role model. Yet Biff shares this knowledge with no one; instead this secret becomes the controlling element of his own life. When Biff does attempt to tell the truth, not about Willy's affair but about his own life, Willy and Happy both resist him. "Let's hold on to the facts tonight, Pop," Biff says, indicating that "the facts" are slippery in their hands.

The outright lies members of the Loman family tell, that is, come more easily because they also exaggerate some facts and minimize others. Although many of their stories may be eventually founded in truth, that truth is so covered with their euphemistic interpretations that it is barely recognizable. The stories the family has told have become nearly indistinguishable from the real circumstances of their lives.

Trying to separate reality from fantasy, Biff says, "facts about my life came back to me. Who was it, Pop? Who ever said I was a salesman with Oliver?" But Willy refuses to acknowledge the substance of the question: "Well, you were." Biff contradicts him, as determined to acknowledge the truth as Willy is to deny it: "No, Dad, I was a shipping clerk." Willy still declines to accept this fact without the gloss of embellishment: "you were practically" a salesman.

Later, the conversation among the three men reveals that similar embellishments continue to characterize their lives."We never told the truth for ten minutes in this house!" Biff proclaims. When Happy protests that they "always told the truth," Biff cites a current family lie: "You big blow, are you the assistant buyer? You're one of the two assistants to the assistant, aren't you?" But Happy continues the family habit: "Well, I'm practical-ly."

This inability to acknowledge the truth affects the family on many levels but most particularly in terms of their intimacy with one another and their intimate relationships with others. Biff hasn't dated anyone seriously, and Happy is most comfortable with prostitutes. While waiting for Willy at a restaurant, Happy assures Biff that a woman at another table is "on call" and urges her to join them, especially if she "can get a friend." Although Happy is clearly a participant in this encounter, he says, "Isn't that a shame now? A beautiful girl like that? That's why I can't get married. There's not a good woman in a thousand." Although Happy and Biff would probably classify their mother as a "good woman," they follow their father's example in seeking out women they won't marry to gratify their egos and then in treating those women as disposable.

Linda eventually responds to her sons with scathing disrespect in part because of the way they respond to other women, but primarily because she assumes they chose to accompany prostitutes rather than to fulfill their dinner plans with their father. "You and your lousy rotten whores!" she says. "Pick up this stuff, I'm not your maid any more," she continues, and then asserts, "You're a pair of animals!" Linda, of course, doesn't realise that Willy, too, whom she accuses her sons of deserting, is guilty of infidelity. Willy's emotional stability is threatened, she believes, in part because of the way his sons respond to him. She fails to consider the possibility that Biff's instability and the immaturity of both Biff and Happy has been affected by Willy's model.

The most profound secret of the play, however, is of course Willy's apparent obsession with suicide. He has been involved in several inexplicable automobile accidents, and he has perhaps planned to asphyxiate himself by attaching a rubber tube to their gas water heater. Linda has discovered this tube and has revealed her discovery to her sons, but she forbids them from addressing the subject directly with Willy, for she believes such a confrontation will make him feel ashamed. This secret is hence ironically acknowledged by everyone except the one whose secret it is — Willy.

When he does finally succeed in killing himself, his act can be interpreted as a culmination of secrets, secrets which are compounded through lies because they have been created through lies. Welland suggested that Willy's suicide results from his affair — "To argue that in these days of relaxed social morals one minor marital infidelity hardly constitutes grounds for suicide is, paradoxically, to add weight to the theme in the context of this play: for Willy Loman it is enough." His affair is certainly one factor in his decision, but it is a factor because he had been found out by his son, and because others are now starting to question him. So although these secrets include his affairs and Biff's knowledge of this aspect of his life, they also include his failure as a salesman and the subsequent failures of his sons.

Major Themes within Death of a Salesman

Death of a Salesman addresses loss of identity and a man's inability to accept change within himself and society. The play is a montage of memories, dreams, confrontations, and arguments, all of which make up the last 24 hours of Willy Loman's life. The three major themes within the play are denial, contradiction, and order versus disorder. Each member of the Loman family is living in denial or perpetuating a cycle of denial for others. Willy Loman is incapable of accepting the fact that he is a mediocre salesman. Instead Willy strives for his version of the American dream—success and notoriety—even if he is forced to deny reality in order to achieve it. Instead of acknowledging that he is not a well-known success, Willy retreats into the past and chooses to relive past memories and events in which he is perceived as successful.

For example, Willy's favourite memory is of Biff's last football game because Biff vows to make a touchdown just for him. In this scene in the past, Willy can hardly wait to tell the story to his buyers. He considers himself famous as a result of his son's pride in him. Willy's sons, Biff and Happy, adopt Willy's habit of denying or manipulating reality and practice it all of their lives, much to their detriment. It is only at the end of the play that Biff admits he has been a "phony" too, just like Willy. Linda is the only character that recognizes the Loman family lives in denial; however, she goes along with Willy's fantasies in order to preserve his fragile mental state.

The second major theme of the play is contradiction. Throughout the play, Willy's behaviour is riddled with inconsistencies. In fact, the only thing consistent about Willy is his inconsistency. From the very beginning of Act I, Scene 1, Willy reveals this tendency. He labels Biff a "lazy bum" but then contradicts himself two lines later when he states, "And such a hard worker.

There's one thing about Biff—he's not lazy." Willy's contradictions often confuse audiences at the beginning of the play; however, they soon become a trademark of his character. Willy's inconsistent behaviour is the result of his inability to accept reality and his tendency to manipulate or re-create the past in an attempt to escape the present. For example, Willy cannot resign himself to the fact that Biff no longer respects him because of Willy's affair. Rather than admit that their relationship is irreconcilable, Willy retreats to a previous time when Biff admired and respected him. As the play continues, Willy disassociates himself more and more from the present as his problems become too numerous to deal with.

The third major theme of the play, which is order versus disorder, results from Willy's retreats into the past. Each time Willy loses himself in the past, he does so in order to deny the present, especially if the present is too difficult to accept. As the play progresses, Willy spends more and more time in the past as a means of reestablishing order in his life. The more fragmented and disastrous reality becomes, the more necessary it is for Willy to create an alternative reality, even if it requires him to live solely in the past.

This is demonstrated immediately after Willy is fired. Ben appears, and Willy confides "nothing's working out. I don't know what to do." Ben quickly shifts the conversation to Alaska and offers Willy a job. Linda appears and convinces Willy that he should stay in sales, just like Dave Singleman. Willy's confidence quickly resurfaces, and he is confident that he has made the right decision by turning down Ben's offer; he is certain he will be a success like Singleman. Thus, Willy's memory has distracted him from the reality of losing his job.

Denial, contradiction, and the quest for order versus disorder comprise the three major themes of Death of a Salesman. All three themes work together to create a dreamlike atmosphere in which the audience watches a man's identity and mental stability slip away.

The play continues to affect audiences because it allows them to hold a mirror up to themselves. Willy's self-deprecation, sense of failure, and overwhelming regret are emotions that an audience can relate to because everyone has experienced them at one time or another.

Individuals continue to react to Death of a Salesman because Willy's situation is not unique: He made a mistake—a mistake that irrevocably changed his relationship with the people he loves most—and when all of his attempts to eradicate his mistake fail, he makes one grand attempt to correct the mistake.

Willy vehemently denies Biff's claim that they are both common, ordinary people, but ironically, it is the universality of the play which makes it so enduring. Biff's statement, "I'm a dime a dozen, and so are you" is true after all.

Miller's Manipulation of Time and space

Miller often experiments with narrative style and technique. For example, Miller includes lengthy exposition pieces that read as stage directions within The Crucible. At first glance, it seems that an audience must either read the information in the programme or listen to a long-winded narrator. Upon further inspection however, it becomes apparent that Miller's inclusion of background material allows actors and directors to study character motivation and internalize the information, thereby portraying it in the performance. Miller provides audiences with a unique experience when it comes to Death of a Salesman.

In many ways, the play appears traditional. In other words, there are actors who interact with one another, there is a basic plot line, and the play contains standard dramatic elements such as exposition, rising action, conflict, climax, and so forth. However, Miller's manipulation of time and space creates a very non-traditional atmosphere that is unsettling but effective because it mirrors Willy's mental state, thereby allowing the audience to witness his mental instability and take part in it. Stage directions call for a complete house for the Lomans. An audience will not simply watch the action take place in the kitchen but can observe several rooms within the home. This sounds as if it would be distracting since an audience can view several things at once. After all, what should the audience look at? If more than one character is on stage, whom should the audience pay attention to? Miller solves this problem through lighting. Only characters that are talking or involved in direct action are lit on stage, all other rooms, characters, and props remain in shadow.

The result is a vast number of rooms and props that can be utilized immediately. The audience does not have to wait while a new set is erected or an old one torn down, but instead moves directly and instantaneously into the next scene. Such movement without the benefit of time delays or dialogue transitions produces a disjointed and fragmented sequence of events, much like a dream. In fact, the stage directions in Act I describe the house as follows: "An air of the dream clings to the place, a dream arising out of reality." Miller does not stop there. Even though the action of the play can shift from one part of the house to another without delay, the action is still limited to the present. Willy's dreams, memories, or recollections of past events must be revealed in a manner that is distinct from actions taking place in the present. This is important for two reasons: First, the audience must be able to differentiate between the present and the past in order to follow the action of the play; second, Willy's increased agitation must be apparent to the audience, and there is no better way to reveal it than to have the audience observe his inability to separate the past from the reality of the present.

Miller achieves this effect by manipulating the space and boundaries of the rooms. When action takes place in the present, characters observe wall boundaries and enter and exit through the doors. During Willy's recollections of the past, characters do not observe wall boundaries, and the action generally takes place in the area at the front of the stage, rather than inside the house. As a result, the audience can distinguish present events from Willy's memories. For example, in Act I, Scene 3, Willy pours a glass of milk in the kitchen, sits down, and begins to mumble to himself. He is in the present. He then remembers a past conversation with the teenage Biff and resumes the conversation. Since this is a past event, Willy directs his speech through the wall to a point offstage. This cues the audience that Willy is digressing in the past.

Sound is also used to create a dreamlike state for both Willy and the audience. A flute melody is associated with Willy, Ben has his own music, laughter cues the Woman, and so forth. Once the sound is introduced with the appropriate character, the audience automatically associates the sound with that same character. As a result, Miller is able to prompt reactions and expectations from the audience, whether they are aware or not. For example, in Act II, Scene 14, it appears that things have finally been settled between Willy and Biff. Even though Biff is leaving in the morning, he and Willy have reconciled. This puts the audience at ease, but once Ben's music is heard, it is evident that the play has not reached its final conclusion. In fact, Ben's appearance may create anxiety for the audience because it suggests an alternate, more disturbing, end to the play.

As the play progresses, the action shifts to the front of the stage. In other words, the audience becomes increasingly aware that the majority of the action is taking place inside Willy's head. It is difficult enough to watch an individual lose his or her identity. It is extremely unsettling and disturbing to be forced to experience the individual's memories, illusions, or perhaps delusions resulting in mental instability. Miller takes that into consideration and then pushes his audiences to the extreme. As Willy's mental state declines, the audience is forced to watch and to react. As a result, the play may be called Death of a Salesman, but it is a death observed and experienced by every member of the audience.

Tragic Myth of the play

Perhaps the dominant theme in the drama of the twentieth century is an attempt to recover—or, more precisely, to restate—a tragic apprehension about the human condition. A pervasive concern about the ultimate meaning of human suffering is reflected, in one way or another, in the work of all of the major playwrights of the twentieth century: in that of Ibsen, Strindberg, Chekhov, Shaw, Claudel, Synge, Lorca, and O'Neill, as well as in that of Pirandello, Brecht, Sartre, Camus, and more recently, Wilder, Williams, Beckett, Genet, Albee, and others.

The American drama has been particularly concerned with the modern face of suffering. Since its emergence, barely a half-century ago, the American drama has attempted, rather consistently, to record the kinds of crises which have characterized our times. The great American masterworks—Mourning Becomes Electra, The Time of Your Life, The Skin of Our Teeth, A Streetcar Named Desire, and others—have been concerned with the response of mankind to rapid technological advance. But the American dramatist has encountered serious difficulties in his search for a mode of expression appropriate to this theme. For he has been handicapped by a critical problem affecting communication: by the absence of a body of natural myths—symbolic interpretations of the life of man. Unlike Aeschylus, Shakespeare, Corneille, or subsequent playwrights in the interrelated European traditions, the American dramatist has been unable to employ as the instrumentation of his vision the great natural legends which are the residue of centuries of civilized growth.

The absence of conventional patterns of mythic interpretation has made it necessary for the American dramatist to devise new ways of seeing, interpreting, and re-creating reality. In terms of his ability to formulate coherent mythic patterns, perhaps the most effective dramatist in the American group is the "middle" playwright Arthur Miller.In his major works, All My Sons, Death of a Salesman, The Crucible, and A View from the Bridge, Miller seems to demonstrate a superiority to other American dramatists in the symbolic interpretation of universal dimensions of collective experience. Indeed, perhaps the most nearly mature myth about human suffering in an industrial age is Miller's masterwork, Death of a Salesman. In this work, first performed some thirteen years ago, Miller has formulated a statement about the nature of human crises in the twentieth century which seems, increasingly, to be applicable to the entire fabric of civilized experience. The superiority of Death of a Salesman over the other worthy American dramas such as Mourning Becomes Electra, A Streetcar Named Desire, or Miller's own work, The Crucible, is the sensitivity of its myth: the critical relationship of its central symbol—the Salesman—to the interpretation of the whole of contemporary life.

In this image, Miller brings into the theater a figure who is, in our age, a kind of hero—a ritual representative of an industrial society. It is its intimate association with our aspirations which gives to the story of Loman an ambiguous, but highly affecting, substratum of religious, philosophical, political, and social meanings. The appearance of the Salesman Loman as the subject of moral exploration stirs the modern spectator at that alternately joyful and painful periphery of consciousness which is the province of tragedy. The enactment of his suffering, fall, and partial enlightenment, provokes a mixed response: that anger and delight, indignation and sympathy, pity and fear, which Aristotle described as "catharsis."

Miller writes that, in Loman, he has attempted to personify certain values which civilized men, in the twentieth century, share. The movement of tragedy from the ground of the lawless Titan Prometheus to that of the common man Loman does not represent, for Miller, a decline in values; on the contrary, it is evidence of a hopeful development. For Loman, a descendant of the nineteenth-century protagonists of Ibsen, Chekhov, Shaw, and others, reflects Western civilization's increasing concern with a democratic interpretation of moral responsibilities. Death of a Salesman attempts to explore the implications of a life for which men—not gods—are wholly responsible.

Some of the problems with the interpretation of this play have grown out of the author's own statements about his intent; that is to say, Miller seems to have created in Death of a Salesman a new form which transcended his conscious motive. Death of a Salesman, despite the presence of those social implications which Miller notes in his later essays, is a myth, not a document; that is to say, it is not, in the conventional sense, a problem play. Unlike Miller's earlier work, All My Sons, Death of a Salesman is not concerned with such human failings as may find permanent social, political, or even psychological remedy. Death of a Salesman, like The Crucible and A View from the Bridge, is, rather, a study of a man's existence in a metaphysical universe. It is, like Agamemnon, Oedipus the King, Hamlet, and King Lear, a mythic apprehension of life. Willy Loman, like the traditional tragic protagonist, symbolizes the cruel paradox of human existence. His story [according to Miller's introduction to Collected Plays,] stripped to its mythic essentials, is familiar:

An aged king—a pious man—moves toward life's end. Instead of reaping the benefits of his piety, he finds himself caught in bewildering circumstances. Because of a mistake—

an error in judgment—a tragic reversal has taken place in his life. Where he has been priest, knower of secrets, wielder of power, and symbol of life, he now finds himself adjudged defiler, usurper, destroyer, and necessary sacrifice. Like the traditional hero, Loman begins his long season of agony. In his descent, however, there is the familiar tragic paradox; for as he moves toward inevitable destruction, he acquires that knowledge, that sense of reconciliation, which allows him to conceive a redemptive plan for his house.

As in traditional tragedy, Loman—the ritual head of his house—seeks to discover a design in the paradoxical movement of life; to impose upon it a sense of meaning greater than that conferred upon it by actuality. The play asks the ancient questions: What real value is there in life? What evil resides in seeming good? What good is hidden in seeming evil? What permanence is buried beneath the face of change? What use can man make of his suffering?

Miller describes this drama as a study of circumstances which affect human destiny in the moral universe:

I take it that if one could know enough about a human being one could discover some conflict, some value, some challenge, however minor or major, which he cannot find it in himself to walk away from or turn his back on. The structure of these plays, in this respect, is to the end that such a conflict be discovered and clarified. Idea, in these plays, is the generalized meaning of that discovery applied to men other than the hero. Time, characterizations, and other elements are treated differently from play to play, but all to the end that that moment of commitment be brought forth, that moment when, in my eyes, a man differentiates himself from every other man, that moment when out of a sky full of stars he fixes on one star. I take it, as well, that the less capable a man is of walking away from the central conflict of the play, the closer he approaches a tragic existence.

In turn, this implies that the closer a man approaches tragedy the more intense is his concentration of emotion upon the fixed point of his commitment.... The assumption—or presumption—behind these plays is that life has meaning.

Now the significant element in this statement is the playwright's suggestion that the ordinary actions of common men have ultimate meaning; indeed, that they are the concrete expression of conflict in the moral universe. The implication of this proposition is indeed profound.

For it assigns primary responsibility for the conduct of the universe to man. Miller's position is, thus, opposed to that commonly assigned to Ibsen. Certainly, it is in contradiction to Realism, which is concerned primarily with the meaning of action and being in a material world. It is, similarly, at variance with the philosophy posited by so-called Christian dramatists such as Claudel and Thornton Wilder, who assign the larger role in the conduct of the universe to a divine power. Miller's position is, at this point, Sophoclean in nature. For like Sophocles, he suggests that the critical role in the moral universe is that of man himself.

Now Miller's Classic stance is not singular in modern theater. A study of the masterpieces of the last fifty years, both in Europe and in America, shows this Classic concept of human responsibility to be common to many examples of Contemporary drama. Miller's position is roughly parallel to that of Jean-Paul Sartre, who in an earlier discussion of Contemporary French theater, wrote:

For them [the young playwrights] the theater will be able to present man in his entirety only in proportion to the theater's willingness to be moral. By that we do not mean that it should put forward examples illustrating the rules of deportment or the practical ethics taught to children, but rather that the study of the conflict of characters should be replaced by the presentation of the conflict of rights....

In each case, it is, in the final analysis and in spite of divergent interests, the systems of values, of ethics and of concepts of man which are lined up against each other.... This theater does not give its support to any one "thesis" and is not inspired by any preconceived idea. All it seeks to do is to explore the state of man in its entirety, and to present to the modern man a portrait of himself, his problems, his hopes and struggles.

Throughout the critical writings of the Contemporaries, in the essays of O'Neill, Saroyan, Wilder, Williams, and Miller, as well as in the work of Europeans such as Sartre, Camus, Anouilh, and others, this dramatic motive is articulated: to illumine the moral choice which lies hidden beneath the face of actuality, to show modern man the present image of human destiny.

Now to say that Miller and others are in process of evolving a Contemporary tragic myth is not to suggest that Death of a Salesman is an imitation of the Greek tragic form. Indeed, Miller states quite clearly [in his introduction to Collected Plays] that changes in the perception of universal law, as well as alterations in the very idea of man, would make Greek tragedy invalid as an expression of our time. He writes that he seeks, rather, to evolve a form which may stand in the same kind of relationship to the moral crises of the twentieth century as did Greek, Shakespearean, or French tragic drama—each to its own epoch. While Miller and others appear, then, to have adopted certain characteristics belonging to traditional tragedy, they have rejected others. Death of a Salesman appears to imitate Classic tragedy primarily in its acceptance of the principle of the ultimate responsibility of the individual. That which appears to differentiate this work from traditional forms is its relocation of the tragic environment. For Death of a Salesman, like other examples of the Contemporary genre, elevates to meaning a new protagonist: the common man. Perhaps of greater importance is the fact that it removes the ground of the tragic conflict from outer event to inner consciousness. Death of a Salesman, like Mourning Becomes Electra, The Hairy Ape, A Streetcar Named Desire, and others, may be described as a tragedy of consciousness, the imitation of a moral crisis in the life of a common man.

Miller [in his introduction to Collected Plays] traces this idea, in part, to the German expressionists, particularly, to Bertolt Brecht. Professor John Gassner finds aspects of this "underground drama" in the nineteenth-century innovators, not only in the work of the playwrights, Ibsen, Strindberg, Chekhov, and Shaw, but also in that of stream-of consciousness novelists such as Dostoevsky, Tolstoy, and Henry James. But while the Contemporary dramatists are indebted to these sources, the idea of form as the imitation of consciousness is much older than the late nineteenth century Clearly, Miller and others have borrowed heavily from Shakespeare and his antecedents in the liturgical drama; moreover, their interpretations of the internal struggle have some of their roots in both Classic and Neoclassic tragedy

The concept of tragedy as a crisis within the consciousness appears to have emerged clearly in the Romantic Period, particularly in the Sturm und Drang movement; in the theater of Goethe, Schiller, Coleridge, Wagner, and Nietzsche. Oddly enough, the idea continued to dominate the theater of the so-called "Realists." It gained a systematic dramaturgy in Expressionism; it has, throughout this century, intensified its hold upon the Contemporary imagination. We may, thus, read the history of Western drama—Classicism, Neoclassicism, Romanticism, Realism, and Expressionism—as a continuous development; the gradual narrowing of theatrical focus upon the moment of crisis within the individual consciousness.

The adoption of this concept by modern dramatists has accounted for major alterations in form. The new form is not a representation of ordinary modes of action, an imitation of events-in-themselves. It is, rather, concerned with the representation of consciousness, with the imitation of a single moment of experience. We may describe Death of a Salesman, for example, as a kind of theatrical illusion. For it is intended, according to Miller, as the apparition of a key image, the imitation of the "way of mind" which characterizes the Salesman Willy:

The first image that occurred to me which was to result in Death of a Salesman was of an enormous face the height of the proscenium arch which would appear and then open up, and we would see the inside of a man's head.... The Salesman image was from the beginning absorbed with the concept that nothing in life comes "next" but that everything exists together and at the same time within us; that there is no past to be "brought forward" in a human being, but that he is his past at every moment and that the present is merely that which his past is capable of noticing and smelling and reacting to.

I wished to create a form which, in itself as a form, would literally be the process of Willy Loman's way of mind. Death of a Salesman, as vision, follows an aesthetic, rather than a logical, mode of development. For it represents the protagonist's attempt to reconstitute the progression of his experience. Loman, as the protagonist, has an extremely complicated identity; for he is actor—observer creator. He is the very ground of reality—the shape of experience itself; at the same time, he is the observer of that unique vision. He is required, finally, to be a creator, the architect of a new poetic universe, in which all components of his vision are united, in a harmonious entity.

We may describe this kind of structure as a theatrical realization of the "stream-of-consciousness." Miller's "stream-of-consciousness" differs in certain particulars from that of other dramatists such as Williams and O'Neill; it is, in many ways, close to that of novelists such as Virginia Woolf. For, like Woolf, Miller does not divide his vision of reality into discrete units—pictures with rigid boundaries. He, rather, conceives Willy's mind as a place "out of time," as a state in which all boundaries have been erased, in which all things are coexistent. He writes [in his introduction to Collected Plays]: "Above all, in the structural sense, I aimed to make a play with the veritable countenance of life. To make the one the many."

Now, the need to give such an ambiguous poetic perception a concrete form in the theater has, obviously, presented the playwright with certain difficulties, which other American dramatists have shared: How can "consciousness" be connoted on the stage? As in traditional tragedy, Miller projects his vision of experience by employing the method of poetry. Death of a Salesman, like Prometheus Bound, Oedipus, King Lear, or for that matter, like Ghosts, The Cherry Orchard, The Ghost Sonata, The Hairy Ape, Our Town, or A Streetcar Named Desire, is, thus, a kind of poem; that is to say, it represents the exposition of a key image, through the simultaneous realization of component figures. We have noted

Miller's own comment on the central image of Willy's head, which opens up to reveal his "way of mind." He describes the play as a veritable "sea of images": shapes in the protagonist's vision: The play's eye was to revolve from within Willy's head, sweeping endlessly in all directions like a light on the sea, and nothing that formed in the distant mist was to be left uninvestigated. It was thought of as having the density of the novel form in its interchange of viewpoints, so that while all roads led to Willy the other characters were to feel it was their play, a story about them and not him....

There are no flashbacks in this play but only a mobile concurrency of past and present, and this, again, because in his desperation to justify his life Willy Loman has destroyed the boundaries between now and then. Death of a Salesman is an aesthetic progression: a reconstruction of the movement of consciousness: the perception of facts, events, and ideas; fears, passions, and superstitions; hopes, dreams, and ambitions, in their various stages of maturity and immaturity.

Clearly, this definition might easily apply to other Contemporary arts, particularly, to the novel, the long poem, the modern dance, or the cinema. The significant factor which distinguishes Death of a Salesman from these related forms is the fact that it was written to be spoken and performed by live actors before a live audience.

Miller speaks of drama as a symbolic ritual, which projects the spectator's consciousness into the mind of the protagonist, and which, in turn, introjects the suffering, enlightenment, and triumph of the protagonist into the consciousness of the spectator. Miller, like other Contemporary dramatists, regards spectacle as a critical element of theatrical language. For it provides the poetic vision with its sensuous fabric, with its texture. Miller, like other playwrights who have followed the theories and practice of Wagner, has given considerable attention to the articulation of an appropriate dramaturgy for the interpretation of his tragic myth. Much of the text of Death of a Salesman is given to the articulation of the sensuous form of the poetic image. The playwright's description of the setting follows:

A melody is heard, played upon a flute. It is small and fine, telling of grass and trees and the horizon. The curtain rises. Before us is the Salesman's house. We are aware of towering, angular shapes behind it, surrounding it on all sides. Only the blue light of the sky falls upon the house and forestage; the surrounding area shows an angry glow of orange. As more light appears, we see a solid vault of apartment houses around the small, fragile-seeming home. An air of the dream clings to the place, a dream rising out of reality.... The entire setting is wholly or, in some places, partially transparent.

The roofline of the house is one-dimensional: under and over it we see the apartment buildings. Before the house lies an apron, curving beyond the forestage into the orchestra. This forward area serves as the back yard as well as the locale of all Willy's imaginings and of his city scenes. Whenever the action is in the present, the actors observe the imaginary wall-lines, entering the house only through its door at the left. But in the scenes of the past, these boundaries are broken, and characters enter or leave a room by stepping "through" a wall onto the forestage.

Death of a Salesman is, then, an example of that kind of form, which Professor Francis Fergusson has described as "poetry in the theater." It is a myth, which projects before the spectator an image of the protagonist's consciousness. The playwright attempts to reveal a tragic progression within the consciousness of the protagonist. He employs, as the instrumentation of vision, a complex theater symbol: a union of gesture, word, and music; light, colour, and pattern; rhythm and movement. We may now ask: What is the nature of this myth? In what sense is it tragic?

Miller follows O'Neill in suggesting that suffering in the modern world is often deceptively masked, inasmuch as it has been clearly removed from the context of the purely physical. The Contemporary protagonist Loman suffers from such an ambiguous evil, from a malady which modern arts and letters have determined the moral sickness of the twentieth century. Miller describes this sickness as the "disease of unrelatedness."

Its symptoms are a sense of alienation, a loss of meaning, and a growing despair. We have seen this illness personified in the protagonist throughout the Contemporary drama: in O'Neill's Yank, Williams's Blanche, in Wilder's Cain in The Skin of Our Teeth, as well as in the protagonists of Odets, Saroyan, Hellman, Hansberry, and, more recently, Albee and others. While other dramatists are often equivocal in their assessment of causes, Miller is quite clear about the roots of this sickness. He traces modern suffering to the ancient cause: ignorance. Death of a Salesman attempts to trace Loman's progress from ignorance, through the cycle of suffering, to enlightenment. As in Classic tragedy, the price of this "Odyssey" is death, but, through his personal sacrifice, the protagonist redeems his house and promises to his posterity yet another chance.

Miller's transposition of the tragic movement to a "modern key" seems effective. If there is a problem with his myth, it would seem to emanate from his choice of Loman as protagonist; that is to say, with the idea of a truly common man as tragic hero. For at first glance, Willy Loman, as a symbol of modern man, seems to have critical shortcomings. To begin with, he does not seem to have sinned greatly enough to satisfy the needs of tragic shock and terror. In this respect, Tennessee Williams's protagonists, with their sexual crimes, more nearly approach the Greek interpretation of man sickened by the horror of transgression.

Miller's hamartia is more subtle than that of Williams, but perhaps even more Classic in its ultimate implications. For Miller, like Sophocles, insists that tragic catastrophe is the result of ignorance rather than the end of willful transgression. Loman's crime in the universe may be likened to that of Agamemnon or Lear; it is the appearance of indifference, the absence of sympathy, and the lack of a sense of moral law. For Miller, moral ignorance is, at once, the most serious—and most common—indictment against humanity in our time.

But there is, yet, a second and even more serious objection which may be raised against Loman as hero; and that is that he does not seem to measure up to the stature of a great and good man. Against the outline of Oedipus, Lear, or Faust, Loman appears a small man, a mere failure, who does not have sufficient grace to warrant universal concern. Again, appearances belie the truth. For Loman, Miller holds, is the measure of certain changes in value associated with the rise of a democratic society. It is, according to the playwright, Loman who is the symbol of the most powerful moral force in the modern world: the common man.

It is, the playwright continues, the outcome of the crisis within his consciousness, which will, with certainty, determine the disposition of the moral dilemma which still grips the human race. But Miller, the American, goes even further in the justification of his protagonist.

For, he declares, not only must a Contemporary tragic myth mirror the shape of transgression and the nature of power in our age, it ought, also, to be the measure of our ethical advance over prior civilizations. If the Greek hero mirrored a society, which condoned slavery, and the Renaissance protagonist represented an aristocratic minority, Willy Loman is the measure of democracy's promise of unlimited human possibility. He is the representative of an open order where all values—even virtue—may be gained at any moment when man is willing to risk commitment.

It is clear that, for Miller, Loman is a virtuous man; that is to say, he wins virtue, in a moment released from the boundaries of time and causality. Miller, like the Existentialists, defines virtue, heroism, and nobility, in anti-Aristotelian terms; that is to say, Loman's character is not a static arrangement of fixed virtues. On the contrary, the protagonist gains ultimate value in the universe at the same instant when he commits himself to the search for truth, in that "Existential moment" which the play itself represents.

Loman, the Contemporary hero, embarks upon a most courageous "Odyssey": the descent into the self, where he engages his most dangerous enemy, himself. The fact that he does so late in his life does not, in the Contemporary context, diminish his value. For Loman, like Lear, is a hero who comes late in the tragic progression to enlightenment.

Miller attempts to take his tragic cycle to its natural conclusion by giving a sign to the protagonist's victory. In Death of a Salesman, as in traditional tragedy, the sign is itself a paradox. Loman's suicide, like Oedipus's self-blinding or Antigone's self-murder, is obviously intended as a gesture of the hero's victory over circumstances. It is an act of love, intended to redeem his house. Willy's wife indicates this interpretation in the Requiem:

Forgive me, dear, I can't cry. I don't know what it is, but I can't cry. I don't understand it. Why did you ever do that? Help me, Willy, I can't cry. It seems to me that you're just on another trip. I keep expecting you. Willy, dear, I can't cry. Why did you do it? I search and search and I search, and I can't understand it, Willy. I made the last payment on the house today. Today, dear. And there'll be nobody home.... We're free and clear.... We're free.... We're free.... We're free....

Arthur Miller's Death of a Salesman is, perhaps, to this time, the most mature example of a myth of Contemporary life. The chief value of this drama is its attempt to reveal those ultimate meanings which are resident in modern experience. Perhaps the most significant comment on this play is not its literary achievement, as such, but is, rather, the impact which it has had on spectators, both in America and abroad. The influence of this drama, first performed in 1949, continues to grow in World Theater. For it articulates, in language, which can be appreciated by popular audiences, certain new dimensions of the human dilemma. The playwright's own words would seem to summarize the achievement of this myth about modern life: The ultimate justification for a genuine new form is the new and heightened consciousness it creates and makes possible— a consciousness of causation in the light of known but hitherto inexplicable effects.

Memory and Dramatic Form in Death of a Salesman

Arthur Miller's evolution from imitator to innovator, which occurred between the publication of his first two works, is the clearest example of that general change in style that both unites and separates the turn-of the-century dramatists and those of the present: the emergence out of dramatic form of a new formal structure for those epic elements that had previously only been given thematic expression. If this process, which is central to the developmental history of the modern theater, has, up to this point, been presented mainly in terms of comparison between the two periods—by contrasting Ibsen and Pirandello, Chekhov and Wilder, Hauptmann and Brecht—in Miller's case, as with Strindberg's earlier, it can be illuminated by the works of a single author.

In All My Sons (1947), Miller tried to preserve Ibsen's analytical approach to social dramaturgy by transferring it into the American present. An inexorable analysis slowly reveals the long-hidden crime committed by the head of the Keller family: his delivery of defective airplane parts to the Army, a deed that involves him in another—the suicide of his son Larry—which has also been kept secret. All the secondary aspects of the action needed to narrate the past as a dramatic event are at hand— the return of Larry's former fiancée and her brother, for example. Their father, an employee of Keller's, was wrongfully imprisoned for Keller's offense. Even Ibsen's often heavy-handed use of the set is preserved in this work: an element of the decor gives visible presence to the ongoing internal effects of the past, while also laboring to symbolize the deeper meaning of the play.

In this case it is the tree that long ago had been planted for Larry. Felled by the previous night's storm, its shattered stump stands in the backyard where the play is set. If All My Sons had not been followed by Death of a Salesman, it might possibly have been discussed here as an example of Ibsen's powerful influence in the Anglo Saxon world, an influence that begins with George Bernard Shaw and lives on today. As it is, however, the play can be regarded as a work from his apprentice years, as if Miller, engaged in giving scenic form to a "wasted lifetime" and in particular to a traumatic past, had, while following in Ibsen's footsteps, come to understand the manner in which dramatic form resists this thematic and the costs attached to making the former serve the latter. What was shown here earlier with respect to John Gabriel Borkman must have become clear to Miller as he worked on All My Sons: the contradiction between a remembered past conveyed by the thematic and the spatial-temporal present postulated by dramatic form; the resulting need to contrive a supplementary action with which to motivate the analysis; and, the disharmony produced by the fact that this second set of events dominates the stage while the real "action" emerges only in the confessions of the characters.

In his second play, Miller tries to escape these contradictions by surrendering dramatic form. Fundamental here is the fact that he does not disguise the analysis as action. The past is no longer forced into open discussion by a dramatic conflict; the dramatis personae are no longer portrayed as masters of the past to satisfy a formal principle when in fact they are its helpless victims. Instead, the past achieves representation in the same way that it emerges in life itself—of its own accord, in the mémoire involontaire (Proust). Therefore, the past remains a subjective experience and can create no illusory bridges between the individuals whom the analysis brings together—individuals whom it had left in lifelong separation. Thus, instead of an interpersonal action that would call forth discussion of the past, the present generated by the thematic discloses the psychic state of the individual overpowered by memory.

Willy Loman, an aging salesman, is presented in this manner; the play begins as he slips completely under the thrall of memory. The family has recently begun to notice that he talks to himself. In fact, he is actually talking to them, not in the real present but in the past he remembers, which no longer leaves him alone. The present of the play is constituted by the forty-eight hours that follow Loman's unexpected return from a business trip. The past had continuously gotten the better of him as he sat behind the steering wheel of his car. He tries in vain to arrange a transfer to the New York office of the company he has represented for several decades; his constant references to the past reveal the state he is in, and he is fired. Finally, Loman commits suicide so that his family can benefit from his insurance policy.

This actional framework, which is situated in the present, has little to do with that found in Ibsen's Drama or even in All My Sons. It is not a dramatic event that closes on itself; and it does not require that the past be conjured up in dialogue. The scene between Loman and his employer is characteristic in this respect. The latter is unwilling to join in a conversation that would give presence to the salesman's career and to his own father, who is supposed to have been favorably disposed toward Loman. He finds an excuse to leave the room and hurries out, leaving Loman alone with his ever more vivid memories.

These memories in turn create a means (one already long familiar to the cinema under the name flashback) of introducing the past into the space beyond dialogue. The scene shifts constantly in the play staged for Loman by his mémoire involontaire. Unlike the Ibsenesque courtroom procedure, remembrance occurs without being spoken of—that is, entirely on the level of form. The protagonist regards himself in the past and, as self-remembering I, is absorbed into the formal subjectivity of the work. The scene presents only the epic object of this subjectivity, the remembered I itself, the salesman in the past, his conversations with the members of his family. The latter are no longer independent dramatis personae; they emerge as references to the central I, in the same manner as do the character projections in expressionist dramaturgy.

One can readily grasp the epic nature of this play of memory by comparing it to the "play within a play" as it appears in the Drama. Hamlet's play, which presents the imagined past in order to "catch the conscience of the king," is built into the action in the form of an episode. It constitutes a closed sphere that leaves the surrounding world of action intact. Because this second play is a thematic piece that does not need to conceal the fact of its performance, the time and place of the two actions are not in conflict— the dramatic unities and the absoluteness of the events are maintained. In Death of a Salesman, on the other hand, the past is not played as a thematic episode; the present and its action constantly overflow into the play of the past. No troupe of actors enters;

without saying a word, the characters can become actors enacting themselves because the alternation between immediate/personal and past/remembered events is anchored in the epic principle of form operative here.

The dramatic unities are likewise abolished—indeed, abolished in the most radical sense: memory signifies not only a multiplicity of times and places but also the absolute loss of their identity. The temporal-spatial present of the action is not simply relativized in terms of other presents; on the contrary, it is in itself relative. Therefore, there is no real change in the setting, and, at the same time, it is perpetually transformed. The salesman's house remains on stage, but in the scenes remembered, its walls are of no concern—as is the case with memory, which has no temporal or spatial limits. This relativity of the present becomes particularly clear in those transitional scenes that belong to the outer as well as the inner reality. Such is the situation in the first act when the memory figure, Ben, Willy's brother, appears on stage while he and his neighbour, Charley, are playing cards:

WILLY: I'm awfully tired Ben.

CHARLEY: Good, keep playing; you'll sleep better. Did you call me Ben?

WILLY: That's funny. For a second there you reminded me of my brother Ben.

The salesman says nothing that indicates he sees his dead brother in front of him. His appearance could be a hallucination, but only within dramatic form, which by definition excludes the inner world. Yet, in this play, present reality and the reality of the past achieve simultaneous representation. Because Loman is reminded of his brother, the latter appears on stage: memory has been incorporated into the principle underlying scenic form. Because interior monologue (dialogue with a figure evoked by memory), stands side by side with dialogue, the result is a Chekhovian speaking at cross purposes:

BEN: Is Mother living with you?

WILLY: No, she died a long time ago.

CHARLEY: Who?

BEN: That's too bad. Fine specimen of a lady, Mother.
WILLY (to Charley): Heh?
BEN: I'd hoped to see the old girl.
CHARLEY: Who died?
BEN: Heard anything from Father, have you?
WILLY (unnerved): What do you mean, who died?
CHARLEY: What're you talkin' about?

To give dramatic form to this sort of continual misunderstanding, Chekhov needed the supporting theme supplied by deafness. In Death of a Salesman, on the other hand, it arises formally out of the side-by-side existence of the two worlds. Their concurrent representation sets in motion the new principle of form. Its advantage over the Chekhovian technique is obvious. The supporting theme, the symbolic character of which remains vague, does introduce the possibility of mutual misunderstanding, but it also hides the real source of this misunderstanding—the individual's preoccupation with himself and with a remembered past, a past that can appear as such only after the formal principle of the Drama is abolished.

It is this past, once again present, that finally opens the salesman's eyes as he desperately tries to understand his own misfortune and, even more, the failed career of his elder son [Biff]. While sitting across from his sons in a restaurant, a scene from the past suddenly surfaces in his memory and, therefore, becomes visible to the audience as well: his son finds him in a Boston hotel room with his mistress. At this point, Loman can understand why his son later wandered from job to job and why he thwarted his career prospects by stealing: he wanted to punish his father.

In Death of a Salesman, Miller did not want to reveal this secret, the failure of the father (which was borrowed from Ibsen and central to All My Sons), through a judicial procedure invented for the sake of form. He gave credence to Balzac's comment, under the sign of which both Ibsen's and Miller's characters stand: "We all die unknown." Because memory takes its place beside the (always) present of the dialogue, which constitutes the sole representational possibility of the

Drama, the play successfully presents a dramatic paradox: the past of a number of characters is given visible presence but only for a single consciousness. In contrast to the analysis that is part of the thematic in Ibsen, this play of the past, founded on the principle of form, has no effect on the other characters. For the son, this scene remains a permanent and heavily guarded secret. He is unable to reveal to anyone the shattering effect it has had on his life. Because of this, his mute hatred breaks into the open neither before his father's suicide nor after it. And in the Requiem, which closes the play, it is precisely the unsuspecting quality of the remarks made by Linda, the salesman's wife, that makes them so moving.

LINDA: Forgive me, dear. I can't cry. I don't know what it is, but I can't cry. I don't understand it. Why did you ever do that? Help me, Willy, I can't cry. It seems to me that you're just on another trip. I keep expecting you. Willy, dear, I can't cry. Why did you do it? I search and search and I search, and I can't understand it.

Point of View in Arthur Miller's Death of a Salesman

In Death of a Salesman Arthur Miller wrote far better than he seems to have realized, at least if we may judge by his critical essays on the play. This is true of both the play's content—its analysis of American values— and of its technique. Miller's recent After the Fall uses the same nonlogical, subjective memory structure as the earlier play, and uses it far more consistently and skillfully, and yet is far less effective in engaging the self identification by the audience for which expressionism strives. And this is not only because the experience examined in After the Fall is less common than the disaster of Willy Loman, but because the very hesitancies of technique in Death of a Salesman, its apparent uncertainty in apportioning realism and expressionism, provide a dramatic excitement of a more complex kind than Miller achieves in his later, more consistent plays.

To claim to understand a play better than its author does may sound egotistic, but we may take comfort from the fact that Miller himself says in the preface to his Collected Plays:

A writer of any worth creates out of his total perception, the vaster proportion of which is subjective and not within his intellectual control.... if it is art [that the playwright] has created, it must by definition bend itself to his observation rather than to his opinions or even his hopes.

It is the contention of this paper, therefore, that by keeping close to actual observation Death of a Salesman presents a far more accurate weighing of American values than Miller's subsequent analyses suggest, and that the blurred line between realism and expressionism is not the weakness some critics have claimed, but, on the contrary, one of the play's most subtle successes. The realism in Death of a Salesman is fairly obvious, and reflects the influence on Miller of Henrik Ibsen, the Ibsen, that is, of the middle phase, the great realist reformer. In All My Sons and Death of a Salesman Miller adopts Ibsen's "retrospective" structure, in which an explosive situation in the present is both explained and brought to a crisis by the gradual revelation of something which has happened in the past: in Death of a Salesman this is, of course, Willy Loman's adultery, which by alienating his son, Biff, has destroyed the strongest value in Willy's life.

This structure is filled out with a detailed evocation of modern, urban, lower middle class life: Miller documents a world of arch-supports, aspirin, spectacles, subways, time payments, advertising, Chevrolets, faulty refrigerators, life insurance, mortgages, and the adulation of high school football heroes. The language, too, except in a few places, which will be considered later, is an accurate record of the groping, half inarticulate, cliché-ridden inadequacy of ordinary American speech. And the deadly realism of the picture is confirmed for us by the way that American audiences have immediately recognized and identified with it in the theater.

However, even in his realist plays, Ibsen has details which, while still being acceptably probable, have also a deeper, symbolic significance: one thinks of such things as the polluted swimming baths in An Enemy of the People, the eponymous wild duck, or, more abstractly, the hair and pistols motifs in Hedda Gabler. Such a deepening of realism is also a technique in Death of a Salesman. Consider, for instance, the value that Willy and his sons attach to manual work, and its glamorous extension, sport, their belief that it is necessary for a man to keep fit, to be able to handle tools and build things.

Willy's handiness around the house is constantly impressed on us: "He was always good with his hands," Linda remembers, and Biff says that his father put more enthusiasm into building the stoop than into all his salesmanship; in his reveries Willy again teaches his boys how to simonize a car the most efficient way, and is contemptuous of his neighbour Charlie, and Charlie's son Bernard, be cause they lack the manual skills; Willy's favourite son, Biff, is even more dextrous than his father—in high school he was a star athlete and, as a man, he can find happiness only as a ranch hand; one remembers that Willy's father was a pioneer type who drove over the country in a wagon, earning money by ingenious inventions and the making of flutes. Willy's mystique of physical skill is thus a reflection of the simpler, pioneer life he craves, a symptom and a symbol of his revolt against the constraints of the modern city.

Slightly more abstract, yet still realistic, is the play's use of trees to symbolize the rural way of life which modern commercialism is choking. Willy, we are told, bought his house originally because it stood in a wooded suburb where he could hunt a little, and where his yard was flanked by two great elms; but now the trees have been cut down and his property is so over-shadowed by apartment houses that he cannot even grow seed in his back garden. (The choked seed is a fairly obvious symbol: Willy Loman is trapped in a society which prevents him establishing anything to outlast himself, ruining the lives of his sons as well as his own.) We learn at the beginning that it is dreaming about the countryside and watching scenery, particularly trees, which is the main cause of Willy's recent road accidents; it is to look after timber that Willy's brother, Ben, tries to persuade him to go to Alaska; the "jungle," Ben says, is the place for riches; and at moments of crisis Willy yells, "The woods are burning," a phrase which is nonsensical unless seen in context of the other tree references.

The last example is already diverging from realism: that is, it is not a phrase habitually used in American life; it needs the context of the play to give it meaning. And when we find Miller directing that, whenever Willy remembers the past, the stage be drenched in a green, checkered pattern of leaves, then it is obvious that the technique has moved from realistic symbolism to outright expressionism.

The set for the play, designed by Jo Mielziner but to Miller's specifications, and influenced, no doubt, by the set for O'Neill's Desire under the Elms, is a bizarre but wholly successful mingling of realism and non realism. Its skeletal house shows several rooms simultaneously (like mediaeval staging); the house is sparsely furnished with just enough properties to suggest a sense of place and environment, with the result, as the first stage direction suggests, that "an air of dream clings to the place, a dream rising out of reality"; and the house has in front of it a bare, neutral forestage, used (as in the Elizabethan theater) to represent any place demanded by the story, with necessary props being carried on and off by the characters themselves. The skeletal framework of the house also gives it a sense of fragility which is intensified by surrounding it with the menacing silhouettes of tall apartment houses, producing an effect of claustrophobia, of rural wood menaced by asphalt jungle.

The set is expressionistically lit to reinforce this impression. The apartment silhouettes are bathed in angry orange; when Willy remembers the past, the house is dappled by the green of vanished trees; when Biff and Hap pick up two women and neglect their father, the directions request a lurid red; and at the end, when Willy insanely tries to plant seed by night, the "blues" of the stage direction simultaneously suggests moonlight and his mood of despair. Music is similarly manipulated: the rural way of life is represented by flute music, telling "of grass and trees and the horizon"; it is heard only by Willy whenever he dreams of the life he should have led or of the early days when his suburb was still in the country. It is associated, of course, with Willy's pioneer father, the flute maker; and in the modern world has degenerated to Willy and

Biff's unbusiness like habit of whistling in elevators, and, at a yet further remove, to the mechanized whistling of Howard and his children as played back on a tape recorder. The tape recorder scene is, in fact, a brilliantly compact piece of symbolism, functioning like the "mirror scene" in some of Shakespeare's plays (or Brecht's "Grundgestus") to epitomize the action of the whole play: not only does it illustrate the mechanization of family life, but Howard's idolizing of his children and bullying of his wife exactly parallel Willy's, showing a resemblance between the two men which undercuts left-wing clichés about employer and worker; and, when Willy knocks it over and cannot stop it, the machine serves as both cause and illustration of Willy's mental breakdown: he has one of his schizophrenic attacks, and the mechanical voices, so like those of his own home life, are an equivalent to the clamorous subconscious of which he has also lost control.

The crucial hotel bedroom scene, in which Biff discovers his father's adultery, is heralded by a shrill trumpet blast, and Willy's final disaster is conveyed by musical shorthand: his decision to commit suicide is accompanied by a prolonged, maddening note, which collapses into a crash of discords, to represent the car crash offstage, and then modulates into a dead march to introduce the requiem scene. Certain characters and situations also have what amounts to leitmotifs: besides the flute music, we are told there is a "boy's music"; raucous sex music for the scene of Biff's discovery and the barroom scene where Biff and Hap pick up women; and a special music to herald the appearances in Willy's memory of his elder brother, Ben.

The presentation of Ben is an important clue as to exactly how, and why, Miller is using expressionism in Death of a Salesman. He is distinctly less "real" than the other characters of the play, stiffer, with a more stilted way of speaking: in the original production, Elia Kazan had the part acted unnaturally, like an automaton. Ben seems less "real" than the others because he is not so much a person as the embodiment of Willy's desire for escape and success: Willy calls him "success incarnate." This is proved by the fact that he does not only appear in memory scenes but is summoned up at the end to "discuss" Willy's plan of suicide; obviously, he here represents a side of Willy's own mind. It is interesting to note, therefore, that the stage directions emphasize that Ben always appears at exactly the moment Willy thinks of him, which is not true of the other characters in the memory scenes. The figure of Ben, then, represents not Ben as he actually was, so much as Ben as his image has been warped in the mind of the rememberer, Willy; and this reveals the peculiar nature of expressionism in Death of a Salesman.

Miller is not using expressionistic techniques in the way they are used by the German writers of the 1920s, to dramatize abstract forces in politics or economics or history. He is using the techniques solely as a means of revealing the character of Willy Loman, the values Willy holds and, particularly, the way his mind works. Miller's reason for blending realism and expressionism in Death of a Salesman is that this combination reflects the protagonist's actual way of thinking: "I wished to create a form," says Miller, "which.. would literally be the process of Willy Loman's mind." It is Willy Loman's character, therefore, which is the chief link between the two dramatic modes, and this is possible, of course, because Willy is technically a schizophrenic: overwork, worry and, particularly, repressed guilt have resulted in a mental breakdown in which present and past mingle for him inextricably, where, in Miller's own phrase, time is "exploded."

As Miller points out, this is not a "flashback" technique (the film of Death of a Salesman failed precisely because it tried to turn the memory sequences into flashbacks); what it does is to present a past distorted by the rememberer's mind—a subjective, not objective record; and the memories have an extra tension because they occur simultaneously with events in the present, more like a double exposure than a flashback. Note, for instance, how the memory scenes appear gradually, usurping the present bit by bit in the card game with Charlie when Willy is talking to the remembered Ben and the actual Charlie simultaneously, or the gradual emergence of the repressed hotel bedroom scene which is brought to a climax when Biff's and Happy's pick-ups enter in the present. This simultaneous presentation of past and present, dream and reality, gives the play a metaphoric quality, a Cocteau-ish "poetry of the theater," which (in my opinion) compensates for the so often criticized banality of language. Ambiguity, irony, and tension occur in the action and stage pictures, not in the wording where they might, more conventionally, be expected. It is a metaphor in time.

The form of the play, then, depends on the gradual admission by Willy to himself of his own guilt; it differs from the public exposés of Ibsen's form in that Willy's adultery is never openly discussed between him and Biff, and Linda and Hap never learn of it at all: the sole importance is that Willy himself should recognize it. Normal chronology is ignored, therefore: the order of events depends on the way that memories of the past swim up out of Willy's memory because of their emotional association with things happening in the present. For example, Willy's worry about having nearly crashed his car in the present brings up memories of happy experiences with cars in the past; as Willy eases his feeling of inferiority to Charlie by mocking Charlie's lack of skill with tools, this conjures up the memory of Ben, Willy's ideal of practical success, and leads with emotional but not chronological logic to reminiscences of their pioneer father. Note, particularly, that certain things always "trigger" this kind of mental relapse in Willy because they are so associated with his guilt: silk stockings, for instance, or the sound of women laughing; and the blurring of mental realities is represented visually by characters stepping across the wall lines of the skeletal setting. Miller says: "The structure of the play was determined by what was needed to draw up [Willy's] memories like a mass of tangled roots without end or beginning." This provides a sense of climax because "if I could make him remember enough he would kill himself."

However, Miller's explanation of his purpose fails to account for an important inconsistency in the use of expressionism. The play does not divide neatly into realistic scenes in the present and expressionistic memory scenes in

Willy's mind; some of the expressionistic scenes deal with events in the present when Willy is not even there, and cannot therefore be said to be distorted through his schizophrenia. Consider the scenes downtown in Howard's office or the barroom, before Willy arrives, which are represented nonrealistically on the unlocalized forestage; or, most strikingly, the unrealism of the Requiem scene, where characters break the wall lines to come downstage, and the forestage itself represents a graveyard. This cannot be a distortion of Willy's mind because Willy is already dead.

The rationale behind the mingling of realism and expressionism is thus uncertain. The result is intriguing. The extension of expressionism to non-memory scenes means that we see even events which Willy did not experience as though through Willy's eyes, as Willy might have experienced them. The play's technique thus forces the audience to become Willy Lomans for the whole duration of the play, to sympathize with his predicament in a way they could not do in real life. It allows them to see more than Willy does, but not to see more than he might have seen; they are expected to criticize Willy, but the technique forces them to criticize him from within, as Willy criticizes and condemns himself. Miller tells us some interesting facts about the genesis of the play which are relevant here:

The first image that occurred to me which was to result in Death of a Salesman was an enormous face to the height of the proscenium arch which would appear and then open up, and we would see the inside of a man's head. In fact, The Inside of His Head was the first title. It was conceived half in laughter, for the inside of his head was a mass of contradictions.

The last sentence is particularly important because it reflects on the values of the play in a way which has not yet been analysed: if we see all the play as Willy might have experienced it, even those scenes in which he does not actually appear, then all the values of the play, good as well as bad, will be restricted to values which Willy might himself have held. The frame of values will be relative to the potential of a character like Willy's, adjusted to the limits of his imagination.

This important "point of view" in the play has been invariably neglected: discussions of Death of a Salesman assume that it presents Miller's own values, and Miller's defence of Willy as a tragic hero has done nothing to rectify the error. Obviously, Death of a Salesman is a criticism of the moral and social standards of contemporary America, not merely a record of the particular plight of one man. And, also obviously, it presents Willy as a victim of the deterioration of the "American dream," the belief in untrammelled individualism. The word "dream" is a key word, recurring frequently in the play; and the deterioration of American individualism is traced through the Loman generations in a descending scale, from the Whitman-like exuberance of Willy's father, through Ben, Willy himself, to the empty predatoriness of Happy, who is, he admits, compulsively competitive in sex and business for no reason at all.

The ideal of self-dependence has become the vicious competition of the modern business community, of which Willy, as a salesman, is the lowest common denominator. Miller has explained Willy's surname as standing for "low man on the totem pole," the bottom of the heap; and, interestingly, Willy's ideal, the old salesman in green slippers, is called "Dave Singleman." The two names contrast Willy's actual exploitation and the dignified independence to which he aspired. Willy's philosophy is the personality cult of Dale Carnegie, the "win friends and influence people" theory which exploits human relations for purposes of gain.

"Be liked and you will never want," Willy advises his sons; and his famous distinction between being "liked" and being "well liked" seems to rest on whether or not the liking can be exploited for practical ends. Such using of friendliness falsifies it and invokes a law of diminishing returns, as Willy's lonely funeral shows. The attitude also encourages empty dreams, reflected economically in advertising and time payments; it is essentially parasitic, producing, building, planting nothing; and the logical extension of its unrestrained competition is Biff's downright theft. The psychologists explain theft as a form of love substitute; and it is true that Biff's stealing only becomes obsessive after his disillusion with Willy; but much more important is the fact that in the past Willy not only condoned but tacitly encouraged Biff's stealing of a football and lumber from a building lot. Willy's bluffing advice to Biff: "Remember, start big and you'll end big," is startlingly like the dictum of the late notorious Dr. Stephen Ward: "If you want to succeed, start at the top!"

So far, then, the play presents a rather conventional, if very powerful, expression of left-wing attitudes to capitalism which have been common since the 1930s. However, Death of a Salesman cannot be simplified into mere propaganda. The naïve interpretation of Willy Loman's plight as the result of exploitation of workers by capitalists is qualified in the play in several important ways. In the first place, Willy's employer, Howard, is not presented as a conscious monster but as a man very like Willy himself, with the same narrow love for his family, the same love of gadgetry, the same empty friendliness. Handy-dandy, which is the master, which is the man?

The resemblance of the two men suggests that the basic error must be sought in human nature, not just in a particular economic system. Secondly, Willy's plight is shewn to be at least partly the result of his own character; he fails not only because of the pressure of the competitive system, but also because of his incorrigible inability to tell the truth even to himself, his emotional, nonlogical mode of thought, which allows him flatly to contradict himself, and of which schizophrenia is merely an intensification: where once he confused reality and wish fulfilment, he now confuses reality and an idealized past. Thirdly, the play balances the failure of Willy and his children with the success of Charlie and his son, Bernard, who thrive in the very same system: Charlie and his son do not cheat, they merely work hard; they prosper yet remain kindly, unpretentious, sensitive, helpful.

Their presence in the play destroys any interpretation of Death of a Salesman as left wing propaganda. In fact, the exaggerated nature of Bernard's success suggests that Miller partially shares the "American dream" himself; and he has been accused of making a merely vulgar distinction between successful materialism in Charlie and Bernard and unsuccessful in Willy. However, no consideration of the positive values in Death of a Salesman is fair unless it takes into account the play's peculiar point of view. This is the area where the distinction between Miller's observation and the limitations of the Loman sensibility through which the whole play is strained becomes most delicate to trace. The positive values suggested in the play are only such as Willy himself might have arrived at; and it is my purpose to suggest that, deliberately or not, Miller presents them as necessarily limited ideals. The futile philosophy of Willy Loman is opposed by three main alternatives in Death of a Salesman: the pioneering adventurousness of Ben, the sensible practicality of Charlie, and the loyalty of Linda—to list them in order of progressive importance. The values represented by Ben need not detain us very long. Their inadequacy is apparent.

Miller's work, as a whole, does reflect a certain admiration for the pioneer virtues of courage and self-reliance, but this is matched by an awareness that such attitudes are dangerous in modern society: the aggressiveness which is admirable in combating raw nature becomes immoral when turned against one's fellow men. It is the latter, critical attitude, which predominates in Miller's picture of Ben, who advises Biff: "Never fight fair with a stranger, boy. You'll never get out of the jungle that way." Clearly, if Willy had gone with Ben to Alaska, he might have been a richer, but he would not have been a better man.

The values represented by Charlie are more important. Charlie is presented as an almost completely sympathetic figure, but Miller includes a few details which prevent any acceptance of Charlie's career as ideal. In the first place, it is suggested, by Charlie himself, that he has had to pay a certain price for his business success, the price of not caring: "My salvation is that I never took an interest in anything." In human terms, Willy's ideal of business, represented by old Dave Singleman, though it is disastrously inaccurate, is more generous than Charlie's calm assurance that "the only thing you got in this world is what you can sell"; it is not without significance that, whereas Willy's idols are the millionaire inventors Edison and Goodrich (one remembers that Willy's father was an inventor), Charlie's is the buccaneer financier, J. P Morgan. This difference in human warmth between Willy and Charlie comes out in Charlie's tight-lipped reticence, remarked on by Willy as a contrast to his own inability to refrain from chatter.

However, the conclusive rebuttal of Charlie's acceptance of the business world comes in the Requiem: his defence of Willy in the "Nobody dast blame this man" speech, which romanticizes the salesman whose job requires him to dream great things, is immediately rejected by Biff, who maintains that Willy was to blame because he lacked self knowledge, because his dreams were all the wrong dreams, because he let himself be caught in an inhuman system. For all his sympathetic qualities, therefore, Charlie's position is shown to be a compromise: he has succeeded by fitting his character into the existing system, meeting business on its own cold terms. But Biff argues that such a system is too small for a man as imaginative and emotional as Willy. The implication of the Requiem is not that Willy ought to have behaved like Charlie, but that he should not have been in business at all.

The most powerful positive value in the play is the value of family loyalty. There is no doubt of Willy's love for his family, particularly for his son, Biff. It is the betrayal of this loyalty which ruins Willy's life, rather than commercial failure, and it is in the name of family love that he finally kills himself, dying "as a father, not as a salesman" (John Gassner, Introduction to Death of a Salesman in Treasury of the Theater). But, perhaps because he romanticizes his own father, whom he never knew, Willy has a false ideal of fatherhood, exposed most blatantly at the very moment when he decides to sacrifice himself for Biff: "Ben, he'll worship me for it." Parental love which is really a disguised form of egotism is a recurrent theme in Miller's work, and the explanation he finds for it is revealed in Willy's reply when Charlie tells him to forget about Biff: "Then what have I got to remember?" As the captain in Strindberg's The Father says, children are a materialist's only hope of immortality. But this puts an unfair pressure on the children which perverts a true family relationship. It is not just Willy's egotism, which qualifies the family love in Death of a Salesman, however; it is also the fact that it is used as an excuse to ignore other, wider loyalties. And this surely is the great limitation of Linda.

Linda is the most sympathetic character in the play. Her famous "attention, attention must be paid" speech is terribly moving in the theater, perhaps too moving: Miller has said that his great temptation as an artist is that he finds it too easy to write pathos. And Linda is so sympathetic not only because she is the loyal, downtrodden wife, but also because her attitude seems to sum up many traditional American values. In this connection, I believe no one has yet remarked on the resemblances between Death of a Salesman and Robert Frost's poem The Death of the Hired Man. Quite apart from the echo in their titles, the situations of the two pieces are strikingly similar: in the Frost poem, the hired man, old Silas, has come "home" ("Something you somehow don't have to deserve") to die: like Willy he is worn out:

And nothing to look backward to with pride And nothing to look forward to with hope. His employer, Warren, seems at first like Howard in the play, unwilling to keep Silas on because he is too old and unreliable; but Warren's wife, Mary, urges pity in lines which are close to Linda's in both their sentiments and their cadence:

He never did a thing so very bad He don't know why he isn't quite as good As anyone. He won't be made ashamed To please his brother, worthless though he is and she says they must befriend him as they once looked after the hound that came a stranger to us Out of the woods, worn out upon the trail, recalling Linda's plea that Willy not be allowed to die like an old dog. Mary is also like Linda in her insistence on maintaining the old man's self-respect; Silas's promises to ditch the meadow and clear the top pasture for Warren are like Willy's boasts of future prosperity, face-savers which neither he nor the others really believe; and Willy's inability to accept help from Charlie as a matter of pride is paralleled by Silas's refusal to appeal to his rich brother who is a neighbouring bank director. Like Willy, old Silas is so exhausted that he rambles in his mind, mixing past and present like a dream: "those days trouble Silas like a dream." In particular, Silas harks back to arguments he had with a young college boy who helped with the haying four years before. They argued about how necessary education is to a man, and Silas feels he got the worst of the argument; he wishes he could at least have taught the boy the practical skill of building a load of hay.

The feeling here is a mixture of Willy's attitude to Biff and his reluctant admiration for Bernard. There are several other details where the poem has similar sentiments to the play but in slightly different arrangements: the openings are very similar, in each case an unexpected return, a request for kindness by the loving woman, and the man's affection overlaid by indignation at having been abandoned in the first place, irritably denying his real feeling of responsibility; there is the same Christian-name intimacy, firmly establishing the domestic scale of both play and poem—though the nicknames and diminutives of the play serve the further purpose of conveying the immaturity of Willy's world, on a par with his use of schoolboy slang and the characters telling each other to "grow up"; finally, the most tenuous resemblance is the way that the values represented by the women are associated in both play and poem with the values of unspoiled nature, though this is overt in the poem, implicit in the play. The similarity of the two works, particularly their titles, suggests that Miller was directly influenced by Frost; but even if this is not so, the analogy is still useful in that it highlights the traditional, rural, humane values which Frost hymned his whole career and which the society of Death of a Salesman denies. The "hired man" is cared for and pitied; the "salesman" is pitilessly discarded.

Her appeal to these traditional values and her downtrodden, loving loyalty are, however, apt to blind audiences to the essential stupidity of Linda's behaviour. Surely it is both stupid and immoral to encourage the man you love in self-deceit and lies. We are told in the stage directions that Linda has the same values as Willy but that she lacks his energy in pursuing them: it was she who persuaded him not to risk Alaska. Linda does not really believe his dreams—at least not at the point where we meet her, whatever she may have done earlier; but, without any higher ideals than Willy, she humours him to keep things going. The easygoing negativeness of Hap is the same moral sloppiness pushed one degree farther (Biff is his father's son, Hap is his mother's). After thirty-five years of marriage, Linda is apparently completely unable to comprehend her husband: her speech at the graveside (I don't understand; the house is paid for) is not only pathetic, it is also an explanation of the loneliness of Willy Loman which threw him into other women's arms.

Interestingly, the basic falsity in Linda reveals itself in the rhetoric of her "attention, attention must be paid" speech, with its epizeuxis, inversions, and unnatural cadences. And there is a similar falsity of tone in the other much criticized speech of the play, Charlie's "Nobody dast blame this man." Whether Miller intended it or not, the falsity of both Linda's loyalty and Charlie's acceptance of business is revealed in the strained language of their rhapsodies. And a more extreme example of the same false rhetoric, very suggestive when we remember that Ben is always distorted to suit Willy's mind, is the notorious: "When I was seventeen I walked into the jungle, and when I was twenty-one I walked out. And by God I was rich." The falsity of these passages, standing out awkwardly from the drabness of speech elsewhere in the play, is, I would suggest, totally appropriate. The values represented by Ben, Charlie, and Linda, though they are more positive than Willy's Dale Carnegie-ism, are in no sense ideal. They are merely values which Willy could have imagined, in rhetoric Willy would applaud.

Death of a Salesman, in fact, offers almost no sure values. Arthur Miller appears to recognize this when he says it is a contribution to the "steady year-by-year documentation of the frustration of man," and he moves to a more positive position in his next play, The Crucible. But even in Death of a Salesman there is one positive gain: Biff at least comes out of the experience with enhanced self-knowledge: "I know who I am, kid." "It is not a proud knowledge, rather an admission of limitation and weakness: Biff admits he will never be a big success in the eyes of the world. But such an admission is the beginning of truth; in religious terms it would be called humility (the preface to Collected Plays and After the Fall confirm that Miller's interests are finally religious).

Moreover, this humility gained by Biff is related to the sacrifice made by Willy. It has been objected, and admitted by Miller, that Willy's stature as a tragic hero is questionable because he dies still self-deceived. But the new truth is there in Biff, and the extension of expressionistic technique beyond Willy's death unbroken into the Requiem binds together the two experiences.

The extension of the point of view into scenes where Willy does not appear enables the audience at the end to associate Biff's acceptance with Willy's disaster as a single, coherent, and, I would argue, tragic experience; though the technique is closer to Everyman than to Oedipus Rex, and the audience's identification with the hero's fate is secured by empathy—emotional manipulation of stage techniques—rather than the more usual method of moral sympathy and admiration.

The Articulate Victims of Arthur Miller

Both All My Sons and Miller's best-known play, Death of a Salesman (1949), presumably dramatize Wasp families, since Miller does not specify racial or religious origins. Mary McCarthy has scolded Miller for concealing the Jewishness of the Loman family (Sights and Spectacles), and Leslie Fiedler has claimed that Miller creates "crypto-Jewish characters.. who are presented as something else" (Waiting for the End). Miller has countered that "Jewishing" the families would undercut their all-American typicality, and Miller views the drive toward success as all-American (Collected Plays). In Death of a Salesman Miller uses an appropriately informal syntax and many casual repetitions to suggest an all-American quality. It is hardly relevant to claim, as does George Steiner, that "the brute snobbish fact is that men who die speaking as does Macbeth are more tragic than those who sputter platitudes in the style of Willy Loman." Macbeth today can be food for farce, not tragedy, as illustrated by the success of McBird and the failure of Macbeth. And platitudes can be meaningful if the total play rises above them.

Whatever Miller may have written afterwards, Death of a Salesman is larger than Willy Loman, and a variety of dialogue contrasts with his platitudes. Leonard Moss mentions a hundred odd repetitions of the word "man," about a hundred of "boy" and "kid" (with its easy, undiscriminating bisexual affection), about fifty variants of the verb "to make." But this flatness is relieved by Charley's cynical urban idiom, Uncle Ben's rugged phrases, Linda's sententious or sentimental outbursts, Happy's wise-guy banter, Biff's lyricism about Nature, and, most important of all, the range of Willy Loman's clichés. Like Buechner's Woyzeck, Willy's feelings overflow his language. But Woyzeck is sparing of words, and Willy is lavish. He himself admits: "I talk too much.... I joke too much!" And Miller dramatizes the "too much" in comparison with the dialogue of the other characters. As in Woyzeck, there is no raisoneur or norm character; there are only different inadequacies expressed through different idioms. Unlike Buechner, Miller does not use folk songs and the Bible to cement his modern Tower of Babel.And yet, the moral logic of the play reveals the bankruptcy of Willy's language.

The original title of Death of a Salesman was The Inside of His Head, and Miller's dramatic achievement has been the skillful manipulation of Willy's last hours to reveal what goes on inside his head. In act 1 four extended memory scenes are climaxed by Biff's discovery of the woman in his father's hotel room. Near the end of act 2 Willy has a fantasy of asking his dead brother Ben for advice about his own suicide. Through blocking, lighting, and music, Miller sets off these verbal excursions into Willy's memory and fantasy, so that we never confuse them with the suspenseful present.

We are able to shuttle between past and present because of the "partially transparent" Loman house. Jo Mielziner's set for the original New York production of Salesman is a descendant of Strindberg's set for The Ghost Sonata. Perhaps under Strindberg's influence, O'Neill built similarly in Desire under the Elms; Williams continued the mode in Glass Menagerie and A Streetcar Named Desire. And Salesman is the last of the series.

The English critic Dennis Welland has summarized the thematic importance of these transparent settings: "The cataclysms that cause the fall of the frontage of the houses of Eugene O'Neill's Ephraim Cabot and Ezra Mannon, of Tennessee Williams's Amanda Wingfield and Stanley Kowalski, and of Miller's Willy Loman, are psychological rather than meteorological.... The 'exploded' house set is integral to the impression at which all these plays aim, for not only does it mirror the family combustion that has come more and more to dominate the American theater, but it is peculiarly suited to their dramatic idiom."

Particularly astute is Welland's recognition that the exploded house is background for an exploding idiom. Desire, Salesman, and Menagerie abound in expletives and sentence fragments. Without the blatant subjectivism of expressionist drama, these plays nevertheless seek to make a similarly general statement, transcending realism.

Miller has called attention to his "expressionistic elements to create a subjective truth" in Death of a Salesman (Introduction, Collected Plays). And the father of such elements is Strindberg in his Dream Play. Miller has often acknowledged his debt to Ibsen rather than Strindberg, and yet The Dream Play is the ancestor of Death of a Salesman, where dream is theme, refrain, and technique. Rather than a tragedy of failure, as the play is often described, Death of a Salesman dramatizes the failure of a dream. The intrusion of Willy's past and fantasy into his present resembles a dream, and the word "dream" recurs, from the early scenic direction: "An air of the dream clings to the place, a dream rising out of reality," through the introduction of Willy's sons: "[Biff's] dreams are stronger and less acceptable than Happy's," to the triple evocation in the Requiem:

BIFF: He had the wrong dreams.

HAPPY: He had a good dream.

CHARLEY: A salesman is got to dream, boy. It comes with the territory. Miller's play is as much about the salesman's dreams as about his death, but death lies immanent in Willy's dreams. Though Willy is prey to the American dream of success, and to the tribal dream of success through heirs, the dream itself is vague in detail. Only obliquely does Willy's success dream come "with the territory," through salesmanship; rather, Willy feels that success will come in some undefined way, through the most insistent phrase in the play—being "well liked." The phrase is Willy's, but it is echoed by Linda, Biff, and Happy. Only Charley challenges this central aspect of Willy's dream, and he does so with a pithy Jewish inflection: "Why must everybody like you? Who liked J. P Morgan? Was he impressive? In a Turkish bath he'd look like a butcher. But with his pockets on he was very well liked." While Willy tries to win friends and influence people, Charley insists that money talks; each of them voices a different aspect of the success dream. Willy is sufficiently sure of his dream to reject Charley—advice and money.

But at the same time he is so insecure in his dream that he carries on a lifelong debate with his brother Ben. Both Charley and Ben—a small businessman and a ruthless adventurer—are foils for Willy, and their respective idioms contrast with his simple clichés of success through popularity. Charley's salty prose has been quoted, and Ben speaks in active epigrams: "Never fight fair with a stranger, boy." But monosyllabically and boisterously, Willy preaches popularity more loudly than he is able to practice it.

Though Willy sometimes claims to be well liked, he confides to Linda that people laugh at him instead of liking him. Even his infidelity is the result of making a woman laugh. Certainly he often makes us laugh—in large part by the juxtaposition of his ephemeral dream against the irritating concreteness of his Chevvy, Studebaker, and Hastings refrigerator. We may not know what Willy sells, but we know what he buys: "The refrigerator consumes belts like a god dam maniac." The death of the salesman is foreshadowed in the comic deaths of his installment-plan purchases, which we witness only through dialogue.

A sequence of shiny, treacherous machines is suggested through the play's abrupt opening and Willy's first memory scene. In these two important early scenes, Biff's boyhood popularity is contrasted with Willy's laughableness. The memory scene begins when Willy praises Biff for polishing his car, but he soon gives advice about the girls with whom Biff is "makin' a hit." At the end of Willy's recollection of Biff's day of success, Willy boasts and complains in typical self-contradiction: "Oh, I'll knock 'em dead next week. I'll go to Hartford. I'm very well liked in Hartford.You know, the trouble is, Linda, people don't seem to take to me." As he describes how people laugh at him, a woman's laugh is heard, introducing Willy's memory within a memory. Unlike the girls who pay for Biff, Willy's Woman has to be bought with silk stockings, while Linda mends her stockings at home. When Willy returns to his first memory, all is soured—Biff is failing math, he steals, the mothers complain that he is too rough with the girls. The emotional shift— conveyed entirely by dialogue—foreshadows the play's climactic confrontation between Willy and Biff.

The opening scenes of act 2 not only develop the precarious quality of Willy's dream; they also set up father-son foils to Willy-Biff. Old man Wagner's son Howard is successful by inheritance, and his idiom reflects his security. Charley's son Bernard is successful by hard work, and his idiom reflects his studiousness. Both sons succeeded within the framework of American capitalism. Yet Biff is a failure because he remained a slave to his father's "phoney dream" even after he has rejected his father as a "phoney fake." His idiom reflects his immaturity; even his name is a boy's nickname.

In the swift sequence of scenes in Howard's office, Charley's office, Frank's chophouse, Miller skillfully disintegrates Willy's dream for us (though not for him). The scene in Howard's office offers a paradigm for the whole play:

Howard is no more faithful to his father's memory than Willy is to the memory of his father's flutes; Howard is as blind and provincial about his children as Willy is about his; Howard speaks inconsiderately to his wife, as Willy does to Linda. The tape recorder is a symbol of both Howard and Willy, with ready-made phrases uttered mechanically. Howard and Willy show two sides of American progress: one is failure and the other success, with little to choose between them.

In Howard's office Willy evokes the memory of the great salesman, Dave Singleman, whose name denies "a dime a dozen." Singleman is singular, unique. He achieved the popularity to which Willy aspired; it is his death, narrated by Willy, that evokes the play's title: "When he died—and by the way he died the death of a salesman, in his green velvet slippers in the smoker of the New York, New Haven and Hartford, going into Boston—when he died, hundreds of salesmen and buyers were at his funeral." And that is the kind of funeral Willy envisions for himself. After leaving Biff his insurance, Willy addresses the fantasy figure of his dead brother Ben: "Ben, that funeral will be massive! They'll come from Maine, Massachusetts, Vermont, New Hampshire! All the old-timers with the strange license plates—that boy will be thunderstruck, Ben, because he never realized—I am known! Rhode Island, New York, New Jersey—I am known, Ben, and he'll see it with his eyes once and for all." Geography and repetition sound lyric notes for Willy, but the old-timers with the strange license plates are dead, if they ever existed; only the family and faithful Charley come to Willy's actual funeral.

The imaginary funeral underlines the poverty of Willy's imagination. Compare his listing of states with the vision of Genet's Solange for the funeral of a maid: "The funeral will unfold its pomp. It's beautiful; isn't it? First come the butlers, in full livery, but without silk lining. They're wearing their crowns. Then come the footmen, the lackeys in knee breeches and white stockings. They're wearing their crowns. Then come the valets, and the chambermaids wearing our colors. Then the porters. And then come the delegations from heaven". Pomp and circumstance create a mythology, so that servitude bursts its bonds to achieve royalty—in the imagination of a maid. Willy's linguistic poverty, by contrast, reflects both the poverty of his world and the poverty of his dream. Henry Popkin has described Willy's world as "full of aspirin, arch supports, saccharine (all the wrong cures for what ails Willy), Studebakers, Chevrolets, shaving lotion, refrigerators, silk stockings, washing machines."

But the first three items are (perhaps) remedies, and most of the others break down. Willy's life embodies the contradiction between these concrete trivialities and his grandiose verbal projections. In past, present, and fantasy, Willy usually expresses himself through repetition and cliché, a formulatic chant which is unaffected by the stubbornness of things. "An air of the dream" may "rise out of reality," but Willy's vague dream is at odds with concrete reality. He has achieved neither popularity nor success as a salesman, and he has failed as gardener, carpenter, and father.

Willy's opening words suggest his immaturity: "Oh, boy, oh, boy." To the figure of Ben he confesses that he feels "kind of temporary" about himself. His repetitions of "the woods are burning" indicate some perception of the Inferno in which he lives, but his perception is limited. Willy's hell may be paved with good intentions, but even they appear to be rationalizations after the fact; Willy dreams of success for Biff because he himself is a failure. Willy refuses Charley's charity because he himself cannot accept the truth of his failure. Though he has been toying with the idea of suicide, Willy actually kills himself only when he can disguise his death as a gift to Biff.

Miller and others have written many pages about Willy Loman, the low man. Consistently conceived, Willy does not speak out of character. But Miller disturbs his own thematic consistency by his climactic scene— Willy's memory of Biff's discovery of a woman in his Boston hotel room. Willy's dream, vague in detail, is the American dream of success. Though Willy dies without recognizing the triviality of his dream, the play makes us aware of that triviality. Before the climax, Miller dramatizes Biff's recognition of the impossibility, if not the insubstantiality, of Willy's dream. We see Willy rejected by Howard, and we hear of Biff's parallel rejection by Oliver.

The scene of Biff's self-recognition is a recognition of the phoniness of his father's dream. Rhythmically colloquial—"He thinks I've been spiting him all these years and it's eating him up"—pointedly economical—"We've been talking in a dream for fifteen years"—the dialogue is nervous with questions, interruptions, and muted repetitions.

WILLY: What happened? He took you into his office and what?

BIFF: Well—I talked. And—and he listened, see.

WILLY: Famous for the way he listens, y'know. What was his answer?

BIFF: His answer was—(He breaks off, suddenly angry). Dad, you're not letting me tell you what I want to tell you!

WILLY, (accusing, angered): You didn't see him, did you?

BIFF: I did see him!

WILLY: What'd you insult him or something? You insulted him, didn't you?

BIFF: Listen, will you let me out of it, will you just let me out of it!

HAPPY: What the hell!

WILLY: Tell me what happened!

BIFF, (to Happy): I can't talk to him!

The repetitions of "listen" stress Willy's inability to listen to any contradiction of his dream. Uttered without strain, Biff's "I can't talk to him" summarizes the scene and Biff's whole life. Biff's recognition scene dovetails neatly with Willy's next memory scene, but the two are not related thematically. A phoney dream of success should be exploded by a scene about the phoniness of success, and not about illicit sex. The final tableau of the scene leaves us with a strong impression of Willy's self-contradiction—begging on his knees as he threatens Biff with a beating. But there are flaws in the woman's dialogue—she insists that Willy open the door and she pointlessly questions Biff: "Are you football or baseball?"

As the climax violates the thematic drive of the play, so the Requiem violates its form. Death of a Salesman is not rigidly contained by Willy's mind, but the Requiem is jarringly and flagrantly outside his mind. More important, the epilogue provides us with few new insights, and those are confusing. We have already heard the divergence of Willy's sons in their judgment of their father; Happy remains subject to Willy's dream while Biff attains self-recognition in Oliver's office; this bifurcation scarcely needs to be spelled out again. Charley, on the other hand, changes surprisingly; having repeatedly urged Willy to give up his phoney dream as a traveling salesman, Charley is suddenly sentimental about that dream. Earlier, he had said to Willy: "The only thing you got in this world is what you can sell," but by the Requiem the "what" gives way to a shine and a smile—an utterly incongruous coupling on the sharp tongue of the cynical businessman.

It is Linda, however, whose words in the Requiem are most confusing. We have witnessed her devotion to her husband, and we can sympathize with her grief. However, it is difficult to understand her lack of understanding. When Linda found the rubber pipe near the gas jet, she worried, but she did not wonder why Willy wanted to kill himself, discouraged and exhausted as he was. Desperate (and deluded) by the end of the play, Willy finally carries out his threat. Her bereavement evokes our pity, but her astonishment is astonishing. Like Charley's final speech, hers sentimentalizes the tragedy in its flagrant bid for tears.

Though Miller's stage directions specify that Linda "lacks the temperament to utter" the longings she shares with Willy, she is quite articulate—too articulate for her final lack of understanding. Willy treats her badly, but she defends him eloquently. Far from the Jewish Mother who has been detected beneath Linda's syntax, Willy's wife is a tear-making tool for Miller, from her "Attention must be paid" speech, through her remonstrances with her sons, to the final ironic chant: "We're free. We're free.. We're free...." Bound to Willy's dream, she defends it against the temptation represented by Ben.

She claims attention for Willy as a "human being," but she magnifies Willy's importance through her use of generalizations, passive constructions, resonant "that man"s, and her pretentious or sentimental epigrams: "Life is a casting off." "A man is not a bird, to come and go with the springtime." "He's only a little boat looking for a harbor." At such lines, one can sympathize with Willy's efforts to shut her up; and yet she is, more perniciously than Willy realizes, his "foundation and support."

Near the beginning of the play, Willy grumbles: "Figure it out. Work a lifetime to pay off a house. You finally own it, and there's nobody to live in it." Linda almost echoes him at the end: "I made the last payment on the house today. Today, dear. And there'll be nobody home." What neither of them learns is that a house is not a home when clichés boomerang transparently. Ironically, however, much of the play's strength lies in the carefully rhymed poverty of Willy's language. His mass-produced phrases belie his claim to special attention. His sentimental fantasies are inevitably punctured by concrete reality. But rather than risk complete deflation, he risks—and loses—his life. Somewhat superfluously, Miller told an interviewer that he was not Willy Loman but a writer; "Willy Loman is there because I could see beyond him." And it may well be that Willy's durable stage thereness rests on the fact that all of us see, and especially hear, beyond him. Willy's vocabulary is totally familiar—endearingly so because it is so limited. Willy's questions seem totally familiar—again endearing because limited. It is easy to pity and even love Willy, who is our father, brother, cousin, friend. But never me.

Compared to O'Neill's Hickey, Willy is bankrupt of words. Hickey begins by being well liked and successful; he has the gift of gab, and he spends it lavishly. Willy is not frugal of words, but he has so few of them that he keeps repeating his small stock. Hickey's relentless flow of words finally turns us against him, but we remain attached to Willy because we can talk and think rings around him. Death of a Salesman triumphs because Willy falls short of us, but within touching distance.

A Study in the Social Influence of Drama

Business is not only the business of America—as President

Coolidge announced—but also of American drama. There are two major ways in which this economic focus has been reflected on the stage: an overwhelming number of instantly forgettable comedies written for entertainment, and a small but serious number of plays that analyse society in a spirit of protest or reform. If the popular Broadway fare of the twenties and thirties is any guide, the drama of social criticism had little direct effect on the public, who even in the Depression flocked to see their dreams come true in plays where the heroes gained heiresses or riches by guile or good fortune, and any attack on the business world was conservative, attempting to reestablish the "old-fashioned" values that everyone respects as long as they do not have to live by them. Using the mainstream of Broadway as a barometer to measure the attitudes of the public, the American myth of success can be shown to have prospered in spite of events, which even such critically acclaimed plays as Waiting for Lefty or The Adding Machine had little wide influence.

The question as to whether drama can change society is an old one, and the traditional answer is no. Playwrights "but echo back the public voice" [says Samuel Johnson] like "lay preachers, peddling the ideas of their time in a popular form" (Strindberg). Yet, looking at the fate of the American dream and the Protestant work ethic, it can be demonstrated that it is indeed possible for the stage to do more than passively mirror established social views. As a corollary, it can be suggested that Odets's or Elmer Rice's failure to alter public consciousness relates to their approach rather than the intrinsic nature of the stage. Waiting for Lefty dealt with a specific injustice and proposed a definite course of action while The Adding Machine presented economic exploitation as a universal existential condition.

The metaphysical level of The Adding Machine in fact gives the impression of almost justifying the society Rice attacks; and it would be fair to say that the more general a play's social criticism is, the nearer it comes to being a protest against life itself with a Beckettian "nothing to be done" as the only response. At the other extreme the specificity of

Waiting for Lefty tied it to a particular circumstance, and—as the Becks have found out more recently with productions like Paradise Now, which was intended to end with a naked audience pouring out into the streets to start "the permanent revolution"—there will be no discernible effect unless the audience come to the theater already prepared to act, in which case the play might be said to have reinforced their attitudes, but not changed them.

However, in the decade after 1945 three now familiar plays approached "the business of America" from a new angle. Instead of the rhetoric of the thirties which attacked dishonest business practices or set profiteering bosses against exploited masses, the morality of business is exposed and a single figure, the salesman, is used to represent the economic system as a whole—following the claim of sales-manuals that we are all salesmen at bottom: "no matter what you do, whether you sell, buy, design, manufacture or manage, your success will depend on your ability to sell". O'Neill first drew the outlines of this symbolic salesman in The Iceman Cometh, written in 1940 though not produced until 1946. Miller explored the mental contours in Death of a Salesman three years later, and Gelber extended the image in 1957 with The Connection. In all three plays the salesman is the carrier of the American Dream, which is rooted in the origins of the country.

The relationship between religion and commerce had been formulated originally by Weber and Tawney, but in applying this general theory to contemporary American society these plays anticipated later sociologists and also acted as catalysts for the change in cultural attitudes that characterized the sixties. It was a decade after Miller and O'Neill before academics began to analyse society in their terms: Wyllie's The Self-Made Man in America and Lynn's The Dream of Success appeared in 1954 and 1955, Whyte's Organization Man in 1956, Herberg's Protestant, Catholic, Jew in 1960, while popularizing works like Berton's The Big Sell only followed in 1963. If the inspiring name of Horatio Alger is now a derisory noise, these plays can be shown to be instrumental in changing its status.

The popularity of Death of a Salesman, the one modern

play on every high school English curriculum, and The Iceman Cometh, the only O'Neill work selected by the American Film Theater, indicates the current widespread acceptance of the social views they present. But their influence was not immediate. In each case critics either mistook the surface level of the play's metaphor for the whole meaning or—when a deeper symbolic level was seen—lost the social reference in a metaphysical interpretation. The fact that Hickey is a salesman, for instance, went unmentioned, while Brooks Atkinson's judgment that Willy "represents the homely, decent, kindly virtues of middle class society"(New York Times, 11 February 1947) was typical. Criticism of The Connection shows the same misunderstanding, either condemned as a defence of dope or praised as "a play about the possibility of redemption"; and this time lag between appearance and understanding suggests that the social influence of drama is subliminal, not direct.

These plays deal with images and, when men come to see themselves and the type of life they lead in terms of an image, the intellectual act of recognition separates their self-concept from it. The awareness of what they are itself makes it impossible for them to be that image, and the nature of society changes. One would normally expect to find social criticism expressed in naturalistic conventions. But the stress in these plays falls on the psychology of selling, and even if the salesman carries sample cases, inside are not material objects but the dreams those materials stand for: popularity, prosperity, security, and success.

The treatment of salesmanship in O'Neill, Miller, and Gelber is characterized by a particular combination of expressionistic and naturalistic elements, so that the subject is not specific (as in Waiting for Lefty) nor existential (as in The Adding Machine) but an image of modern society. Death of a Salesman is the most obvious example where the naturalistic present merges into expressionistic memory sequences, and Willy's situation closely parallels Mr. Zero's. The links with Elmer Rice's expressionism are obvious in Miller's intention "to create a form which would literally be the process of Willy Loman's way of mind" (Introduction, Collected Plays)—even some of the details are exact repetitions, Willy's stress on completing "a twenty-five year mortgage" echoing Zero's "canned—after twenty-five years" when (like Willy) he hoped for promotion to the "front office"—but the nauralistic stress on environmental conditioning relates this to contemporary society. Willy is not man in the abstract, but nor is he—in light of what Miller called the "symbolic designs which function as overt pointers towards the moral to be drawn from the action"—just a victim of society. He is its symbol.

O'Neill counterbalances naturalistic and expressionistic approaches in a similar way. On the surface Harry Hope's "Bedrock Bar" is a faithful copy of Jimmy-the-Priest's "grisly, vermin-infested three-storey establishment" where in 1912, the year of the play's action, O'Neill, like his character Paritt, took refuge from a guilty conscience and tried to commit suicide. But the schematic organization of the figures on stage and the repetitions turn the play into an allegorical morality. O'Neill summed up the general theme of his work as "the death of an old God and the failure of science and materialism to give any satisfying new one," but in a press conference after the premiere of this play he pointed to a specific aspect of this, calling the United States "the greatest failure" because of the nature of its material success: "we are the greatest example of 'For what shall it profit a man if he shall gain the whole world and lose his soul?'

We had so much and could have gone either way." The patterning of characters underlines this critique of American commercialism, all the figures being mirror images of Hickey, and the cross references transform him from an individual character to "the Salesman." They also present salesmanship in terms of prostitution, unrealizable ideals which impose self-destructive guilt, or quack doctors who fill the cemeteries with their "miraculous cure." On the political level the salesman is seen as "the peddler pimp for nouveau riche capitalism," while the anarchy of laissez faire free trade make him a kind of commercial Bakunin: "the great Nihilist Hickey" running "a movement that'll blow up the world."

At the point in the play where the inmates of the saloon

are attempting to turn their dreams into reality (which on a basic level is what any customer is offered, even if, like Hickey, the salesman realizes that the dream will not stand the light of day) we are given a graphic image of the spiritual emptiness of materialism, the contrast between the outward respectability of consumer society and its inner psychological state. Willie Oban, for example, is "shaved and wears an expensive, well-cut suit, good shoes and clean linen but his face is sick and his nerves in a shocking state of shakes."

The characters' sobriety—that hallmark of the businessman—is stressed, but so are the rigidity and deathly qualities associated with it. Each feels "like a corpse" and they "look dead." At other points in the play the characters' appearance represents the degradation, absence of moral value and impermanence of materialism. Clothes are "flashy" but "worn" or "seem constructed of an inferior grade of dirty blotting paper," shoes are "wrecks of imitation leather"; while a whole catalogue of objects—"phoney rings," "five-and-ten-cent-store spectacles," "badly fitting store teeth"—parodies "the good life" as an artificial, cheap, and unsatisfactory substitute for real human needs. On another level the characters are down and out, dropouts or outcasts, the opposite of the bourgeois ideal represented by the salesman-figure, and so stand for positive values. As O'Neill reminded the actors during rehearsal, "remember, goodness can surmount anything. The people in that saloon were the best friends I've ever known."

O'Neill once projected a sequence of plays on the emptiness of the American Dream, and at least two of his later works could be seen as part of such a cycle: More Stately Mansions and The Iceman Cometh. Simon, the hero of More Stately Mansions, a corrupt businessman, gains the insight that when devoted to money and power "human life is a silly disappointment and when finally the bride or bridegroom cometh, we discover we are kissing Death" and The Iceman clearly takes this as its starting point. The world described is one of "greedy madness" in which everything is commercialized and the Boer War is no more than a money making spectacular for the St. Louis Fair. Hickey is the epitome of this world, "the Great Salesman" who arrives "bringing the blessed bourgeois long green," but the communist dream is no alternative. The "Tomorrow Movement" are shown to be "as stupidly greedy for power as the worst capitalist they attack," while the people do not "want to be saved from themselves, for that would mean they'd have to give up greed, and they'll never pay that price for liberty." Reactionary or revolutionary interpretations of equality and progress were simply different sides of the same coin to O'Neill, who stated that he was going on the theory that the United States instead of being the most successful country in the world is the greatest failure.. because it was given everything.. [yet its] main idea is that everlasting game of trying to possess your own soul by the possession of something outside it too.

O'Neill's major sociological criticism is directed against the connection between materialism and religion. In his use of revivalist rhetoric—"Now I've seen the light" or "I wouldn't say this unless I knew, Brothers and Sisters. This peace is real! It's a fact! I know! Because I've got it! Here! Now! Right in front of you!"— Hickey takes after his father, the "preacher in the sticks of Indiana" who sold the hayseeds "nothing for something" by fast talk and playing on their fears, and O'Neill implies that American commercialism is rooted in the puritan origins of the country.

On the surface Willie Oban's fathering of his lewd ballad on Jonathan Edwards is humorously incongruous, but on the deeper level the buying of love parallels the protestant ethic, in which prosperity is seen as an open sign of divine approval and virtue is measured by material success. The pervasiveness of this assumption and its specific application to salesmen can be seen in turn-of-the-century sales manuals: "the Creator made man a success-machine.. and failure is as abnormal to him as discord to harmony".

The Iceman Cometh has lent itself to a metaphysical interpretation because of the obviousness of its symbolic superstructure, and Hickey is certainly a parody Christ who brings death. O'Neill's intention to create a "nobler" theater dealing with "the death of an old God and the failure of science and materialism to give any satisfying new one for the surviving primitive religious instinct to find a meaning for life in" is well known, but it is a mistake to take an author's description of his theme to represent his own belief. Against this should be set the equally well known comment, "the relation between man and man.. does not interest me at all. I am only interested in the relation between man and God." To see The Iceman as O'Neill's despairing view of a damned creation overlooks both his religious sense and the details of his imagery. The view may be bleak, with illusions as the only escape from an intolerable existence, but Nature is conspicuously absent from this play.

Even "the sunlight in the street outside does not hit the windows" which are "so glazed with grime one cannot see through them." This is the world men have created, and it is not life but specifically Hickey, the salesman, who makes Larry a "convert to death." Nor is it simply the author, but his salesman (commercialism) who transforms the biblical Last Supper with all the material trappings of middle-class celebration— red ribbons, candles, gifts. It is Hickey who substitutes cake for the bread, now "desiccated" and "dust-laden" by neglect, and turns the wine of communion into champagne, that symbol of material success and social achievement. Miller has no need to go over the same ground in Death of a Salesman only three years later, and one of his major images simply assumes the relationship between Puritanism and commerce that O'Neill explored. Ben, who won "diamond mines" in the African jungles, and Willy, who believes that diamonds can be gained "over the lunch table at the Commodore Hotel," are obviously the Arabs of Russell H. Conwell's famous sermon, one of whom sold his farm to search the world for diamonds, while the other, who bought the farm, found "acres of diamonds" in his back yard.

Hickey is the salesman per se: "His expression is fixed in a salesman's winning smile". and he has "the salesman's mannerisms of speech, an easy flow of glib, persuasive convincingness." Willy is not only "the Salesman" (with a capital S) with "the Salesman's house" as his setting, but also "a human being." Miller has taken the same representative characteristics as O'Neill, but views them from beneath, as it were, instead of from above. Where Hickey's "smile of self-confident affability and hearty good fellowship makes everyone like him on sight," Willy jokes "too much" and his claim to be "very well liked" is a symptom of insecurity. Where Hickey presents his restlessness and the way he "always had to keep on the go" as positive, admiring the "drummers around the hotel" who "kept moving," the same quality is given a different value in Willy, who feels "kind of temporary" about himself.

The overall career of the two salesman-figures is strikingly similar. Both betray their families by falling into temptation while on the road, both are betrayed by their dreams, both make a subconscious connection between "salvation" (in which moral and monetary success are equated) and death, both are implied to be insane, and Hickey's last wish is "to go to the Chair" while Willy commits suicide. But where O'Neill outlined the salesman in terms of general qualities, Miller uses specific manifestations of modern commercialism to characterize Willy.

Instead of revivalist rhetoric he uses aphorisms taken from Dale Carnegie: "Be liked and you will never want"; "The man who makes an appearance is the man who gets ahead"; "Personality always wins the day"; "It's not what you do it's who you know it's contacts contacts." Where O'Neill makes his salesman a death figure, Willy is a reversed Horatio Alger, old and worn instead of young and eager, fired instead of promoted, whose riches in this consumer world of designed obsolescence turn to rags. Hickey is the archetype, "the Iceman of Death," while Willy is typical—"a hard-working drummer who landed in the ash-can like all the rest of them." The same development is obvious in the use made of "dreams"— the most frequently repeated word in each play. Miller's characters are defined by "massive dreams" or "turbulent longings" and they sum up their "whole lives" as "lotta dreams and plans," while O'Neill's characters only exist in terms of "dreams about their tomorrows and yester days" and "a pipe dream is what gives life" to them all. But where O'Neill presents dreams as a common denominator of humanity, being in essence "the pursuit of happiness," Miller only deals with those dreams that relate to the egoism of success and the cult of personality: "It's the only dream you can have—to come out number-one man." Similarly, the values represented by O'Neill's salesman are the moral basis of American materialism—the stress on being up to the minute, living in the present, facing reality, "free now to be yourselves," and the downplaying of morality with the rejection of "guilt and remorse"—while in the myopic vision of Miller's characters "all kinds of greatness" are reduced to $15,000 a year. O'Neill having established coordinates, Miller can chart the territory

O'Neill's moral vision and Miller's extension of it into the American images of individualistic capitalism, Ben the entrepreneur and Dave Singleman the middleman, taken together give us a complete picture of the salesman which is paralleled in a remarkable manner by some modern "inspirational" sales manuals.

The assumption of such books that "salesmanship continues to be one avenue by which men can still rise from rags to riches" is that held by Willy who, in his exaggerations of his sales prowess, could be said to be following their principle: "Accent the positive.. substitute the word 'opportunity' for the word 'problem' every time." The authors urge that "you yourself should be sold" on what you sell, and typically give their own careers as proof—a technique that Hickey follows in presenting himself as an advertisement for his product. Willy's sporting slang and his idealization of Biff—"the tallest a star like that" is devastatingly close to such sales manuals' exhortations as "You can be a star. You can stand head and shoulders above the crowd."

Even the view that Hickey is only symbolically a salesman in that he sells dreams or views of reality should perhaps be reevaluated in the light of what is called "the direct approach, one which sells benefits.... This in effect tells [the buyer], 'I can help you to be a hero,'" which is no different from Hickey's working method of "pretending you believed what [the customers] wanted to believe about themselves." Those quotations are from an exhilaratingly entitled book, The Power of Enthusiastic Selling, published in 1962.

If our reaction today is a cynical smile, the popularity of these plays has contributed to our altered perspective; and the specific influence of O'Neill's connection between religion and materialism and Miller's view of the American "success images" can be indicated by the Maysles brothers' cinema verité film of 1969, Salesman. This documents six weeks in the lives of four salesmen and the breakdown of one, Paul, whose failure forces him to confront his dreams of riches and independence. In their comments the filmmakers constantly draw comparisons with the plays. For instance David Maysles claimed that what attracted him was specifically "the idea of guys out on the road. Like Hickey.. Paul Brennan, for instance, is very much an O'Neill character, the way he romanticizes everything." In lecturing at the University of Texas the Maysles brothers even drew the same moral from their film as O'Neill had from The Iceman Cometh, stating that their "attitude to success could be summed up in the line, 'for what shall it profit a man, if he shall gain the whole world and lose his own soul?'" And they compared the action of their film explicitly with Death of a Salesman:

AM: If anyone were doing Salesman in fiction he would absolutely insist that somebody die in the play [Arthur Miller] does. DM: It is the death of a salesman and that really is death in his face which may be more than any kind of physical death.

Even the salesmen being filmed saw themselves in terms of the plays, and one of them, Paul, concluded a letter to the Maysles brothers with a direct comparison: "This is one part I will always be proud of. Lead on Macbeth and tell Arthur Miller I am ready." Apart from providing a grotesque panorama of the emptiness of the American wasteland—the moral and mental vacuum in its consumer society where, as one of the salesmen says, the people are "really dead, you know? No no enthusiasm"—the film concentrates on the connection between religion and commerce in the same terms as O'Neill. These salesmen sell the Bible, and at the annual convention the firm's theological consultant, who is billed as "the world's greatest salesman of the world's best seller," assures them of the "esteem [and] self satisfaction knowing what you are doing about your Father's business." But the equation of sanctity and salesmanship cuts both ways. The commerce that is deified degrades the Bible, and what is featured as an "inspiration in the home" is transformed into a commodity by the process of selling:

It's the only thing I know you secure in a lifetime that doesn't depreciate. A car after three years is worth nothing. A Bible like that is really something that will really build up a heritage in the home as if it were equity in a mortgage and don't worry, they don't repossess the Bible.

We are back with Hickey's father selling "those Hoosier Hayseeds building lots along the Golden Street." As for the American myth of "success," the Maysles's film follows Miller very closely in dealing with the motivation of salesmen, and at the sales convention each drummer outbids the other for Willy's Horatio Alger dream of ending up "with diamond mines": I-uh-my wife just talked me into buyin' a big house. And she wants to have a few more kids and all this kind of rot. So, I'm going to make 35,000 dollars this coming year.... I expect to make 50,000 not thirty-five. Or better. And I think I can do it.

Each is determined "to come out number-one man," and at the opening of the film Paul parodies the security of run-of-the-mill jobs, rejecting them in favour of the success ethos:

Me fathah's on the fahrce. He gets a pinshun.... He'll get his reward at the other end. He retired.... He lives about two weeks after and died. (He breaks up laughing.) But the customer in sales terminology is literally a "prospect," and the poverty of the public, their numbness and apathy, destroy Paul's vision of wealth and working for oneself. He finds it increasingly impossible to make sales, and by the end of the film his repeated story about his "fathah" and his "pinshun" is told wistfully. It becomes a self-consciously ironic condemnation of his own aspirations. He is fired, "eliminated" as "the sour apple spoilin' the barrel"—which reminds one inescapably of Willy's protest: "You can't eat the orange and throw the peel away—a man is not a piece of fruit!"—and the final shot underlines the emptiness behind the facade of material progress, the spiritual death in the ideals of "personality" and "success": "Framed in the doorway, fear in his eyes, he stares nowhere." As a documentary, Salesman shows how acutely O'Neill and Miller perceived the figure and fate of the salesman.

But the fact that the film was made at all can be attributed to the influence of Death of a Salesman and The Iceman Cometh, the subject having been chosen because "selling the Bible represented a metaphor of our time, which had ramifications reaching to every avenue of our culture"; and the plays even conditioned the raw material of "the document" in so far as they had moulded the salesman's awareness of their role. On one level, then, the film is a demonstration of how drama, by analyzing social reality accurately, can in turn mould society's perception of itself. Since what we conceive as reality is an image, the judgment of art can become self-fulfilling. Gelber's play The Connection rounds out this exploration of the business world on the American stage, even though it has not discernibly affected public attitudes—perhaps because the correspondence between stage and society is not so clear. The two earlier plays make an obvious distinction between a realistic level of action and thematic symbols, presenting pipe dreams as simply a way of describing illusion or the figure of "success incarnate" as an open hallucination, and explicitly spelling out the meaning of both Ben and the booze of Hope.

But Gelber's whole play is a metaphor, though on the surface it appears entirely literal. We are told that the cast are addicts not actors, and that the characters have been bribed with the promise of "a fix" to allow a documentary film to be made of their existence. There are two photographers who underline "that's the way it is. That's the way it really is"; a character introduced as the author complains that the addicts are not following his scenario; and the character who claims to be producing this improvisation informs the audience that "no matter what they tell you they will be turned on by a scientifically accurate amount of heroin" after the interval. So much of the dramatic effect of The Connection hinges on persuading the audience that the drugs—marijuana and heroin—are real narcotics and in no sense symbolic, that the true theme only becomes clear when the play is seen in the context of Death of a Salesman and The Iceman Cometh, which— significantly—was revived on the New York stage in 1956 just one year before The Connection was written. The similarities, in fact, are striking.

Both The Connection and The Iceman Cometh have been compared to Gorki's Lower Depths, and the addicts wait for "the big connection" just as O'Neill's drunken bums wait for "the Great Salesman." Hickey, the hardware drummer, has become Cowboy, the hard-drug pusher, and both are explicitly selling "death" disguised as peace. But Gelber takes the "territory" covered by Miller and O'Neill for granted and presents their conclusions ironically. Instead of analyzing the roots of the business ethic through family background, Gelber simply sums it up in a name: Cowboy, for instance, conjures up the American myth of individuality and expansion, while the other pusher referred to, Leonard the Locomotive, stands for the railways that civilized the West. Similarly, O'Neill outlines the relationship between modern salesmanship and hell-fire preaching in straight terms because he is making an original point, while Gelber can turn this, as an established concept, into a basis for humour.

Cowboy picks up a decrepit Salvation Army Sister "under a flag symbolizing American freedom of speech and religion" near the central police station—a parody figure whose psalm-induced ecstasies are as empty an attempt to escape existence as the addict's needle. The correspondence between religion and drug taking is exact. Baptism is equated with "a fix" and the "high" of heroin is described mockingly in salvationist rhetoric: "I've seen the light. Praise the Lord! I am redeemed! From my eternal suffering, I am redeemed! Like a pawn ticket." For Gelber, not only does American commercialism present itself as a religion but religion itself has become commercialized, and "Sister Salvation" speaks in sales jargon: an addict "looks like a good prospect to save." Gelber also picks up the basic identity between customer and salesman established by O'Neill and Miller, but inverts it. Hickey and Willy are the primary consumers of the ideals they peddle. Here all the "users" are seen as salesmen. Cowboy is presented as "a good businessman" who has "work hours" just like the "day jobs" of legitimate society; and each of his customers, in the sense that all have to produce in order to pay for what they consume, is said to be "a pretty conniving businessman. " The addicts are selling their "scene" to the audience and Jaybird, the author, is selling his view of life in his play.

As the producer says: "Why are salesmen put down? I'm selling an idea. What's so immoral about that?" A salesman, as the middleman between manufacturer and consumer, is literally "the connection" in a capitalist economic structure, and when one of the photographers asks about "the big connection.. the man behind the man," the answer given is that "the man is you. You are the man. You are your own connection."

As in O'Neill, the dropouts represent society The underground anti-society of the drug culture in fact epitomizes our everyday world, and its principles are the same: "Everything that's illegal is illegal because it makes more money for more people that way.... We all pay our dues whatever we do." Gelber deliberately presents drug taking as a norm, in contrast to popular treatments of the subject, which are dismissed "as exotica and often as erotica." It is not only normal in the sense that almost everyone on stage, including the author, the musicians, photographers, and Sister Salvation is given a fix, but also symptomatic of modern life: "The twentieth century has developed anti-social habits.

There isn't a day that goes by without some item in the daily papers involving insanity." The audience are also assumed to be customers for their own brand of narcotics. An actor seated in the audience claims that he made a financial arrangement with one of the characters during the interval—"I gave Sam five bucks and I want a story"—and the story he is given satirizes the average theatergoer's desire for vicarious excitement in the form of sex or crime. Entertainment is referred to as "a habit," so is sport. Everyone, Gelber implies, is "hooked": on sex stories, new clothes, or chlorophyll; addicted to aspirins, vitamins, or "the next dollar." Ideals are also presented as drugs—not only the obvious "opium of religion" but social panaceas, "education, for example," or any "truth"—and the pursuit of happiness in contemporary society is seen as the equivalent of the junkie's yearning for dope: "A fix of hope. A fix to forget.

A fix to remember, to be sad, to be happy, to be, to be." In spite of the breadth of this equation between drugs and every socially determined goal, the picture is not of man in general but of men in a particular placε and time. The play was performed by the Living Theater at a time when Julian Beck and Judith Malina were concerned with promoting revolutionary consciousness, and is intended to have a political effect. As one of the characters says, "You know we live in a white society. Did you ever see black snow?"

The only "action" in the play is the near death of one of the addicts from an overdose, and the author is stated to have "chosen this petty and miserable microcosm because of its self-annihilating aspects" (italics mine). If consumer society, as Gelber presents it in his reversed mirror, bears in it the seeds of its own destruction, it is because the search for happiness or enlightenment in this particular culture, like the craving for narcotics, is "the seeking of death"; and Solly, Gelber's "foolosopher" character, sums up the psychology of modern America as a mechanized rat race: "I don't jump into the streets against the lights and just miss killing myself a hundred time a day. That's what happens out there. And in here too".

Those in the addict's pad are outside society, those out in the streets are "in"—the one is a dark mirror of the other, both equally imprisoned by their "habit" (social conditioning) and driven by a death wish (the competitive spirit). And this street metaphor is the key to the play's vision, being repeated in the author's name, Jaybird, with its connotations of "jaywalker" and "jailbird."

The problem in presenting such a general indictment of society is that Gelber cannot give the audience a figure with whom they can identify—the conventional dramatic way of controlling audience-response. Hence his attempt to make the stage action seem real, not illusory. He clearly expects a middle-class audience. If they can be persuaded that actual heroin is being trafficked and taken in their presence, then they may react with shock, horror, perhaps even fear of the legal consequences; and since the addiction on stage is turned into a symbol of consumer society as a whole, Gelber intends their feelings of rejection to be transferred to the conditions of their own daily lives.

Between them, these three plays give a complete picture of the psychology of selling. The Iceman Cometh focuses on the product peddled, happiness in the present or personal improvement, and the pseudo-religious nature of the ideal of progress. Death of a Salesman deals with the motivation, the myth of "success" and its effect on the salesman. The Connection analyzes the restless vacuity and "compulsive" buying of the market-place mentality. All three plays talk of socially determined goals as "dreams," but the American dream is seen as progressively more destructive. In O'Neill it is the recognition of the reality created by the Protestant work ethic with its burden of guilt that is deadly, driving men alternatively to suicide, existential despair, or the debilitating drink of "pipe dreams."

Miller presents only one "phony dream," the ethos underlying American commercialism—other ideals, the retreat to a simple life on the land or maternal love that cements a family into a viable social unit, being indicated as realizable alternatives, though in fact the context makes them sentimental. For him men literally kill themselves to achieve this dream of success, but even if "a salesman is got to dream" because "it comes with the territory" there are other social positions which allow people like Charley or Bernard to prosper in the system. By the end of the fifties, however, all dreams engendered in the system are seen as equally lethal, and drugs are not simply metaphoric. What was an illusion of the mind has become a socially conditioned addiction reinforced by everything we buy. In a similar way the object for sale changes. Hickey promotes an ideal, even if perverted, and believes he is acting for the improvement of mankind. Willy is associated with contrasting objects that epitomize American materialism: the planned obsolescence of a refrigerator, where advertising substitutes for quality; and silk stockings, the artificial stimulus for dreams of glamour. Cowboy, cynically amoral and characterized by his attitude of "who cares?" traffics in a poison that gives delusions of happiness when shot into the blood stream.

Linked to this is a progressive discrediting of the salesman-figure; from the salesman who is assumed to be the integrating force in society, the "life of the party" (although the reverse is in fact shown to be true), through the salesman as an individual alienated from society and himself, to the salesman as the force that makes it possible for an anti-social and alienated society to exist. O'Neill exposes an admired figure, Miller dissects a victim of the society he represents, and Gelber presents a criminal outcast as the cynical embodiment of the society that (officially) condemns him. Side by side with this change in the salesman goes a development in the view of his customers. Down at heels but kindly drunkards in the early forties have become drug addicts and social rejects by the late fifties, capable of the stealing and murder that was only boasting in the earlier play. The "Hope" who provides free booze has been transformed into a "Leach" (the owner of the pad) who steals "the shit" from his fellow junkies.

The stage picture grows bleaker, the social engineering necessary to improve the situation more radical and more difficult. O'Neill at least implies that God exists, even if all we are shown is the "end of the line" to which the false religion of commerce has brought America, since the parody of the Last Supper and the perversion of the Christ-figure only has point in the context of true belief. Miller himself seems to think his alternatives viable, even if to us they appear empty romanticism, even though they cannot save either Willy or the ironically named Happy. Gelber too offers an alternative, although it is too nebulous to be formulated explicitly—the music played by a negro jazz quartet that forms an atmospheric background to his play, jazz being the creation of harmonic self-expression and free relationships outside structures and forms. But there is no real hope of regeneration from the musicians. As blacks they may not be a part of Anglo-Saxon America, but jazz is the sound of the drug culture and one of the junkies is a negro. Miller can still believe that truthful drama is able "to transform those who observe it" and that good will come of it. Gelber's metaphor confronts us with a choice of evils. If this addictive society continues, death from an overdose is inevitable, yet withdrawal symptoms themselves can be lethal, and the breaking of obsessive habit patterns is agonizing (in political terms, a total revolution) if not impossible.

It seems to take time—in the case of these examples over a decade— for the subliminal impact of drama to seep through to public consciousness, and it is difficult to measure the degree of influence a particular play might have had if a change of vision does occur. But the viewpoint of these plays is the attitude that characterized the sixties; the rejection of middle-class commerce and comforts by the young, the abandonment of the Protestant work ethic, and the search for alternative societies in Woodstock, communes, and fundamentally or orientially inspired religious cults—which roughly parallel the respective solutions of Gelber, Miller, and O'Neill. Further deductions about the social effectiveness of drama can be drawn from the differences in style and approach between the three plays.

Usual theories assume (following Brecht) that the tone should be rational and "alienating," that the author's moral stand should be clear, and that the message should be directly stated (à la Brieux), of a sort which can be argued in a preface (as with Shaw), or summarized in general principles (as in Brecht's epilogues and songs). Social dramatists also tend to assume avant garde forms are the most appropriate, rejecting naturalism as an expression of the social order they wish to change on the new-wine-in-old-bottles principle. These assumptions, at least in the contemporary American context, seem questionable. As the Maysles's film indicates, it was The Iceman Cometh and Death of a Salesman that had the greatest effect. The Connection has not gained a similar public standing, even though stylistically Gelber's play is the most original; his political position is clearer, being more extreme; and his attempt to manipulate his audience is not only the most direct, but works by an exaggerated form of alienation which comes close to antagonism.

By contrast, Miller and O'Neill provide characters who are explored in familiar ways which draw audiences into the play through progressively revealing the past or exposing hidden motive, "pre-existing images," and stories which are conventionally interesting—clichés even: the boy who takes revenge on an over demanding mother because she "made all the decisions"; the boy who "went wrong" because he caught his father with another woman; the melodrama of suicide. Gelber's play, though apparently intended for the middle-classes, was produced by the Living Theater with its notorious revolutionary line and might be said to have preached only to the converted. O'Neill and Miller gained a wide public hearing and caught the popular imagination, which is always conservative in taste, because they did not initially appear to be attacking society—although the way in which the 1951 film version of Death of a Salesman was treated shows that by then the producers were both alive to and nervous about its subversive implications.

Another element that also determined the relative effect of these "salesman-plays" is timing, which on occasion has been known to turn very ordinary plays and even operas into rallying points for existing revolutionary sentiment. By the time The Connection reached the stage the view of commerce and the American Dream presented by the earlier plays had already begun to percolate through society; and allowing ten years for subliminal impressions to filter through into general awareness before they issue in changed social attitudes, when the effects of Gelber's play might have been expected the movement of which it was a part was fading. Today the intimate relationship between religion and trade, for instance, is so firmly accepted that advertisers can even use it to sell their products: "Toyota," we are told, "saves."

Death of a Salesman as Psychomachia

In a footnote to an article on " Point of View in Death of a Salesman," Brian Parker observes that "the play's technique of presenting all events and characters as though strained through Willy's mind resembles the Morality technique in which characters and events are allegories of the central character's psychomachia." Parker does not develop this idea, but it is an important one, for the drama can be interpreted as a psychomachia, and doing so will shed light on the perennial objection to the play, that it is a confused mingling of expressionism and naturalism. The drama, for all its modernistic techniques, can be read very much like Everyman. Willy is, like that medieval hero, a generator of other personalities which are to a large extent fragmented aspects of himself. Angus Fletcher, in his study of allegory, makes some interesting remarks that can be applied to a reading of Willy's character:

The allegorical hero generates a number of other characters who react against or with him in a syllogistic manner. I say "generate" because the heroes in Dante and Spenser and Bunyan seem to create the worlds around them. They are like those people in real life who "project," ascribing fictitious personalities to those whom they meet and live with.... the finest hero will then be the one who most naturally seems to generate sub-characters—aspects of himself—who become the means by which he is revealed, facet by facet. This paper will attempt to show that all the characters in the play are not only filtered through Willy's perceptions, but represent aspects of his splintered mind. As Fletcher observes, "the fragmentation of the allegorical hero enables a writer to deal with a highly complex moral world by creating a composite protagonist who is not by any means as restricted as he appears." Miller dramatically presents the complex moral world of mid-nineteenth-century American values and beliefs, for each of the characters embodies an abstract quality. Linda, the devoted wife, represents that pernicious American value, security. Biff, the all-American boy turned thief, embodies the vanished frontier, the lost promise of America, while Happy, whose name is the most ironically allegorical, represents the sterile materialism and sensuality that have eroded the frontier spirit. Ben, as a number of critics have noted, is the character who most obviously functions as an element of Willy's mind, representing the fantasy of success through the ruthless Darwinian spirit, while Charley, a sort of double for Ben, embodies the domestication of capitalism within the city. Charley's son, Bernard, and young Howard are, as sons and fathers, mirrors in which Willy sees his own and his sons' failures. All the characters in the drama, then, are mirrors or doubles for Willy, for all represent aspects of not only his failure, but the failure of America to achieve its promise.

The drama is, as Miller makes clear in the subtitle, "certain private conversations," that is, private conversations with Willy's mind and with those characters who shape and have been shaped by his values. This is not to suggest that Linda, Biff, Happy and Charley do not exist as actual characters who have as much reality in the drama as Willy has. It is instead meant to suggest that Miller believes and has attempted to express the notion that we shape our perceptions of reality in as many ways as possible. Thus, Willy convinces himself that he is the crucial salesman in New England, that he is handsome, a loving husband and devoted father, and that his sons are able to "lick the civilized world." All these conceptions are, of course, delusions, but, unfortunately, they are believed to some degree by all the family members. Their motivation in believing these fantasies is made clear when both Happy and Linda warn Biff to tell his father what he wants to hear, not what has actually happened. Happy and Linda, like Biff, are less to be blamed than Willy, for it is Willy who has forced his family to play the parts that he has designed for them. They are all characters in a dream, Willy's dream of reality. The initial stage directions make this explicit: "An air of dream clings to the place, a dream rising out of reality."

Linda, according to a recent critic [Guerin Bliquez], prods Willy to his doom by "helping him shirk the responsibilities of the kind of knowledge needed to hold himself and his family together." But Linda is much more a victim of Willy than vice versa. In his introduction to the Collected Plays, Miller observed that "Linda is made by Willy though he did not know it or believe in it or receive it unto himself." When Willy remembers receiving a job offer in Alaska from Ben, he immediately hears Linda's voice: "Why must everybody conquer the world? You're well liked, and the boys love you, and someday—why, old man Wagner told him just the other day that if he keeps it up he'll be a member of the firm." In this episode Linda clearly represents not so much an actual woman holding her husband back, but an aspect of Willy's own mind, an aspect that is afraid of risks and uncertainties. Willy, however, chooses to remember that it was Linda who persuaded him to remain a salesman, but we have only his rationalizing memories of the event. His quick acquiescence to Linda's position reveals that Linda functions primarily as an echo of Willy's own position; she embodies his need for security even at the price of mediocrity. Ironically, Willy assures Linda that she is his "foundation and support," and to a large extent she is, for her existence testifies to Willy's domestic success. The house, appliances, cars and insurance prove that Willy has achieved the necessary social status in a society which confuses a facade for substance.

Ben, on the other hand, represents Willy's dreams of financial success through ruthless strength: "The man knew what he wanted and went out and got it." But Willy was not willing or able to take the risks that great success demanded; therefore, he magnifies the cunning required and dangers faced—from the darkest jungles of Africa to the arctic terrors of Alaska—in order to justify his own hesitations and failures.

If Linda and Ben embody Willy's dreams of domestic and financial success, Biff is a living reminder of Willy's failure as both. Biff represents the great American dream gone wrong. He could have recaptured the pioneer spirit of his grandfather, the itinerant inventor, but he has been fatally infected by

Willy's values. Although Biff recognizes his father as a fake, he also needs to recognize that he, too, in embracing his father's beliefs, is also a fake. The climax of the play for Biff occurs in Bill Oliver's office, for it is there that he is forced to recognize the fact that he has lived and believed the fantasy that Willy has created of and for him. Biff had let Willy shape him so that he became the embodiment of Willy's dream of parental success. But Biff, on some level, realized this and his thefts had been pathetic attempts to break the mold of perfection that Willy's mind had created.

Willy's materialism and philandering find expression in his other son, Happy, who confesses that he finds pleasure in seducing the fiancées of executives because "maybe I just have an overdeveloped sense of competition or something." Like Biff, Happy has been warped by Willy's belief in success at any price. His promiscuity and insensitivity reach their pinnacle in the "celebration" dinner when he deserts his father for a woman he has just picked up—an event that parallels what Willy did to Biff in that Boston hotel room.

The scene in the hotel room, which returns to Willy with violent force in the restaurant, represents Willy's failures as a husband and father. When Bernard probes close to the buried incident by asking Willy if Biff met him in Boston, Willy turns on him: "What are you trying to do, blame it on me? If a boy lays down is that my fault?" By refusing to accept responsibility for Biff, Willy is also refusing to accept responsibility for himself. When Biff explodes at Willy: "You—you gave her Mama's stockings! Don't touch me, you—liar! You fake! You phony little fake! You fake!" he expresses the self-accusations that Willy has carried and will carry to his death. Willy has failed, as American society, in Miller's eyes, has failed, to be true to its pioneer heritage. The myth of the American dream—an easy, soft life and an easy, painless death, as represented by the old salesman Dave Singleman—has been replaced by the reality of Willy's death.

The short Requiem that concludes the play has been criticized for its sentimentality and the artificiality of its speeches. The purpose of the Requiem, however, is made clearer by recognizing the drama as a psychomachia. All the characters who had previously functioned as parts of Willy's dream or nightmare are now supposedly free of him. In fact, Linda's final words are, ironically, "We're free." But each of the characters continues to embody the values that Willy demanded of them.

They are not free of Willy any more than he could be free of them and of his need to control them. This interconnectedness of human beings reveals Miller's major theme and further explains his reason for using both expressionistic and naturalistic techniques. In an interview with Ronald Hayman, Miller compared Death of a Salesman with the later After the Fall by stating: I have worked in two veins always and I guess they alternate. In one the event is inside the brain and in the other the brain is inside the event. In Death we are inside the head. That's why I've needed two kinds of stylistic attack. Miller is more explicit about his stylistic techniques in his introduction to the Collected Plays. There he concludes that the first image that occurred to me which was to result in Death was of an enormous face the height of the proscenium arch which would appear and then open up, and we would see the inside of a man's head. In fact, "The Inside of His Head" was the first title.

Miller continues in the introduction to remark that the major tension in the play is between the past and the present, but it can more accurately be said that the major tension in the drama is between the self and the others. Willy descends into himself and encounters his wife, his sons, his older brother and his neighbors, but it becomes clear to us, if not to him, that all these people are not others who have been respected by Willy as individuals in their own right. Rather, he has shaped all of them, with disastrous results.

Willy does not recognize this, however, for he has always viewed other people as mirrors of himself. He does not understand what he has done to Linda or Happy, but he is forced to recognize what he has done to Biff. The drama revolves around the exploration of one mind's grappling with its responsibilities for others, and because of that the technique utilized has to be expressionistic, for we have to be inside Willy's mind to understand and appreciate its rationalizations. But just as Miller recognized the interrelationship between the individual and society, so does he reveal that in any treatment of one man's mind we will encounter larger social issues, thus the naturalistic element in the drama. Willy's mind is the mind of mid-twentieth-century America, obsessed with security, status, financial success, athletic and sexual prowess, and public recognition.

The drama, then, utilizes both expressionism and naturalism in order to capture an extremely complex moral vision, for when we view or read the play we are both immersed in one mind which is many minds, and yet we are allowed the aesthetic distance so that we can objectively evaluate that mind's and our society's values. Miller's basic theme, that we are all morally responsible for one another, becomes artistically embodied in the technique of psychomachia. In Willy Loman we see what has become of a man and a nation that have not learned to accept their responsibility for others. When Miller first saw the play produced, he noted: Then it seemed to me that we must be a terribly lonely people, cut off from each other by such massive pretense of self-sufficiency, machined down so fine we hardly touch any more. We are trying to save ourselves separately, and that is immoral, that is the corrosive among us. Miller captured this theme in his utilization of psychomachia, for Willy is both self and society, the embodiment of an America that is spiritually dying.

Willy Loman and the Soul of a New Machine: Technology and the Common Man

As Death of a Salesman opens, Willy Loman returns home "tired to the death." Lost in reveries about the beautiful countryside and the past, he's been driving off the road; and now he wants a cheese sandwich. But Linda's suggestion that he try a new American-type cheese—"It's whipped"—irritates Willy: "Why do you get American when I like Swiss?" His anger at being contradicted unleashes an indictment of modern industrialized America: The street is lined with cars. There's not a breath of fresh air in the neighborhood. The grass don't grow any more, you can't raise a carrot in the back yard.

In the old days, "This time of year it was lilac and wisteria." Now: "Smell the stink from that apartment house! And another one on the other side." But just as Willy defines the conflict between nature and industry, he pauses and simply wonders: "How can they whip cheese?"

The clash between the old agrarian ideal and capitalistic enterprise is well documented in the literature on Death of a Salesman, as is the spiritual shift from Thomas Jefferson to Andrew Carnegie to Dale Carnegie that the play reflects. The son of a pioneer inventor and the slave to broken machines, Willy Loman seems to epitomize the victim of modern technology. But his unexpected, marvelingly innocent question about whipping cheese reveals an ambivalence toward technology livelier and more interesting (and perhaps truer to the American character) than a simple dichotomy between farm and factory, past and present. Death of a Salesman engages an audience's attitudes toward technology: fear of the new and unfamiliar; marvel at progress; and the need, finally, to accommodate technology to cultural mythologies by subordinating it to personality. Willy's contradictions clearly indicate his alienation, but they recall Walt Whitman, too (that other restless Brooklynite who could sing enthusiastically of leaves of grass, lilacs, and locomotives in winter). "Do I contradict myself?" Whitman asks near the end of Song of Myself; "Very well then I contradict myself, / (I am large, I contain multitudes.)"

In "Passage to India," Whitman says that after the engineers, inventors, and scientists have accomplished their work, Finally shall come the poet worthy of that name, The true son of God shall come singing his songs.

I do not claim the status of Whitman's divine poet for either Arthur Miller or Tracy Kidder, the author of The Soul of a New Machine. But both are fine connectors who invoke the spirit of Whitman, Thoreau, and Emerson as they help us integrate technology with cultural mythologies and thus triumph over it in the popular imagination. Indeed, the great American writers of the nineteenth century define, in part, the tradition into which some contemporary writers try to fit modern technological enterprise.

Miller endows Willy Loman with a Whitmanesque urge to appropriate technology to his personal vision, not just consume it. This quality complicates Willy's relationship with technology, and thus the whole notion of his pathetic victimization. Willy's Whitmanesque impulses help define the need to appropriate technology to American cultural values, and to allay the fear, voiced by Norman Mailer in Of a Fire on the Moon, that "The art of communication has become the mechanical function, and the machine the work of art." By defining the problem and impulse, Death of a Salesman creates a context for interpreting Kidder's attempt, in The Soul of a New Machine, to bring computer technology into the American popular culture and literary tradition.

The Soul of a New Machine does not answer the question of how they whip cheese, but it explains how some people build computers: with intelligence, imagination, enthusiasm, and sheer hard work. Kidder casts his "new journalism" report of how the Data General Corporation developed "Eagle," a 32-bit minicomputer, as a high tech frontier tale.

Tom West, the computer engineer-manager and folksinger who leads the Data General team, the Eclipse Group, seems to be the new American Adam, an aggressive business manager and dropout at the same time. As a success story, a story of men and women who refuse to be defeated by machines, The Soul of a New Machine seems to refute the failure dramatized in Death of a Salesman. Except that as Eagle goes out the door— renamed by marketing men the "Eclipse MV/8000"—a few of its builders go with it. The verge toward Salesman is an irony I'll return to later. Rather than show easy resolutions to the conflicts between individualism, technology, and corporate impersonality, Kidder recasts some of the fundamental questions. Death of a Salesman and The Soul of a New Machine impose arbitrary limits on a huge topic. As Leo Marx argues in The Machine in the Garden, the goal of establishing an American "society of the middle landscape, a rural nation exhibiting a happy balance of art [including science] and nature," goes back at least to the eighteenth century. "But no one, not even Jefferson, had been able to identify the point of arrest, the critical moment when the tilt might be expected and progress cease to be progress." We all set personal, arbitrary limits on acceptable technology. Wilbur Moore, an old black mechanic, once told me that western civilization fell into decline when Chevrolet went from six- to eight-cylinder engines. Tom West, the Data General engineer, draws the line at digital wrist watches: Anyone who dared to consult such a chronometer and in [West's] hearing say, "the exact time is..," could expect to receive the full force of his scorn, for being such a fool as to think that a watch was accurate just because it had no hands. One winter night, while stirring logs in his fireplace, West mutters, "Computers are irrelevant."

As the limits of technology shift, so do our means of coping with it and incorporating it into the popular culture. Steve Goodman's song, "The City of New Orleans," wistfully ritualizes the end of a passenger train, while the homes, farms, and fields the train passes on its last run endure. The conflict between technology and nature has been nicely revalued. Corvette Summer, an otherwise unremarkable movie, concludes with an interesting variation of the obligatory car chase. The bad guy runs his car off the end of the pavement on a highway construction site. The car, as I recall, careers down an embankment, rolls over, and comes to rest, demolished, on another pavement. As the driver staggers from the wreck, the car's horn blares mournfully The driver shoots the car dead with one well-placed bullet.

If you can kill a machine, with remorse as a cowboy does his crippled horse, you have managed a marvelous control over it; and you have brought it into the typology of the American West. Walt Whitman, who according to Leo Marx "comes [the] closest [of our nineteenth-century writers] to transmuting the rhetoric of the technological sublime into poetry," can turn a locomotive into a sexual object: "Thee in they panoply, thy measured dual throbbing and thy beat convulsive." If you can sodomize a machine, if only in the imagination, you have asserted a peculiar but persuasive control over it.

Whitman haunts Death of a Salesman, especially in the scene in boss Howard's office, in which Willy is fired. This is a critical moment in Willy's life, as he goes in to plead for a New York job after spending thirty-four years on the road. It is the play's most blatantly anti-business scene: "it's a business, kid," young Howard explains to old Willy just before he sacks him, "and everybody's gotta pull his own weight." On the surface, it is also the play's most obviously anti-technology scene, for throughout most of it Howard is preoccupied with his new toy, a wire recorder. It "records things," Howard explains enthusiastically:

I tell you, Willy, I'm gonna take my camera, and my bandsaw, and all my hobbies, and out they go. This is the most fascinating relaxation I ever found.

As Willy's life falls apart, the voice of Howard's five-year-old son, recorded on the wire, intones the capitals of the states: "The capital of Alabama is Montgomery; the capital of Arizona is Phoenix; the capital of Arkansas is Little Rock.The episode is a savagely comic, yet pathetic, mockery of Whitman's America, evoked through its place names, and his celebration of common people.

But in the middle of this scene Willy celebrates Dave Singleman, the old drummer who at the age of eighty-four could still make his living with pride and dignity by going up to his hotel room, putting on his green velvet slippers, and calling the buyers on the phone. Singleman is a troublesome figure; he works and lives alone, and we do not know how much Willy has exaggerated his success over the years. But Willy links Singleman with his own father (also a loner) and commerce with the American frontier:

Oh, yeah, my father lived many years in Alaska. He was an adventurous man. We've got quite a little streak of self-reliance in our family I thought I'd go out with my older brother and try to locate him, and maybe settle in the North with the old man. And I almost decided to go, when I met a salesman in the Parker House. His name was Dave Singleman.

Most persuasively, Willy apotheosizes Singleman in an unexpectedly eloquent, genuinely Whitmanesque passage that includes an image of technology, the train: Do you know? when he died—and by the way he died the death of a salesman, in his green velvet slippers in the smoker of the New York, New Haven and Hartford, going into Boston—when he died, hundreds of salesmen and buyers were at his funeral.... In those days there was personality in it, Howard. There was respect, and comradeship, and gratitude in it.

The reference to "personality" does not sway Howard because he is not listening. But we are listening as the speech—Willy's longest in the play—swells out of the painful conflicts between boss and employee, parents and children, men and machines. Speaking with the eloquent desperation of a person clinging to his job and vision—his very identity— Willy captures Whitman's sweep and rhythm, his balance of particular and generalization, place and motion. Purpose, movement, and activity infuse Willy's naming of places, as the names define both the cities and the railroad that serves them. He invokes Emerson's spirit of self-reliance, the wilderness, and the newer frontier of American commerce that he must endow with epic qualities. The speech conveys the "enterprise and bravery" of commerce that even Thoreau admires (with some irony) as the Fitchburg train breaks the peace at Walden Pond. It may be that Willy never recognizes [as Gerald Weales writes] "that there is more than one way to kill a salesman." But it is apparent, too, that there is more to "personality" than is dreamt of in the philosophy that Dale Carnegie propounds in How to Win Friends and Influence People.

Willy puts us back in touch with that idealized New England cult of personality called transcendentalism. Willy, the apparent victim of technology—he will kill himself in a car wreck—shows us how we can, and perhaps must, integrate technology and personality with a rich cultural past. This is one reason why, as Linda insists, "attention must be finally paid to such a person": Willy's metaphoric quest distinguishes him from the rest of the characters in the play and many in the audience. Howard, by contrast, is a forties' version of the unthinking consumer of fashionable technology, the first in line at Sears to buy "Pac Man." But video games should not be singled out for derision. They are, after all, offshoots of pinball games; and pinball has a long tradition in popular culture as a point at which people and machines connect.

There is, for example, a wonderful moment in William Saroyan's The Time of Your Life when Willie, a marble-ball maniac, beats the machine in Nick's Pacific Street Saloon, Restaurant, and Entertainment Palace. It only takes Willie six nickels (though most of the day) to triumph, and the results are spectacular. The machine's lights flash, some red, some green, and an American flag jumps up. "Oh, boy, what a beautiful country," Willie says as the machine plays " A loud music-box version of the song 'America.' " Several characters stand up and sing along with the machine. " Everybody," the stage directions tell us, "has watched the performance of the defeated machine from wherever he happened to be when the performance began." Willie is "thrilled, amazed, delighted":

Took me a little while, but I finally did it. It's scientific, really. With a little skill a man can make a modest living beating the marble games. Not that that's what I want to do. I just don't like the idea of anything getting the best of me. A machine or anything else.

The Time of Your Life is a beatific, wish-fulfilling fantasy. Even Murphy, a.k.a. Kit Carson, the teller of tall tales, lives out his fantasies about the Old West when, at the end, he shoots Blick, vice squad captain and the only vicious character in the play: I shot a man once. In San Francisco. Shot him two times. In 1939, I think it was. In October. Fellow named Blick or Glick or something like that. Couldn't stand the way he talked to ladies. Saroyan's play did not test American ideas and assumptions the way Death of a Salesman was to do ten years later; Saroyan plays on nostalgia, whereas Miller tests the assumptions on which the nostalgia is based. But the marble game and the echo of the Old West are good examples of the kind of mythic appropriation I have been describing. They depend heavily on familiar cultural idioms and rhythms, revived in twentieth-century circumstances, for achieving comic release and audience awareness. They contribute some ambivalence, too: has the machine really been defeated? Or has it been released to display a hidden array of electronic/mechanical wizardry that delights an audience once it has fulfilled its purpose of challenging the operator?

A colleague told me the story of some enterprising student engineers at Stanford in the early 1970s. For senior projects they had to build devices that could, under their own power, climb a flight of stairs. The winners, this one year, built a robot that climbed the stairs, shot up an American flag, played the " Star Spangled Banner," and then blew itself up. That is a triumph over technology that even Willie, the marble-game maniac, might envy. The students first had to design and build the machine, programming it to destroy itself as a demonstration of their domination over it (and as a comment, perhaps, on America's technological prowess). I offer this anecdote not as an example of programmed obsolescence, but as a literal demonstration of what Tom West says is the compulsive need never to look back: "The old things [i.e., last year's computers], I can't bear to look at them. They're clumsy I can't believe we were that dumb." This need to dominate the machine characterizes the engineers depicted in Kidder's The Soul of a New Machine, and it links them, within modest limits, to the fighter pilots turned astronauts celebrated hyperbolically in Tom Wolfe's The Right Stuff.

Style and self dramatization declare the nature and significance of the human domination of technology. Saroyan's Willie needs to beat the machine to be able to reassert the American myth of individualism and multiplicity (here, ethnic multiplicity): (Indicating the letter "F" on his sweater) See that letter? That don't stand for some little-bitty high school somewhere. That stands for me. Faroughli. Willie Faroughli. I'm an Assyrian. Miller's Willy must also assert his identity when charged by his son to know himself better: "I am not a dime a dozen! I am Willy Loman, and you are Biff Loman!" Here Willy Loman does more than embrace "the American myth, born of the advertisers," that confuses "labels with reality." The myth is deeper than that, for here Willy echoes, like Saroyan's Willie before him, Walt Whitman's bold declaration of self in Song of Myself:

> *Walt Whitman, a kosmos, of Manhattan the son,*
> *Turbulent, fleshy, sensual, eating, drinking and breeding,*
> *No sentimentalist, no stander above men and women or apart from them,*
> *No more modest than immodest.*

Willy Loman, even as he collapses under the weight of his own cultural baggage, feels compelled to fit technology into his inherited vision of American enterprise, to bring it under the control of language inspired by Whitman. Reshaping the technological environment with a vision born of language, making it conform to the culture created and articulated by its people, may finally be the most significant triumph over the machine. This second feat—appropriating the technology into the myth, not just mastering or applying it—makes Kidder's book persuasive and helps overcome our suspicions about the dehumanizing power of computers. Rather than computer technology, The Soul of a New Machine celebrates a few of the people who build computers. To make the technology and the drama accessible, Kidder invokes the kinds of tropes and expressions that I've been describing.

Carl Alsing, the leader of the "Microkids" and, at 35, one of West's trusted old men (as well as his observer, his Boswell), describes a "war" between Data General's Massachusetts and North Carolina research teams as "the big shoot-out at HoJo's." He imagines it as "a pen-and-ink drawing [in which] snarling engineers are shown hurling complexities at each other." The enigmatic Tom West, who rarely talks to his recruits the whole time they are building Eagle, is finally described by a team member as a hired gunslinger—a kind of corporate Johnny Ringo—who cleans up the town but then is run out by the respectable people. "That's a classic American story," remarks Alsing, warming at once to the appropriateness of the analogy.

Such analogies help the engineers order their own experience and give it meaning, and they define, in an important way, Kidder's methods of taking us into the high tech wilderness of computer engineering. Alsing uses the computer game "Adventure" to break in his new recruits on their Data General machine and to introduce Kidder to the engineers' mystical experience of midnight programming. Playing Adventure, "you travel by computer into an underground world, wandering through strange, awful labyrinths, searching for treasure that's guarded and sometimes snatched away by dragons, dwarfs, trolls, and a rapacious pirate who mutters: 'Har. Har.' " A metaphor for the underground world of computer research and development, "The game is a harrowing of hell," because you get lost in a series of mazes that test your very sanity:

I had the feeling I was lost in a forest, and I acted as no smart woodsman would, heading off in this direction, then heading off in that, getting nowhere.

Then I heard Alsing chuckle. "Ahhh, I love it.... What do you do when you get lost?"

"You make maps, of course."

Alsing sat back and nodded, smiling.

Thus Leatherstocking teases and leads the neophyte into the wilderness. The neophyte's experience becomes the bridge between two cultures, as Kidder leads the rest of us into the wilderness, civilizing it and toughening us as he goes.

But even Alsing as Leather stocking is only one sign on Kidder's map into the deep woods. Rather than just make the unfamiliar familiar, the frontier metaphors gradually reveal that technology is a worthy adversary for adventurous spirits. Instead of wolves, hostile Indians, and broken wagon wheels, the new wilderness consists of missing NAND gates, the indecisiveness of logic designers, and the like. Such travails define the new wilderness that must be charted. Indeed, Kidder tells us, "A computer's boards seem to show order triumphing over complexity." That notion seems to be the metaphysical point of computer technology for the Data General engineers, and especially for Tom West.

Branded an underachiever at Amherst College, West dropped out for a year and sang folksongs in Cambridge,

Massachusetts. He knew the chaos of the early 1960s, and he sought out meaning and order. Instead of retiring to Walden Pond or the Maine Woods, West dropped into engineering.

I think I wanted to see how complicated things happen. There's some notion of control, it seems to me, that you can derive in a world full of confusion if you at least understand how things get put together. Even if you can't understand every little part, how infernal machines get put together.

West insists on living a double life as high-powered manager and dropout, sometimes driving directly to work, ready to play the tough manager, after playing his guitar all night. The 32-bit Eagle would process information more quickly and efficiently than its competitors, and it would stretch the capabilities of its young inventors in ways they had never been stretched before. Building the super mini computer, then, gives West the opportunity to reconcile two opposite ambitions: "He was back in Cambridge, as it were, singing folk songs, while at the same time putting money on Data General's bottom line. He could be, for a while, a balladeer of computers."

"Balladeer of Computers" is something of a misnomer. West is a namer, a coiner of phrases, as well as an amateur folksinger. But he does not sing of computers; he sings of people and their work. His figurative language—having "shootouts," "beating up" people, persuading them to "sign up" behind his group's project, "playing pinball" (that is, getting a machine out the door with your name on it so that you win another, more inspiring project to develop), creates a rough-and-tumble world that comes to define the Eclipse Group's workplace and the team members' intensity. West's words, at least to Alsing, have a transforming power. After the Eclipse Group loses its bid to build EGO, its first challenge to the North Carolina team's project, West brings his team out of its depression "into the honesty of pure work," achieving a persuasively New England salvation. Because West finds romance and excitement in the ordinary—a sudden weather change at sea or the challenge of reducing the number of circuit boards in a computer—he manages to turn the Eagle project, a relatively uninteresting computer as far as "sexy" machines go, into an extraordinary event. According to Alsing, "West took a bag on the side of the Eclipse and made it the most exciting thing in our lives for a year and a half."

That describes a kind of effective management that might appeal to Whitman or Thoreau, even Willy Loman, but not to Willy's boss, Howard. The dogged quest for a missing NAND gate, a little circuit that gives a "not yet" signal to an electrical charge, lends almost epic qualities to the builders' debugging efforts. But the successful search ends simply, and in the best folk tradition the engineers underplay their achievement. Rather than give the NAND gate a formal, technical name, as is usually done in formal, bureaucratic organizations, the Eclipse engineers use the vernacular "NOT YET" because that describes exactly what the NAND gate's signal says. The effort to "simplify" reflects West's general approach to technological matters: "No muss, no fuss."

The quest to reduce complexity while creating a commercially successful product makes the building of Eagle a kind of high tech metaphor for Thoreau's experience at Walden. The analogy may be whimsical (Kidder does not go so far as to make it explicit); certainly it is ironic. Tom West retreats each night to his old New England farmhouse, leaving Data General at a distance that cannot be measured in miles or minutes. Nevertheless, it is on the job, or at home when thoughts of work intrude, that solving the practical problems of computer engineering becomes the effective equivalent of attempting to live simply, in tune with nature and oneself.

"Pinball" is the key concept, now in an elaborate, "real world" extension of the inspiration that Willie the marble-ball maniac enjoys. Signing up to work long hours, with no pay for overtime and few company resources, to get a machine out the door with your name on it, is exhausting and frustrating. The stakes are high, however. In playing pinball, the computer designer is playing, finally, for "substantial freedom": freedom to work on the projects he wants, the way he wants, and to put his name on his work. The game is compelling for those who chucked the established ways, as West puts it, because it offers "Some notion of insecurity and challenge, of where the edges are, of finding out what you can't do, all within a perfectly justifiable scenario." Pinball benefits the company materially, but it seems to benefit the individual workers spiritually even more. That is its subversive appeal.

The success of the Eagle project seems to rebut the failure and alienation Miller dramatizes in Death of a Salesman, except that the project does not end the way West thought it would. West leaves the Eclipse Group to take another job in the company, a job that would take him often, appropriately, to the Far East. Most of the young engineers get to play pinball, but most of the older ones—West's lieutenants—leave the company. Stripped of most of his managerial responsibilities at Data General, Carl Alsing, for example, takes a job in California. Echoing Willy Loman, Alsing explains that he felt unappreciated by the company. The verge toward Salesman reminds us that the problem is not with technology per se; rather, it is with organizations that mimic the impersonal responses of machines. Society is still a "joint-stock company" that "loves not realities and creators, but names and customs," as Emerson says.

But the human failure of corporations is not the most important link between Salesman and Soul. The more important connection is the assertion of personal identity within the environment of business and technology. Aside from the insistence on tragedy, what Arthur Miller says in "Tragedy and the Common Man" about the modern hero applies to a person like Tom West as well as to characters like Willy Loman and Willie the marble-ball maniac (a delightfully comic figure): the individual's struggle to claim his whole due as a personality demonstrates the indestructible will of man to achieve his humanity. Robert Pirsig, in Zen and the Art of Motorcycle Maintenance, calls for a reassertion of thought and personality in technological matters, as does Mailer, in another, more flamboyant, vein in Of a Fire on the Moon. Even more flamboyantly, indomitable personality characterizes Tom Wolfe's brethren of "the right stuff," the test pilots who keep alive in the sky the raucous qualities of legendary backwoodsmen. What is finally compelling about Willy Loman and Tom West is their compulsive need to dramatize their work, to redefine it with words that evoke the American past and its values of personality and individualism, and then through their work seek substantial freedom. Miller and Kidder invoke the spirit of Whitman, Thoreau, and Emerson, who before them sought peace with technology while defining a new individualism and freedom. The language of Salesman and Soul connects the individual with a large, often richly contradictory tradition of popular American myth. At least one important form of accommodation of the human to the technological is achieved through this kind of mythmaking. It may be, of course, that computer technology is yet another "improved means to an unimproved end," as Thoreau puts it. But in terms of the writers' abilities to appropriate technology to the popular culture, and to reassert the individual's imaginative control over the machine, the "tilt," the moment when progress ceases to be progress and the system crashes, seems not yet to have occurred.

Tragic Form and the Possibility of Meaning in Death of a Salesman

In his introduction to the Collected Plays (1957), Arthur Miller claims that "the assumption—or presumption—behind" his "plays is that life has meaning." In seeming contradiction to Miller's assumption, many characters in his plays express doubts about the significance of life in general and their own lives in particular. Quentin, the main character in After the Fall, "arrives on the scene weighted down with a sense of his own pointlessness and the world's."

Early in The Price, Victor, the soon-to-be retired policeman who during the depression sacrificed his chance to attend medical school in order to support his apparently broken father, confesses, "I look at my life and the whole thing is incomprehensible to me." And in Death of a Salesman Willy Loman recalls admitting to his older brother Ben that he feels "kind of temporary about" himself. Of course, these characters can be said to be taking for granted, even as they express their doubts, that life can become meaningful. Quentin's sense of pointlessness, Victor's inability to comprehend his life, and Willy's feeling of inconsequential impermanence all imply that somehow life should take on meaning, that, as Miller suggests in "On Social Plays" (1955), "meaning is the ultimate reward for having lived."

In Death of a Salesman Miller denies this "reward" to Willy Loman. He characterizes Willy as essentially meaningless by dramatizing him, as most but not all readers and viewers of the play have recognized, not as a tragic hero but as a pathetic, limited man. But, if Miller has written Death of a Salesman without a tragic hero, we nevertheless need to acknowledge its tragic form. For Miller brings Willy to life through a form that is double-edged. In Death of a Salesman the tragic form, which for Miller is adapted from ritual, is at once an ironic commentary on the smallness of Willy's life and a model of action that supports Miller's assumption, or at least the possibility of assuming, that life has meaning.

Any claim that Death of a Salesman is tragic in shape needs to begin by admitting that the play's central character makes it seem something less than a tragedy. In the first place, the superficial form of the play, the way it blends the workings of Willy's mind with reality, demonstrates that Willy has no more control over his mind than over the wire recorder he accidentally switches on in Howard Wagner's office. Willy is, simply, a man breaking down. Besides lacking mental ability, Willy also lacks moral strength. He allows his sons to steal and is unfaithful to his wife. Whereas theft becomes important particularly in Biff's life, Willy's infidelity dominates his memory His infidelity is the act of, to use The Woman's phrase, the "saddest, self-centerdest soul I ever did see-saw."

His infidelity lays bare the hollowness of his affection for his "foundation and support," Linda. It echoes his own father's desertion and, because Biff discovers him with The Woman, helps splinter the Loman family. But the play shows Willy as less a cause than a result. In Death of a Salesman society is, as the director Elia Kazan wrote in his notebooks for the first production of the play, "the 'heavy.'" And Willy is one of society's victims, one of those "who landed in the ash can."

As Miller explains it, society chews Willy up because he has broken "the law which says a failure in society and in business has no right to live."

In brief glimpses, Willy recognizes that he is a victim. After he is fired, he complains to Charley, "After all the highways and the trains, and the appointments, and the years, you end up worth more dead than alive." Despite such moments of awareness, three of the most painful things about Willy are his nearly total acceptance of the notion that he must succeed within the business world that eventually rejects him, the lying and self-delusion this acceptance leads him to, and the lack of insight into his own life this acceptance also entails. Willy is clearly an unquestioning devotee to the notion that "in the greatest country in the world" one must be a Thomas Edison, a B. E Goodrich, or a Dave Singleman. Moreover, although it may become clear to Willy that he might have done better doing more manual work than that of a "well liked" salesman, he cannot even consider such an alternative because part of succeeding is doing better than one's ancestors.

When he overhears Biff considering being a carpenter, he chides his son, "Even your grand father was better than a carpenter." Through such thoughts Willy ensures, participates in, society's victimization of him. To make matters worse, knowing that he is, at best, a mediocre salesman, Willy must convince himself that he is a great one. Accordingly, from his "overactive mind" comes lie after lie, lies that are at once ineffective because they fail to alter reality and too effective because they are infectious.

As Biff, who has learned how he deluded himself into believing that Bill Oliver had an "arm-on-my-shoulder" appreciation of him, exclaims to Willy, "We never told the truth for ten minutes in this house!" Willy not only lies because of his notion of success; he also blinds himself. When Biff finally breaks down and cries and, thus, finally confesses his love for his father in a way Willy can grasp, we see that Willy is capable of some understanding. But what also becomes clear is that his enlightenment can only be partial because he can see his son only in terms of his notion of success. Indeed, Willy is so firmly caught by his acceptance of this notion that he uses it to justify killing himself. The conclusion one draws from all this—Willy's lack of control over his mind, his lack of moral strength, his victimization by society, his belief in what is for him a misguided definition of success, his resultant lying and self-delusion, and his lack of insight—is that Willy is pathetic. Linda may insist, as she does to her sons, that "there's more good in him than in many other people."

A director such as Kazan may suggest to his leading actor that "This Willy is a fine, tender, capable, potentially useful human" and that "Willy is a good man" and "has worth." An actor such as Lee J. Cobb may bring a "touch of human grandeur" to his dramatization of Willy. And critics sympathetic to the play may feel called upon to show that Willy somehow has the stature of a hero. Nonetheless, though Willy is movingly human, he remains pathetic. In "Tragedy and the Common Man" (1949) Miller writes that "the pathetic is achieved when the protagonist is, by virtue of his witlessness, his insensitivity or the very air he gives off, incapable of grappling with a much superior force." Willy, seen in light of this definition, is clearly pathetic. In fact, Miller seems to admit as much in a 1953 interview:

There is great danger in pathos, which can destroy any tragedy if you let it go far enough. My weakness is that I can create a pathos at will. It is one of the easiest things to do. I feel that Willy Loman lacks sufficient insight into this situation, which would have made him a greater, more significant figure.

And, as Miller's comment suggests, Willy's pathos undercuts his significance. Willy is a pathetic man who fails to give meaning to his life, a boyish man who will never be more than "temporary." will Moreover, because Willy is pathetic, it is tempting to feel superior to him. Like Charley, we want to tell Willy "to grow up." Or like Herbert J. Muller in The Spirit of Tragedy, we feel tempted to call him "little Willy" We are not, however, similarly tempted to recognize him as an equal, let alone as a tragic hero.

Clearly Willy is not Oedipus, Hamlet, or Lear. Except as a victim of society, as an example of unnecessary self-delusion, as a mental case who finally kills himself, he is, as I shall continue to insist, meaningless. But I am also going to insist that he is—like, say, Sophocles' maddened, suicidal, and essentially pathetic Ajax—the central character of a play that derives much of its significance from being, if not a tragedy, an adaptation of tragic form. In other words, while admitting the importance of Willy to the meaning of Death of a Salesman, I think it is a mistake to focus, as many of the critics of the play have done, mainly on the character of Willy.

Although critics with their belief in ideal tragic heroes with tragic flaws and searching intellects were ready to find fault with Willy, Miller must share blame for the overemphasis on the question of Willy's stature. Seventeen days after Death of a Salesman opened in New York, Miller published in The New York Times "Tragedy and the Common Man." No model of clarity, the article argues that a common man can be a tragic hero and, thus, seems meant, though Willy is not named, to claim tragic stature for Willy. The "tragic feeling," Miller contends, depends not upon the hero's rank but "is evoked" by "a character who is ready to lay down his life, if need be, to secure one thing—his sense of personal dignity." Here Miller seems to write of Willy, who does lay down his life for his sense of dignity, mistaken though it is.

But, when Miller writes that "tragedy is the consequence of a man's total compulsion to evaluate himself justly," " one must wonder if he has the self-deluded Willy in mind. At any rate, seeming to have claimed tragic stature for Willy, Miller gave critics cause to focus on the character, and the bulk of them have found, as I do and, indeed, as we have seen Miller do, that Willy is pathetic. In his foreword for The Theater Essays of Arthur Miller (1978), Miller acknowledges his chagrin over his critical statements on tragedy and his bemusement over the critical response to them: "I have often wished that I had never written a word on the subject of tragedy." As will become clear, I, to the contrary, am glad that Miller has written on tragedy because much of what he says helps clarify the importance of form in Death of a Salesman. But in "Tragedy and the Common Man" Miller makes a mistake that has helped blind us to the play's full meaning. His mistake was to seem to emphasize the importance of character over form when his play employs a form in which, as Aristotle points out, the most important element "is the arrangement of the incidents, for tragedy is an imitation, not of men but of action and life, of happiness and misfortune" (On Poetry and Style). Although Miller's later essays put more emphasis on tragic form and its significance, Miller himself has been slow to say that in Death of a Salesman he "was dealing with something much more than Willy Loman, the tactile experience of that one particular character."

And, ignoring the form of Death of a Salesman, critics have tended to conclude that Miller's "drama is unlike both" Greek and Christian drama because "for the most part it rejects a religious framework", that "religious feeling, as normally understood, has absolutely no place in his plays". Because critics have tended to pay attention to Willy rather than to form, too few have noticed that in part "Miller has addressed himself to the world beyond the senses", or, in Miller's words, "beyond the skin, to fate." For it is the informing, ritual-based actions of the play—an action as apparently futile as Willy's planting seeds in a sterile garden, the seemingly truncated tragic action of the entire play, and an action as obliquely brought to bear as the Requiem Mass—that Miller uses both to lay bare the lack of meaning in Willy's life and to suggest the possibility of meaning beyond that life.

Except for Willy's suicide, perhaps the action he performs that is at once most meaningless and yet most meaningful is his planting of the garden toward the end of the second act. Miller starts preparing us for this action early in the play when Willy focuses on what the urbanization of Brooklyn has done to his yard: "The grass doesn't grow any more, you can't raise a carrot in the back yard." Despite this fact, at the beginning of the second act, in a surge of hopefulness over both Biff's and his own possibilities, Willy says to Linda, "Gee, on the way home tonight I'd like to buy some seeds." Linda reiterates what Willy already knows— "Nothing'll grow any more"—but Willy is expansive, his mind already beyond the sterility of his backyard: "You wait, kid, before it's all over we're gonna get a little place out in the country, and I'll raise some vegetables, a couple of chickens." Even after Willy's expectations are more than not realized—even after Biff fails to get a loan from Oliver, Howard fires Willy, and, saddest of all, Willy's sons abandon him at Frank's Chop House—Willy is still thinking of planting a garden. After the waiter helps him off the restroom floor, Willy asks, "Is there a seed store in the neighborhood?" Here the seeds, which earlier represented Willy's hopes, come to his mind because of his failure, his despair: "Nothing's planted," he says: "I don't have a thing in the ground." When his sons return home, Willy, in an act confessing his failure, is planting his garden in the dark.

Besides an admission of failure, this act is yet another sign that Willy is breaking down. And the garden planting relates to the larger action of the play in other ways. For one thing it dramatizes the conflict between the pastoral values of the Loman family and the urban setting that, in boxing them in, seems to help to destroy them. The scene shows Willy asserting too late—and not willfully but compulsively—that possible true self who is good with his hands, who might have been a good farmer, who should have gone, perhaps, to Alaska to manage his brother's timberland in "those grand outdoors." Since the garden planting will be fruitless, the action also reminds us that the Lomans' lives have been fruitless in the sense that nothing has grown to maturity on Loman ground. Willy's failed sons are still boys, and Willy himself has remained a large kid. And, moreover, because the garden planting leads to nothing, it becomes an ironic commentary on the suicide Willy considers as he plants the garden. Still caught, even while acknowledging failure, in his need to succeed, Willy plots yet one more action that will bear fruit, prove his worth, and show that his life had meaning. But, as we shall see when we consider the final scene, Willy's suicide, like the garden he plants, does not bear fruit.

Besides being an action through which Willy unconsciously demonstrates, in small, the futility of his life, Willy's garden planting seems to be a ritual. As Chester E.

Eisinger suggests, Willy in this action "has recourse to sowing his garden, this ancient ritual by which man sustains himself, when all else has failed him." Or as Stuart B. James comments, Willy's "planting of the seeds is his fumbling attempt to reestablish some lost relationship with the earth, some rapport with an order of nature long lost to urban man." The ritualistic element of Willy's planting that these two writers respond to is an element I would like to emphasize. Indeed, I would like to go so far as to suggest that Miller may have had a specific ritual in mind when he wrote this scene—the ritual planting of gardens of Adonis.

In Death of a Salesman, it seems to me, Miller toys with both the myth of Adonis and a related ritual of planting gardens that are not meant to grow except briefly. In a scene in which Willy compares his sons to the "anemic" Bernard, he exclaims, "I thank Almighty God you're both built like Adonises." Adonis, the name of a beautiful male hero/god, is popularly a name for a handsome young man, the name one would use for a supposedly attractive young detective in Dick Tracy or the name one would use (in the 1980s) for a male strip show. Nevertheless, what is interesting about Willy's use of the word is that it brings to mind a myth that has parallels with the play.

Three different versions of the Adonis myth apply here. In one version, when Adonis was born—out of a mother who had earlier been transformed into a myrrh tree— Aphrodite fell so in love with the beautiful baby that she wanted to keep him for herself. She hid the baby in a chest, which she gave to Persephone in Hades, asking this goddess to conceal the chest for her. Persephone, however, opened the chest and she, too, fell in love with Adonis and refused to give him back to Aphrodite. Zeus (in a variant, Calliope) arbitrated the dispute by deciding that Adonis would spend part of the year with Aphrodite and the other part with Persephone in Hades. The second version of the Adonis myth holds that Aphrodite fell in love with Adonis when he was an adolescent. She warned him not to go hunting, but he disregarded her advice and met an untimely death when he was killed by a boar. The third version of the Adonis myth is an adaptation of the second. In this version Adonis returns each year to where his body is buried at the source of the river Adonis (in Syria), each year to be killed again and to turn the waters of the river red.

Three things are notable about these stories: The attractive Adonis is loved, through no effort of his own, by goddesses; he dies young; he is a dying-reviving god. If we examine the character of Biff, we see that there are striking, if not exact, similarities between him and Adonis. First, though not loved by goddesses, young, athletic Biff has easy success with girls. Happy proudly reports to his father, "There's a crowd of girls behind [Biff] every time the classes change." To an unheard statement from Biff, Willy responds, "That so? The girls pay for you?.. Boy, you must really be makin' a hit." It was Biff, moreover, who first introduced the philandering Happy to the "it-gets-like-bowling" pleasures of sex. The second way that Biff resembles Adonis is that he, too, in a way, dies young. For at eighteen he simply gives up his life. Having shown, as Willy sees it, godlike potential as a football player, Biff willfully fails to live up to it. After discovering Willy with The Woman, he dies, as Bernard describes it, a ritualistic death:

> And he came back after that month and took his sneakers remember those sneakers with " University of Virginia" printed on them? He was so proud of those, wore them every day. And he took them down in the cellar, and burned them up in the furnace. We had a fist fight. It lasted at least half an hour. Just the two of us, punching each other down the cellar, and crying right through it. I've often thought of how strange it was that I knew he'd given up his life.

The third similarity between Adonis and Biff is the most convincing. Having in a way died, Biff is somewhat like a dying-reviving god that comes and goes "with the springtime." As Biff explains to his brother, "And whenever spring comes to where I am, I suddenly get the feeling, my God, I'm not gettin' anywhere! That's when I come running home." Drawn by his sense of failure, Biff returns home each spring in a sacrifice of what seems his true self to his father's definition of success.

In addition to apparently adapting the myth of Adonis, Miller also echoes, in the garden planting scene, the related ritual of planting gardens of Adonis. Sir James George Frazer describes this ritual in The Golden Bough:

Perhaps the best proof that Adonis was a deity of vegetation.. is furnished by the gardens of Adonis, as they were called. These were baskets or pots filled with earth, in which wheat, barley, lettuces, fennel, and various kinds of flowers were sown and tended for eight days, chiefly or exclusively by women. Fostered by the sun's heat, the plants shot up rapidly, but having no root they withered as rapidly away, and at the end of eight days were carried out with the images of the dead Adonis, and flung with them into the sea.

Such " Adonis ceremonies," Frazer suggests, "were originally intended as charms to promote the growth or revival of vegetation; and the principle by which they were supposed to produce this effect was imitative magic." Willy in Death of a Salesman is doing his version of this or some similar ritual. He is trying to promote the growth and revival of his family. In a sense, he is trying to bring back to life his own Adonis, Biff. Willy's garden planting is one of a number of ritualistic actions that can be found in Miller's plays. In A View from the Bridge, a play Miller claims is based upon a story with a "myth like feeling," Eddie Carbone's death occurs within a "Pietà-like tableau" in which he dies in the arms of his wife to the accompaniment of "the dull prayers of the people and the keening of the women." In After the Fall, Quentin twice uses the gesture of spreading "his arms in crucifixion."

Clearly Miller is interested in employing gestures with recognizable ritual bases. And from a comment he made on Quentin's Christ-like gesture we learn that in part at least he sees such gestures as ironic. Miller has stated that Quentin is "quite aware," when he spreads his arms, that the gesture "is an archaic reconciliation." In other words the gesture is empty. As Miller says, "It doesn't work. [Quentin] doesn't believe in God. But he's going through what is at that moment the only available gesture which men could go through in order to climb above their suffering." If Quentin's gesture is effective, it is so only in undercutting him by suggesting a possible godliness he not only refuses to achieve but also cannot achieve. In contrast to Quentin's gesture Willy's garden planting is not as self conscious. But like Quentin Willy is, albeit mindlessly, imitating a possible "reconciliation" with experience that, if it were to work, would allow him to move beyond his suffering, his failure. But his gesture, like Quentin's, does not work. His garden planting will not regenerate the Loman family. Instead, his gesture, suggesting as it does large possibilities, ironically underscores Willy's sterile condition.

Miller's apparent use of mythic and ritualistic material associated with the dying-reviving god Adonis points to his modeling Death of a Salesman after Greek tragedy, a form that is itself based on ritual. When asked in 1965 "Which playwrights did you most admire when you were young?" Miller responded, "Well, first the Greeks, for their magnificent form.... That form has never left me; I suppose it just got burned in." And what probably "got burned in" along with the form is the notion that it was based on ritual.

When Miller writes, for example, that he "was told that the plays of Aeschylus must be read primarily on a religious level," he acknowledges familiarity with the theory proposed by Jane Harrison, Gilbert Murray, and Francis MacConald Cornford that the classical Greek tragedies, performed at the "April festival of Dionysus," were, though they contain many non-ritualistic elements, adapted from religious dances that enacted the death of the old-year spirit and the birth of the new-year spirit.

The Greek tragedy seems based in part on the following seven elements from the ritual: the chorus, once the band of dancers who performed the ritual dance; the agon, a struggle between Winter and Summer; the pathos, a death of Winter; the threnos, a lamentation for the dead spirit; the anagnorisis, the discovery and recognition of the new spirit; the peripeteia, a quick turn around in emotion from sorrow to joy; and the theophany, an appearance of the new spirit in all his glory. Harrison contends that "these ritual forms haunt and shadow" each Greek tragedy, "whatever its plot."

And for the most part these ritual elements, although greatly adapted and somewhat shuffled in order, give shape to Death of a Salesman. For example—to mention two of the elements—there is at least one major discovery: Willy's recognition of Biff's love (Biff's realization that both he and Willy have had the wrong dreams is not, as I shall soon suggest, a truly new recognition). A peripeteia occurs when Willy finally sees Biff's love for him and swings from despair to (though it will prove suicidal) joy: "That boy is going to be magnificent!" Adaptations of four other elements can be identified. Of the seven elements, however, one seems not to be in Death of a Salesman—the theophany.

Indeed, the play seems to end with the opposite of a theophany. Rather than showing us a new god or—what could be taken as an equivalent gesture—giving meaning to Willy's life, the play's final scene continues the debunking of Willy. In the first place, rather than clarifying Willy's life, the statements of the characters at Willy's graveside serve only to demonstrate that they are simply too confused by Willy's life to deal with it honestly and meaningfully. Happy, who had earlier disowned his father, oddly clings to the dream that has helped make him dissatisfied with life.

His claim that his father "did not die in vain," that he had had "the only dream you can have—to come out number-one man," suggests his life will be as meaningless as his father's. Charley's "A-salesman-is got-to-dream" speech has been called, perhaps because of its rhetorical power, "the only fitting epitaph" for Willy, but this speech, though showing Charley's sympathy for Willy, suggests, as does Happy's, that the meaninglessness of Willy's life was somehow heroic. And, moreover, the speech is cant; Charley is truer to himself and closer to being meaningful about Willy's life when, earlier in the play, he tells Willy to grow up.

Unlike Happy and Charley, Linda at least confesses her lack of understanding. Besides wanting to deny Willy's suicide—"It seems to me that you're just on another trip"—she confesses her perplexity—"I search and search and I search, and I can't understand it." Her repetition of her recognition that she and Willy have reached a meaningless freedom underscores her inability to make Willy's life make sense. She acknowledges what is also true of Happy and Charley; they are all incapable of seeing meaning in Willy's life.

Biff's role in the final scene is more complicated than those of the others. If any character seems to grow in Death of a Salesman, it is Biff. He seems to find himself during the play, and one critic [John V. Hagopian] has argued that, because he does so, he is, instead of Willy, the main character in the play. Nevertheless, if we examine his remarks carefully, we see that he does little to give either his father's or his own life meaning. In the first place Biff's statement that Willy "had all the wrong dreams," although showing clearer understanding than that of the other characters, deprives Willy's life and suicide of the meaning Willy wanted them to have. The statement also indicates Biff's refusal to make himself—and thus his father—meaningful as what his father would term a success. While Biff denies his father the meaning he wanted, other elements of Biff's stance—his confusion, his lack of true growth, and his continued reliance on what are essentially his father's terms to define himself— deprive even him of meaning. Biff's attempts to praise his father reveal both Biff's continuing moral stupidity and lack of insight.

When he says of Willy, "You know, Charley, there is more of him in that front stoop than in all the sales he ever made," he means to praise his father as having been capable with his hands. But Biff fails to recognize that his statement contains another truth that condemns Willy, for that stoop, made of stolen materials, is a small monument to Willy's lack of moral stature. Such confusion of mind seems typical of Biff. Earlier in the play he expresses his pastoral values in a way that undercuts them: "We should be mixing cement on some open plain." Biff's ability to make meaningful realizations is limited by such confusion. His seeming to have found who he is, is further undercut because his realization is not a new discovery. He actually rediscovers what he already knows—that, whistler in elevators that he is, for him the business world provides only "a measly manner of existence." More than this, Biff's calm assertion that "I know who I am" is an echo of his earlier furious statement, "Pop, I'm nothing! I'm nothing, Pop!" Put in these terms, Biff's view of himself does not so much show growth into a new vision of the world as it indicates a continued acceptance of the vision of the world that led Willy to say, when Biff tells of his failure with Oliver, "No, you're no good, you're no good for anything." Biff remains, though in a different way than Happy, too ready to see himself in his father's terms. Biff, then, at once deprives Willy of meaning and offers no clear alternative to the meaninglessness of Willy's life. Biff is not, in any clear way, a theophany, a character who, in contrast to Willy, takes on meaning.

Not only do the confused statements made at Willy's grave deprive him of meaning, but so also does the dearth of people present at his funeral. Willy's funeral was to have been his theophany, the event that would reconvert Biff into the worshipper he used to be. As Willy plants the garden, he imagines the success, the glory of his death:

> Ben, that funeral will be massive! They'll come from Maine, Massachusetts, Vermont, New Hampshire! All the old-timers with the strange license plates—that boy will be thunderstruck, Ben, because he never realized—I am known! Rhode Island, New York, New Jersey—I am known, Ben, and he'll see it with his eyes once and for all. He'll see what I am, Ben! He's in for a shock, that boy!

In the back of Willy's mind as he creates this fantasy is the funeral of Singleman, to which "hundreds of salesmen and buyers came." But the final scene shows that Willy's expected epiphany does not occur. Instead, only his family and the "only friend I got" attend. The scarcity of people reminds us of Willy's failure to be well-liked and, moreover, emphasizes the lack of familial feeling, on one hand, and the lack of communal feeling between the Lomans and the world, on the other. One critic (Orm Overland) suggests that the Requiem has a "chorus-like effect," but any suggestion that the characters grouped around the grave make up a chorus is ironic. Not only do these characters fail to speak together as one group that has arrived at an agreed-upon conclusion about the meaning of Willy's life, but, in failing even to understand each other, they also come near to failing to speak to one another. They are separate people, and the Lomans are no longer, if they ever were, a family. As Linda says, "There'll be nobody home."

And beyond this disintegrated family is a community they are only loosely connected with—the salesman who called Willy a "walrus," the math teacher whose lisp indirectly led to Biff's failure, the woman who reported Willy's earlier suicide attempt, the insurance investigators who must have suspicions about Willy's fatal "accident," and Howard Wagner, whose adoration for his own family does not extend, even in the form of sympathy, to the man who claimed to have named him. This last scene implies, then, a world of hollow, meaningless relations.

What becomes evident from the thoroughgoing way Miller deprives Willy of meaning in the final scene is that, though Miller provides no theophany, the ritualistic form that suggests the possibility of theophany is on his mind. And through the very name of the final scene—Requiem— Miller both shows that during this scene his mind is clearly on some kind of religious theophany and points up the lack of meaning in Willy's life. By titling the final scene Requiem, Miller calls to at least the reader's mind, if not that of an audience, the Catholic mass that once was said to call for the eternal rest of the dead. Miller is not arguing for Catholicism, but neither is his titling of the last scene casual.

His reference to this ritual brings to mind at least two types of theophany that neither Willy nor the characters at his grave seem to think possible. They do not look forward, as the celebrants of a Requiem mass would, to "the final identification of the Christian with Christ in His death and Resurrection and the beginning of the life of glory." Nor do they imagine a Dies Irae, the judgment of God's wrath. By calling the final scene Requiem, Miller acknowledges that his final scene is an ironic theophany and, moreover, points beyond the more obvious personal, familial, and social implications of the play to the lack of metaphysical meaning in Willy's life.

What we seem to have in Death of a Salesman, then, is a play that insists upon the meaninglessness of its main character and, we might extrapolate, of modern life in general. To use the words of Joseph Wood Krutch from a description of another character in modern drama, "Not only is" Willy's "failure utter, but it is trivial and meaningless as well" (Two Modern American Tragedies). Other critics have reached such grim conclusions about Willy's life and death. Stuart B. James writes that "One of the striking things about" the play "is the metaphysically dead sound it gives off.

All resonance of holiness is gone." Or as Brian Parker says, the play "offers almost no sure values." Miller himself has written about modern drama that "we have abstracted from the Greek drama its air of doom, its physical destruction of the hero, but its victory escapes us." Though meant to describe the work of other dramatists, his comment seems to apply to Death of a Salesman. At least the victory of tragedy surely escapes Willy. And to the extent Miller uses his adaptation of the ritualistic form of tragedy to suggest the possibility of victory, he suggests that possibility, in terms of Willy, only to underscore Willy's meaningless defeat.

This is all fairly bleak, to say the least: Willy Loman is a pathetic man caught in a tragic form that undercuts any pretensions he might have of meaning. But one must wonder, at this point, if one has understood the play fully, for Miller insists that the play is not pessimistic. In his introduction to the Collected Plays he remembers his surprise at the effect the play had on audiences: "In the writing of Death of a Salesman I tried, of course, to achieve a maximum power of effect. But when I saw the devastating force with which it struck its audiences, something within me was shocked and put off. I had thought myself as rather an optimistic man."

And Miller seems to think of Death of a Salesman and tragedy in general as somehow optimistic. In "Tragedy and the Common Man" he argues that it is "a misconception" to hold "that tragedy is of necessity allied to pessimism" but that it is more correct to hold that "tragedy implies more optimism in its author than does comedy" because the "final result" of tragedy "ought to be the reinforcement of the brightest opinions of the human animal." The writer of tragedy, Miller suggests, believes "in the perfectibility of man" or, as he suggests in another essay on tragedy, in man's capability of "flowering on this earth."

The answer is that it is the same thing that Miller uses to undercut the meaningfulness of Willy—the action, the form. If we return, for example, to the garden planting ritual, we see that the ritualistic gesture does more than help us focus on Willy's fruitlessness. It also has, even for Willy, some efficacy. It allows him to acknowledge his own failures—that nothing is planted, that his will has been limited, that his life has not been shaped by himself—while also celebrating, through imitation, the possibility of will, the possibility that, even though he has failed, life can be shaped. Or, put another way, behind the futility of Willy's action is the assertion that, despite everything, life is worth living (and, we might add, even worth dying for). Similarly, the ironic reference to Requiem masses, while clearly not meant as a suggestion that the audience adapt this particular ritualistic response to the world, reminds us that forms exist that, no matter what our belief in them, embody the possibility of making sense, even metaphysical sense, of life. We are given in both the garden ritual and the Requiem forms that at least suggest the "possibility of some kind of reconciliation with existence."

Another such form is tragedy In The Idea of a Theater, Frances Fergusson points to Sophocles' Oedipus—along with Shakespeare's Hamlet, and, though it is not drama, Dante's Divine Comedy—as one of those "cultural landmarks in which the idea of a theater has been briefly realized." Of Oedipus Fergusson writes that its first audience went to it with "ritual expectancy" and that, "when one considers the ritual form of the whole play, it becomes evident that it presents the tragic but perennial, even normal, quest of the whole City for its well-being." Like Fergusson, Miller wishes for such a "realized" theater and views as his model for such theater the form of Greek tragedy. In " Shadows of the Gods," for example, while calling for improvements in modern theater, Miller comments,

"I am not asking for something new, but something as old as Greek drama." Miller values this form because for him it suggests, first, the possibility—though only the possibility—of a metaphysical explanation of the world, second, a unified sense of community, and third, in its ritualistic form the kind of action that allows one to explore, if nothing more, the possibility of coming to terms with both metaphysical and communal problems.

As already suggested, in Miller's mind Greek tragedy is closely related to religion. He approved of the ill-fated Group Theater because it promised to be "a prophetic theater which suggested the Greek situation when religion and belief were the heart of drama." He has pointed out that in his opinion "a Greek could [not] have discussed" tragedy "without the idea in the back of his head of God. It would have been of the first order of importance because what it is, is the relation not of man to man, but of man to God." He suggests that, "if we're going to talk of tragedy at all, we've got to find some equivalent to that superhuman schema that had its names in the past, whatever they were." And he relates his reading of Greek tragedy to his own sense of quasi metaphysical order. He explains that as a student he did not understand why the dramas of Aeschylus could only be lay drama to the modern mind because to him "one did not have to be religious to see in our own disaster the black outlines of a fate that was not human, nor of the heavens either, but something in between."

Miller appreciates not only the religious thrust of Greek tragedy but also the related social, communal thrust. He writes that Greek drama "was religious for [the Greeks] in a more than mystical way. Religion is the only way we have any more of expressing our genuinely social feelings and concerns, for in our bones we as a people do not otherwise believe in our oneness with a larger group. But the religiousness of Greek drama.. was more worldly; it expressed a social concern, to be sure, but it did so on the part of the people already unified on earth rather than the drive of a single individual toward personal salvation." Greek tragedy expressed its social concern in part by showing "man confronting his society, the illusions of his society, the faiths of society." But while questioning society, Greek tragedy, as Miller sees it, asserted the underlying rightness of social community: "In Greece the tragic victory consisted in demonstrating that the polis—the whole people—had discovered some aspect of the Grand Design which also was the right way to live together."

Miller's comments on tragedy suggest that in his mind what allowed Greek tragedy to be a form of metaphysical questing and communal assertion was its ritual basis. He calls Greek drama "a kind of universal mass statement of prayer." It was a ritual enactment that would shed light on the metaphysical order. "The tragic hero," Miller says, "was supposed to join the scheme of things by his sacrifice.... He threw some sharper light upon the hidden scheme of existence, either by breaking one of its profoundest laws.. or by proving a moral world at the cost of his own life." Tragedy, Miller states, "has to do with the community sacrificing some man whom they both adore and despise in order to reach its basic and fundamental laws, and, therefore, justify its existence." Greek tragedy, in other words, was a ritualistic gesture that helped accomplish a "reconciliation with existence."

Miller expresses considerable faith in the form he chooses. He writes in "The Family and Modern Drama" that "there lies within the dramatic form the ultimate possibility of raising the truth-consciousness of mankind to a level of such intensity as to transform those who observe it." But I would not maintain that Miller's use of tragic form in Death of a Salesman means that he accomplishes such a transformation. Far from it. At best, Miller's audience may be somewhat enlightened because, as Miller suggests, "by showing what happens where there are no values, I, at least, assume that the audience will be compelled and propelled towards a more intense quest for values that are missing." What Miller admits here is that his play does not discover these missing values; nor does it accomplish a "reconciliation with existence." Nevertheless Miller's use of tragic form allows him not only "to demonstrate the inevitability of [the] defeat and death" of the meaningless Willy Loman but also "to organize life" with a form that has for him at least the possibility of helping us to come to terms with existence. The play is shaped by a ritualistic form that implies the possibility of grasping a unifying sense— and meaningful sense—of the world. The optimism of Death of a Salesman, tentative though it is, lies in a form that entertains, embodies, keeps alive, a possible way of finding and asserting the answers the play fails to find.

In his introduction to the Collected Plays Miller notes that Death of a Salesman "made only a fair impression in London." But he then proudly adds, but in the area of the Norwegian Arctic Circle fishermen whose only contact with civilization was the radio and the occasional visit of the government boat insisted on seeing it night after night—the same few people—believing it to be some kind of religious rite. And well might they have such a belief, for Miller's play is both a dramatization of the meaninglessness possible in a modern life and a restrained celebration, through the imitation of a ritualistic form, of the possibility that man might still find the "reward" of meaning.

Death of a Salesman: In Memoriam

For all its contemporary relevance, All My Sons was essentially a product of the 1930s. Its emphasis on human brotherhood, its thematic innocence and dramatic simplicities have rather more to do with the moral certainties and confident principles of prewar and wartime America than the anxieties and existential dilemmas of the late 1940s and 1950s—a world of increasing material prosperity but of growing domestic and foreign paranoia. The success of Communism abroad and fear of its subversive policies at home destabilised the political consensus and implicitly initiated a debate about those very American qualities and values, which were presumably at stake. And, with the collapse of a consensus created originally by the economic necessities of the 1930s and the political requirements of war, individuals and groups felt themselves increasingly alienated. The assault on New Deal liberals, the barely concealed anti-Semitism of many of the attacks on supposed subversives, the distrust of intellectuals (associated in the minds of HUAC investigators, right wing politicians and a number of industrialists, with a betrayal of American values) created a condition in which a writer like Miller was bound to find himself increasingly at odds with the model of America which that implied. The first evidence for this, apart from his novel, was Death of a Salesman, which placed the whole question of American values at the centre of his attention. And subsequently came The Crucible, which challenged head-on the corrupting influence of those who would enforce their own model of national purpose and personal morality on others. All My Sons ran for 328 performances.

The New York Drama Critics passed over O'Neill's The Iceman Cometh and awarded it their Circle Award. The movie rights were purchased by Hollywood, the film starring Burt Lancaster and Edward G. Robinson. Offered the opportunity to write the screenplay, Miller declined, choosing instead to begin work on a play which he called Plenty Good Times which was to be a "love story of working people in an industrial city." When this began to lead nowhere he turned to another project which eventually emerged as his most famous play—a classic of the American theater— Death of a Salesman. As he has explained, after All My Sons he wanted to do a lyrical piece, because most of the plays I'd written were not of that kind. So that Death of a Salesman was a more romantic, even nostalgic piece, apart from its social analysis, than I'd ever done on the stage, although it is nostalgia with some irony. It's an attempt to remake the West.. in the middle of office buildings. But the feeling, the emotions of nostalgia, of simplicity, are very strong in that play

The origins of Miller's best-known play lie in a brief short story which he wrote at the age of seventeen and which his mother rediscovered at the time of its first production. Called "In Memoriam," it is based on Miller's own experience with a Jewish salesman when he was working for his father for a few months after graduating from high school. The story is concerned with a single day during which the young narrator accompanies the salesman, carrying some of his samples for him (in this case, coats). The man is old and tired and has to humble himself by asking his young companion for the car fare. The salesman sells nothing and is mistreated by the buyers. The story ends with his reported death and the narrator's sentimental response. In fact, Miller observes in a note scrawled on the manuscript, the man had thrown himself in front of a subway train. Clearly the experience and the story do contain the seeds of the later play. As the narrator observes of the old man:

His was a salesmans profession, if one may call such dignified slavery a profession, and he tried to interest himself in his work. But he never became entirely moulded into the pot of that business. His emotions were displayed at the wrong times always and he never quite knew when to laugh. Perhaps if I may say so he never was complete. He had lost something vital. There was an air of quiet solitude, of cryptic wondering about both he and his name.

He is described as looking out of place in clothes which seemed to have been chosen by someone else and with a name which seemed not wholly to belong to him. "His last name was Schoenzeit, the first I never learned, but it had to be Alfred. He always seemed to need that name." His growing desperation is apparent in his whole manner. "I knew that he felt as though his life was ended, that he was merely being pushed by outside forces. And though his body went on as before his soul inside had crumpled and broken beyond repair." However, it is instructive to note the differences. Unlike the salesman Wiliy was to be located firmly in the context of his family life while Miller was concerned to project his illusions and frustrations onto a national level. He became both a vital character and a patent symbol. And unlike the protagonist of the short story Willy was not Jewish. Indeed, Mary McCarthy was later to attack the play as a story about Jewish characters in which their Jewish identities had been suppressed. Miller has denied this, pointing out that when the touring company, quite coincidentally, was found to consist entirely of Irish actors, including Mary McCarthy's brother, it was greeted by two Boston newspapers as an Irish drama.

Death of a Salesman—the story of an ageing salesman,

baffled by a lifetime of failure in a society which apparently values only success—has proved one of the most powerful and affecting plays in American theatrical history. The confusions and dreams of a single individual on the verge of psychological collapse were made to embody the collapse of national myths of personal transformation and social possibility. Miller's achievement lay in his ability to distil in the person of Willy Loman the anxieties of a culture which had exchanged an existential world of physical and moral possibility for the determinisms of modern commercial and industrial life—the country for the city. The dislocations of Willy's private life—discontinuities which open up spaces in familial relationships no less than in memory and experience—are equally those of a society chasing the chimera of material success as a substitute for spiritual fulfillment.

All the characters in the play feel a need which they can articulate only in terms of the rhetoric of a society which has itself lost touch with its youthful ideals. Aware of a profound sense of insufficiency they seek to remedy or at least to neutralize it in the public world of consumerism and status. For the most part they are blind to the consolation and even transcendence available through personal relationships. The love which they feel for one another is real enough. To some degree it shapes their actions and determines their desperate strategies, which are none the less real for their failure to be realized. But it fails to hold them back from the fate in which they willfully conspire. And this is the basis of the irony which slowly erodes their confidence and their hopes.

And yet the play's success in virtually all societies in the four decades following its first performance shows that it is something more than a dramatization of the American dream, its corruptions and coercions. Willy proved an international figure, as appealing and recognizable to a Chinese audience in 1983 as it had been to an American one in 1949. Willy's dreams are too recognizable, his blindness to the reality and necessity of a proffered love too familiar, for his plight not to demand the attention for which his wife calls. Like most plays it perhaps has its flaws but the human reality of Willy Loman is such that few works have provoked the shock of recognition which has greeted and continues to greet Willy's anguished debate with himself and with the world in which he has never felt at home.

Willy betrays himself and others. Desperate to sustain his self-esteem he has an affair with another woman, buying her attention with a gift of stockings while his wife sits at home mending her own. And when his son, Biff, catches them together he believes that the moment of disillusionment links them together in a more profound way than had the love which he felt but which he could never adequately express. Biff's "failure" thus becomes a living reproach which fuses love and guilt together in such a way as to threaten the spontaneity and integrity of his responses. Increasingly anxious to justify his life and expiate what he sees as his responsibility for his son's willful self-annihilation, he plans a suicide which will create the fortune that his life could never accumulate.

The proceeds of his insurance policy will thus stand as a justification of his dreams while offering some kind of belated restitution to the wife and son he had betrayed. Desperate for love they are to be offered cash. The irony of Willy's life is that he has accepted other people's estimations of his value. He has the power to construct himself as he has the skill to fashion wood but he cannot bring himself to believe in the worth of a sensibility so constructed and a life forged out of nothing more substantial than an honest perception of the real. The play is Miller's requiem for a country which, no less than Willy, had all the wrong dreams as it is a gesture of absolution towards those who allow themselves to be too fully known. Though in a sense it is a story of defeat, its very lyricism implies the persistence of other possibilities and of a relationship with language, experience and the physical world which goes beyond the terrible banality and threatening pragmatism of a dream tainted at source.

Willy is a kind of Everyman. Miller may have taken care to root him in a specific social and historical world but that specificity is raised to another level by the authenticity with which he reproduces the tangled emotions and diffuse longings of those who translate into the language of national myth what has its origin in more fundamental necessities. Willy Loman lives and dies in an attempt to sustain a sense of personal dignity and meaning. Yet if that is a struggle which has its correlative in terms of American notions of self-fulfillment and social status it is equally a battle waged by everyone who tries to locate a sense of significant purpose in a life which seems to consist of little more than a series of contingent events. And if that in turn seems in some final sense a losing game then a certain dignity is perhaps to be derived from the courage with which it is conducted and the poetry which can on occasion be forged out of the prose of experience.

Death of a Salesman is built around the relationship between Willy and his son, Biff. In his notebook Miller wrote himself a memo: "Discover. The link between Biff's work views and his anti W feelings. How it happens that W's life is in Biff's hands—aside from Biff succeeding. There is W's guilt to Biff in re: The Woman. There is Biff's disdain for W's character, his false aims, his fictions, and these Biff cannot finally give up or alter." Here, as elsewhere in Miller's work, the relationship between father and son is a crucial one because it focusses the question of inherited values and assumptions, it dramatises deferred hopes and ideals, it becomes a microcosm of the debate between the generations, of the shift from a world still rooted in a simpler rural past to one in which that past exists simply as myth.

It highlights the contrast between youthful aspirations and subsequent compromises and frustrations. It presents the submerged psychological tension which complicates the clear line of social action and personal morality. The family, so much an icon of American mythology, becomes the appropriate prism through which to view that mythology. The son's identity depends on creating a boundary between himself and his father, on perceiving himself outside the axial lines which had defined the father's world.

Biff and Willy's relationship is bedeviled by guilt. Willy feels guilty because he feels responsible for Biff's failure. Having discovered Willy with a woman in a Boston hotel room, he had refused to retake a mathematics examination, thereby abandoning his chance of reaching university and his access to a better career. But Biff equally feels guilty because he recognizes a responsibility which he cannot fulfill, the responsibility to redeem Willy's empty life. In a telling speech, included in the notebook but excluded from the published and performed versions, Biff outlines his feelings explicitly.

> Willy—see?—I love you Willy. I've met ten or twelve Willy's and you're only one of them.—I don't care what you do. I don't care if you live or die. You think I'm mad at you because of the Woman, don't you. I am, but I'm madder because you bitched up my life, because I can't tear you out of my heart, because I keep trying to make good, do something for you, to succeed for you.

If Biff loves Willy, he also plainly hates him. Like the other characters he is composed of contradictions. Indeed, in his notes, Miller saw the conflict in Biff between his hatred for Willy and his own desire for success in New York as crucial to an understanding of the play as he did "the combination of guilt (of failure), hate, and love—all in conflict" that Willy hopes to resolve "by 'accomplishing' a 20,000 dollar death." Indeed, the ironies of the play flow out of contradiction in Death of a Salesman, much as they do in another sense in Waiting for Godot. Action is immediately aborted, assertions withdrawn, hopes negated. Thus Willy complains of Biff that "the trouble is he's lazy." only to reverse himself a few seconds later. "There's one thing about Biff—he's not lazy."

Happy asserts that money holds no interest for him and that he would be happy with a free life in the West, only to ask immediately, "The only thing is—what can you make out there?" The response to Biff's "Let's go" is the same as that proffered in Waiting for Godot. They do not move. And so Happy regards himself as an idealist while taking 100-dollar bribes, Biff as rejecting a material life while stealing from his employer. For Willy, constant contradiction is a linguistic reflection of the collapse of rational control, but, more fundamentally, for all the Loman men it is indicative of a basic contradiction between their aspirations and the reality of their lives, between their setting and the essence of their dreams. They are denied peace because the philosophy on which they have built their lives involves competition, a restless pursuit of success, a desire to register a material achievement which they can conceive only in financial terms because they have neither the language nor the capacity to assess its significance in any other way. Hence Biff, who tries to retrace the steps of his father into the past and the West, is unable to accept a simple sense of harmony with his surroundings as adequate to the definition of success which his father has instilled in him, though that harmony is precisely what his father longs to achieve. As Biff explains to his brother,

This farm I work on, it's spring there now, see? And they've got about fifteen new colts. There's nothing more inspiring or—beautiful than the sight of a mare and a new colt. And it's cool there now, see? Texas is cool now and it's spring. And whenever spring comes to where I am, I suddenly get the feeling, my God, I'm not getting anywhere! What the hell am I doing, playing around with horses, twenty-eight dollars a week! I'm thirty-five years old, I oughta be makin' my fortune. That's when I come running home. And now, I got here, and I don't know what to do with myself.

And so the lyricism, which is a powerful and crucial dimension of the play, defers to materialism, to a pragmatism which disrupts an incipient harmony and opens up a gap between Biff and his setting which, once closed, would not only offer him a simpler relationship between himself and the natural world but also still the conflict between his sensibility and his actions. He is, however, held back not only by the surviving dream of material success, a dream which he might be able to abandon, but also by the guilt which he feels towards Willy. He continues to feel responsible to a man who has warped his life but to whom his fate is ineluctably joined. In Miller's earliest draft the point is even more explicit:

WILLY: What do you want to be?

BIFF: I want just to settle down and be somebody! Just a guy working in a store, or digging earth, or anything..

WILLY: Then do it, do it.

BIFF: You won't let me do it.

WILLY: Me? When did I control you?

BIFF: You do control me. I've stood in the most beautiful scenery in the world and cried in misery. I've galloped elegant horses and suddenly wanted to kill myself because I was letting you down. I want you to let me go, you understand. I want you to stop dreaming big dreams about me, and expecting anything great of me. I'm manual labour, Pop; one way or the other I'm a tramp, that's all. Can you make your peace with that? I ask one thing. I want to be happy.

WILLY: To enjoy yourself is not ambition. A tramp has that. Ambition is things. A man must want things, things.

In the final version these perceptions no longer need to surface in language. Biff and Willy remain bewildered for most of the play, unable to analyse the pressures at work on them, unable in particular to confess to the guilt, the love and the hate that connect and divide them. Willy's concern with things, meanwhile, is evident in his fascination with his refrigerator and his car but, most significantly, in his acquiescence in his own reduction to inanimate article to be marketed on appearance and image.

In his first stage direction Miller insists on Willy's "massive dreams and little cruelties," but in truth the play is concerned with suggesting that the adjectives might be legitimately reversed. And Biff, like his father, is still trying to buy love. As Miller wrote of the scene in the restaurant in which Biff and Happy abandon their father, "Biff left out of guilt, pity, an inability to offer himself to W." He recognizes that Willy's desire that he should succeed is, in part at least, evidence of his love and, as Miller reminded himself, Biff "still wants that evidence of W's love. Still does not want to be abandoned by him." However, it is a love which threatens to destroy him, since it expresses itself in a desire on Willy's part to bequeath his son the thing he values most of all—his dream. The drama of the play emerges from the fact that Biff now gradually recognizes the necessity for his abandonment. Indeed he has returned home with an intention not that remote from that of Chris Keller or Gregers Werle. "He has returned home," Miller insists in his notes, "resolved to disillusion W forever, to set him upon a new path, and thus release himself from responsibility for W and what he knows is going to happen to him—or half fears will." There is the same passion for truth which springs from guilt and self-interest as had characterized the protagonists of All My Sons and The Wild Duck. But now Miller seems to recognize the necessity for this break with illusion. For here, it is finally not truth which kills, as it had been in All My Sons; it is a continued commitment to illusion. Biff breaks free; Willy does not. In his own eyes his death accomplishes the success that had evaded him in life, and, more importantly, it finally purges him of the guilt that he has felt for what he takes to be his son's failure. Since Biff had abandoned his potential career after finding Willy with another woman, Willy had thereafter felt responsible for his son's failure. And this is the principal tension of the play. In order for Biff to survive he has to release himself from his father and the values which he promulgates; in order for Willy to survive he has to cling to Biff and the conviction that material success is still possible.

Thus guilt becomes the principal mechanism of human relationships. As Miller notes, "Biff's conflict is that to tell the truth would be to diminish himself in his own eyes. To admit his fault. His confusion, then, is not didactic, or restricted to Willy's elucidation of salvation, but towards a surgical break which, he knows in his heart, W could never accept. His motive, then, is to destroy W, free himself." In the final version it is not so clear. He is intent to save Willy's life as well as his own. His motivation is less obvious, his concern for his father largely genuine. And yet, of course, in saving Willy he will be freeing himself, so that the self apparently lies behind all actions. This was certainly to be the conclusion that Miller reached in After the Fall, but here that conclusion is masked by a social drama. For the fault does not only lie in the individual; it also patently lies in self-interest systematized into capitalism. Willy Loman is thrown on the scrap heap by his employer after thirty-six years, and, though Miller has objected that in the persons of his next-door neighbors, Charley and

Bernard, he has created two characters who retain their humanity, it is Charley who advises Willy that human concerns can play no role in business. When Willy objects that he had actually selected his employer's first name when he was born, Charley replies, "when you gonna realise that them things don't mean anything? You named him Howard, but you can't sell that. The only thing you got in this world is what you can sell. And the funny thing is that you're a salesman and you don't know that." It is Charley who boasts that his son's success had been a consequence of his own lack of concern, announcing that "my salvation is that I never took an interest in anything." And, though his own compassionate treatment of Willy would seem at odds with this, the system of which he is the most admirable representative can clearly accommodate itself to individual acts of charity provided that these don't threaten its structure.

The fact is that Charley underwrites the system that destroys Willy. Bernard, a successful lawyer, makes too brief an appearance to know whether his affability towards Willy goes any deeper than appearance. His success is certainly a consequence of hard work but the question of the human value of that success, central to the play's theme, goes largely unexamined. After all, elsewhere in the play Miller seems to be posing the question as to whether material success bears any relationship to basic human needs, but in the person of Bernard he seems to suggest the possibility of having one's cake and eating it.

Biff and Willy feel a profound if unfocussed sense of dissatisfaction with their lives. Beneath the monotony of daily survival is a yearning spirit, a perception of some kind of spiritual need which they can only express through material correlatives or through stuttering encomiums to beauty or belonging. One of the problems of the play, indeed, derives from the fact that their lack of success actually confuses spiritual with financial failure. The more significant question is whether material success would have blunted or indeed even satisfied that need and, though this might have brought Miller perilously close to cliché, his portrait of Bernard—moral, hard-working, successful, attractive—is perhaps in danger of validating the dreams which Willy had had for Biff. Willy had, admittedly, regarded such success as an inevitable product of life in America and had taught Biff to take what he could not earn, and yet in some way the adequacy of that success is not challenged in Bernard's case. Indeed, he seems to represent the apparently untroubled serenity which is the reward of honest toil. Indeed, it was not until After the Fall that he chose to question the adequacy of that portrait, taking as his protagonist a lawyer whose success, like that of Bernard, is marked by his appealing a case before the Supreme Court. Then he was to query the value of success even when it is the product of effort and application. Uncle Ben might be a portrait of a Horatio Alger figure, stumbling over wealth, but Bernard is in many ways an idealised figure. The danger is that he is not only a model for Willy of what his sons might have become; he also becomes a model for Miller.

The dice are loaded against Willy. In the original notes he was literally to have been a little man. Miller chose to transform that into an obesity apparent in the text but ignored when Lee J. Cobb was cast for the central role: "I'm fat. I'm very—foolish to look at, Linda.. as I was going in to see the buyer I heard him say something about—walrus. And I—I cracked him right across the face." Even allowing for the exaggeration of self-pity, this offers a clue to his failure as a salesman. His misfortune was that he chose a career in which appearance was everything, at a time and in a country in which appearance was primary. As Biff was to have said in an early draft, and as is apparent but not voiced in precisely these words in the final version, "The pity of it is, that he was happy only on certain Sundays, with a warm sun on his back, and a trowel in his hand, some good wet cement, and something to build. That's who he really was." As a salesman he has always to dissemble, to smile, to put up a front. He is an actor who has increasingly lost his audience. His life is a falsehood. But perhaps there is a certain naivety in the assumption, no less Miller's than that of one of his characters, Charley, that the situation is fundamentally different for others, for his contrast of the life of the salesman with that of a man who can "tell you the law" seems to be justified by the character of Bernard. The real force of the play suggests otherwise. For Miller implies that Willy had the wrong dreams, not simply that his methods of fulfilling those dreams were wrong. With Eugene O'Neill he seems to suggest that Willy's mistake was to imagine that he could gain possession of his soul through gaining possession of the world. In that respect he was paradigmatic. Charley and Bernard are successful and humane, but they, too, live a life whose intimacies seem lacking. Where is the love between them? The problem is that the light is never swung in their direction and thus it is possible to see in them a vindication of the material success which they represent.

Biff's anger at his father derives partly from Willy's weakness and helplessness, partly from his bitterness, but partly also from his love for him, a love which won't cut Biff loose from his own sense of guilt. To absolve his father would be to admit to his own weakness and culpability. As Miller wrote in his notebook,

> Biff's conflict is that to tell the truth would be to diminish himself in his own eyes. To admit to his own fault. The truth is that though W did overbuild B's ego, and then betrayed him, Biff feels guilt in his vengeance on W knowing that he also is incompetent. Through this confession of his having used W's betrayal, W sees his basic love, and is resolved to suicide.

Again the final version of the play deflects this confession into action, intensifying the force by refraining from discharging its energy through words. Thus Biff, having denounced his father and admitted to his own inability to command more than a dollar an hour, breaks down in tears, "holding on to Willy, who dumbly fumbles for Biff's face." And love, which Miller has said was in a race for Willy's soul, becomes the very mechanism which pulls Willy towards his death. Thus Linda, whose love for Willy has revealed itself in an encouragement of his dreams combined with a practical capacity which has enabled him to sustain his illusions in the face of reality, proves finally to be deadly. Her actions are motivated by a compassionate concern but there is a clear connection between her refusal to challenge those illusions and his death. Nor is she free of responsibility for the warped values of her children. She is simply too passive a force. Her culpability lies in her acquiescence, which is simultaneously an expression of her love. In her own way she is as obsessive as Willy. She has reduced her own life to a single focus—Willy. And so she tells Biff to leave home and completely ignores Happy's announcement of his impending marriage. Doubtless she recognises it for the self deceiving gesture which it is, but she seems to feel no obligation towards her sons. Though she is never swept up in Willy's dreams she refuses to judge them. Her almost complete failure to understand Willy, as opposed to sympathise with and admire him, is thus finally a sign of the inadequacy of that love. It is not strong enough to make demands, to wrestle Willy away from his illusions.

Once to have been called " The Inside of His Head," Death of a Salesman is a memory play. The past we see is as it is recalled by Willy Loman, as he tries to track down the moment when things began to go wrong. And not the least of Miller's achievements lay in the originality of the staging through which he created a theatrical correlative for Willy's tortured mind. The action had to move easily between past and present. The realistic texture of Willy's environment was crucial but so were the distortions created by his memory, the fragments of the past through which he sorted with increasing desperation. The result was a blend of realism and expressionism which dramatised personal psychology in the context of social change.

In a sense the environment—the trees and open spaces of the real or remembered past, the oppressive constrictions of an urban environment—is a principal character in the play and a primary achievement of Miller, his director Elia Kazan, and his designer Jo Mielziner.Instantaneous shifts of scene were achieved through the ingenuity of Mielziner who, in one scene, contrived a small elevator to enable the actors playing Biff and Happy to move directly from a bedroom in the "past" to a kitchen in the present. Writing in the introduction to his Collected Plays Miller has confessed to standing "squarely in conventional realism," but has equally insisted that where necessary he has "tried to expand it with an imposition of various forms in order to speak more directly, even more abruptly and nakedly of what has moved me behind the visible facades of life." The experiments are perhaps seldom radical since until later in his career he was too concerned with establishing the social context and implications of his plays to stray too far from a form which gives physical expression to the wider world. He is fully aware that the innovative power of realism has long since been blunted but he has always been drawn to find some way to relate the private anguish of his characters to the environment which presses upon them and which in part they themselves shape and deform. His resistance to the total determinism of naturalism, however, is in a sense symbolised by his reaction against the totally realistic set and it would not be unreasonable to see the incomplete walls and insubstantial props as evidence of his belief in change and even transcendence.

In Death of a Salesman the production style was necessitated by the need to create a "continuous present." In allowing past and present to collapse towards one another Miller was able to trace causalities and hence identify the possibility of change. However, it was also necessitated by his desire to represent the psychological state of a man whose inner and outer life are in a state of collapse, and it was precisely the fact of Willy's disintegrating mind, of his literal inability to sustain temporal or spatial boundaries, which suggests a pathological state apparently inimical to the tragic status claimed for the play and at odds with a reading that would make it simply a critique of American values.

Eric Bentley even suggested that insofar as it is a tragedy this potentially destroys the social play as the social play destroys the tragedy, Willy being either the victim of his own flawed character or of society, but scarcely both. Such a stance, however, seems to ignore the degree to which tragedy seldom if ever acknowledges an impermeable membrane between the self and its setting, projecting psychological disruptions outwards into the social world and vice versa. However, talk of tragedy was ill-advised. Willy never really shows any evidence of self-knowledge or awareness of the reality of the situation in which he is involved. His dreams, described by Miller as massive, are in reality petty and sustained by sacrificing not only himself but those around him. In fact it is Biff, and not Willy, who provides the moral, though scarcely the theatrical, focus of the play.

He does acquire self-knowledge and develops as a character through understanding the mechanism by which he has suffered and of which he has been a primary agent. As I have argued elsewhere, so long as Biff and Happy are regarded as expressions of Willy's own mind—the one representing a vaguely perceived spiritual need, the other a sexual and material drive—such a split between the dramatic and moral focus is insignificant. Once granted genuine autonomy, however, Biff's moral development merely underlines Willy's inappropriateness as a tragic hero. This is not a weakness in the play, however, but simply an indication that it is not best approached by trying to force it into a category of merely pedagogic significance.

Willy Loman's life is rooted in America's past. His earliest memory was of sitting under a wagon in South Dakota. His father had made and is left without meaning or direction when he can no longer smile, when he no longer commands respect or recognition. He survives but without a sense of himself. His sons are his only chance to succeed by proxy, the only mark he has left on a world resistant to his charm and his human needs alike. But there is an ambiguity to the play's conclusion. Biff has acquired a crucial insight into himself. Presumably the striving is over, and he can now accept that simple harmony with the natural world which had always foundered on his persistent need for a material success which would appease his father and free him from his guilt. Certainly, that is the only real value, which has been identified—a lyricism strongly contrasted with the diminished world of urban America. He can return west to the one place where he was really happy. The problem is that on the one hand his flight to the west had originally also been a flight from responsibility, and on the other it is an a historical move. Like Huck Finn at the end of Twain's novel, he is lighting out for the territory ahead of the rest. But the rest will inevitably follow, and Miller admitted as much a few years later when, in The Misfits, the beautiful mare and its colt are rounded up by trucks and turned into dog food. Biff Loman has become Gay, an ageing cowboy as bewildered by the collapse of his world as Willy Loman had been.

And so Biff, who at the end of Death of a Salesman has supposedly learned the lesson which Willy could not, seems to be committed to the old mistake of seeking in movement and in space what he should perhaps have sought in relationship. Indeed, when Miller returned to the stage in 1964, after a nine-year silence, it was with a play in which grace is the reward of suffering, and meaning the result of a love constantly renewed in the face of acknowledged imperfection. Like Steinbeck in The Grapes of Wrath he ends with a piety whose emotional force is undeniable but whose social utility is more problematic because he can conceive of no mechanism whereby Biff's moment of epiphany can be translated into social action. And that equivocation hangs suspended in the air, inhibiting the sense of completion towards which the play has seemed to move and projecting forward into all our futures a dilemma not so easily resolved by a moment of insight, by a seemingly purposeful action or by an articulate statement of intent. History has moved on and Miller's characters in Death of a Salesman seem close kin finally to Scott Fitzgerald 's in The Great Gatsby.

Corrupted by dreams, which simultaneously denied them access to the potential redemption of human connectiveness, they had reached out for some substitute for the meaning which continued to elude them. They sought it mostly in an endlessly deferred future, a green light which beckoned them on towards a mythical world of romance and affluence. But at the end of the novel the narrator tries to find it in the past, a rural world where the dream was first born and where the corruption first started. Biff does much the same here, for the world of rural simplicity to which he will now presumably return had provided the context for his grandfather's desertion of Willy. It was also where Uncle Ben began his mythic climb to wealth and power, having abandoned his search for his lost father. The frontier bred the disease. And if it also represents a natural world of pure process then even that is under pressure. Like the land surrounding the Loman home it will presumably itself one day make way for the city and its cruelties. And so Biff, like Nick Carraway, seems poised for a deeply ambiguous and even ironic journey. So that if Willy, like Gatsby, believed in the green light, "the orgastic future that year by year recedes before us," a future which "eluded us then, but that's no matter—tomorrow we will run faster, stretch out our arms further And one fine morning," he and Biff alike are also, perhaps, no more nor less than "boats against the current, borne back ceaselessly into the past."

Bibliography

"Miller, Arthur." Biographical Dictionary. New York: Chambers Harrap Publishers Ltd., 1997.

Miller, Arthur. Death of a Salesman: Certain Private Conversations in Two Acts and a Requiem. New York: Penguin Books, 1998.

"Miller, Arthur." Modern American Literature: A Library of Literary Criticism. Vol. 2. ed. Frederick Unger. New York: Charles Scribner's Sons., 1969.

"Miller, Arthur." Twentieth Century Authors: A Biographical Dictionary of Modern Literature. Ed. Stanley J. Kunitz. New York: The H. W. Wilson Company, 1955.

"Miller, Arthur." 200 Contemporary Authors: Biobibliographies of Selected Leading Writers of Today with Criticism and Personal Sidelights. Ed. Barbara Harte, Carolyn Riley. Detroit: Gale Research Co., 1969.